CONTENTS

*The true and complete criticism is the serene historical narration of that which has happened.* CROCE

# SYNGE AND ANGLO-IRISH LITERATURE

# Synge and Anglo-Irish Literature

### DANIEL CORKERY
M.A., D.LITT.

THE MERCIER PRESS
4 BRIDGE STREET, CORK

1931

Printed in the Netherlands

# Synge And
# Anglo-Irish Literature

## CHAPTER I.

### ON ANGLO-IRISH LITERATURE

#### I.

OF Synge as a portent in Anglo-Irish literature we can have no clear idea unless we have formed for ourselves some general view of that literature as a whole.

In our youth and even later it used always to be spoken of as Irish literature ; and this custom old-fashioned folk have not yet given up : to them Thomas Moore's *Melodies* are still Irish Melodies. Generally, however, literature written in English by Irishmen is now known among us as Anglo-Irish literature, while by Irish literature we mean the literature written in the Irish language and that alone ; to have outsiders become familiar with the distinction is simply a matter of time.

Irish literature—that great mass of writing which for us began to exist, say about 1,200 years ago, and which is being still added to—is adequately covered by its description. It is Irish. It is as Irish as Greek literature is Greek or Russian literature is Russian. But what are we to say of Anglo-Irish as descriptive of that literature which had no existence until towards the end of the eighteenth century ? Is that as Anglo-Irish as Greek literature is Greek ? If a stranger, say a Russian, become acquainted with this literature, he will not of course ever think of troubling himself with such a question, he will not think of saying : But is this Anglo-Irish literature at all ? for of course he accepts it as such. Before such a thought can strike him he must in some way have come to know this country, its people, the virtue that is in them. One will not therefore expect enlightenment on such a question from the Russian or any other outsider, least of all from the Englishman; and among ourselves, where it is habitual bodily to take over and use whatever is current in English thought, the question has not been raised. What has been discussed is whether this literature may justly be described as Irish—ridiculous argument to those who know what Irish literature is, whereas by taking the narrower question, whether it can fittingly be described as Anglo-Irish, we may clarify our ideas of the literature such as it is, and consequently our idea of Synge's place in it.

The answer to the question: Is there an Anglo-Irish literature? must depend on what regard we have for what Synge spoke of as collaboration—without perhaps taking very great trouble to explore his own thought. The people among whom the writer lives, what is their part in the work he produces? Is the writer the people's voice? has there ever been, can there be, a distinctive literature that is not a national literature? A national literature is written primarily for its own people: every new book in it—no matter what its theme, foreign or native—is referable to their life, and its literary traits to the traits already established in the literature. The nation's own critical opinion of it is the warrant of life or death for it. Can Anglo-Irish, then, be a distinctive literature if it is not a national literature? And if it has not primarily been written for Ireland, if it be impossible to refer it to Irish life for its elucidation, if its continued existence or non-existence be independent of Irish opinion—can it be a national literature?

To ask ourselves such natural questions is to become at once aware that this literature differs in many ways from the literature of every normal people. If we ask such questions about any other literature—English, French, German, the answers are straightforward; they are what one expects. Every new book written by an Englishman in English is written primarily for his own people; English life and English

2

literature as a whole lie behind it ; the English cosmos is the tree from which the book, like a ripe fruit, has dropped ; and English opinion decrees life or death as its portion.

If we ask ourselves by what standards of criticism is French literature clarified and guided, the answer is at hand. So of German literature, of Russian. But to ask ourselves what standards of criticism help the growth of this Anglo-Irish literature, is to be puzzled. When one examines the matter closely one finds that in periods of national exaltation, when the spirit of the land is quickened by struggle, then, as if suddenly aware of the deficiency, Anglo-Irish literature makes an effort to develop a body of criticism of its own. As soon however as the struggle is over, this literature once again becomes a free agent ; once again begins unduly to reflect movements and fashions in literature which do not take their rise in this country, which have nothing to do with the mental life of this country, fashions which never in the least degree become acclimatised in this country—as French or English fashions become acclimatised, say, in America ; and not alone does it make use of its freedom from any incipient national literary tradition to forage where it will, to take on what colour it will, but once again definitely shows itself scornful of the judgement of this country, such as it may be, shows itself indeed utterly provincial in its overwrought desire to be assessed and spoken well of by the critics of another people. It is therefore not normal, for a normal literature while welcoming the criticism of outsiders neither lives nor dies by such criticism. It abides the judgement of its own people, and by that judgement lives or dies. If this literature then be not a normal literature it is not a national literature, for normal and national are synonymous in literary criticism.

To take another test : a normal literature is written within the confines of the country which names it. It is not dependent on expatriates.[1] The literary annals of almost

[1] This word must serve, although of course it is not the right word to apply to such writers as, for instance, Swift, Goldsmith, Shaw—writers for whom Ireland was never a *patria* in any sense.

every people will, of course, once in a while give account of their expatriate writers. In these cases the expatriation is hardly ever a life sentence, and expatriation itself is a rare phenomenon in the history of the literature. How different with us ! Expatriation is the badge of all the tribe of Anglo-Irish literary men ; and in nearly all cases it is a life sentence. It has ever been in vogue, and is still as bad as ever, or, it may be, worse. Even as I write, who knows if one other— we still have one or two left—may not have taken ship for New York, Paris, or London ? Where to-day are those wild geese of the pen : Padraic Colum, E. A. Boyd, Joseph Campbell, Lyle Donaghy, J. B. Fagan, Frank Harris, Ethel Colburn Mayne, Geoffrey Phibbs, Thomas MacGreevy, J. H. Cousins, Gerald O'Donovan, John Eglinton, Stephen Mac Kenna, Eric Dodds, Conal O'Riordan, Alfred Percival Graves, E. Temple Thurston, Monk Gibbon, Con O'Leary, Austin Clarke, James Joyce, D. L. Kelleher, James Stephens, Lord Dunsany, Seumas MacManus, Sean O'Casey, Patrick McGill, W. P. Ryan, Shane Leslie, L. A. G. Strong, Robert Lynd, St. J. Ervine, C. K. Munro, George Moore, G. B. Shaw, Liam O'Flaherty—others ? [1] Here without any searching into the matter is a list of over thirty names : it would be impossible to make a list quarter as long of home-staying writers. Furthermore it is to be noted that whereas most of those expatriate writers live by the pen there are hardly more than one or two of the home-staying writers who do so ; so that in a way we have no home-staying *writers* at all !

Why our writers have to go abroad is obvious : a home market hardly exists for their wares. Now unless one can show that the demands of the alien market are on all fours with those of the home market, how can this literature be Anglo-Irish ? How can it be a national literature ? The question is not : Can expatriates produce national literature ? but : Can expatriates, writing for an alien market, produce

[1] This list probably is not quite accurate. Sometimes an expatriate writer returns and remains for a little while. The name of W. B. Yeats is not included as it is not his habit to spend the whole of any year abroad.

national literature ? For our literary expatriates differ from those of other peoples. Ibsen lived in Rome, in Munich ; but he wrote for no alien market. Turgenev lived in Paris, but it was for Russia he wrote. So of Rolland, of Unamuno, of Ibanez, of many others. At the present time a colony of American writers, pleading the lower cost of living, make their home very foolishly in Paris ; it is however for America they write. Those expatriates then are not like ours, for whom practically no home market exists. In no sense do our expatriates write for Ireland as Ibsen wrote for Norway or Turgenev for Russia. Some of them, of course, have cut away their own land as summarily as Henry James did his. Shaw, Ervine, Munro, others, are of this class. They however are not the type. The typical Irish expatriate writer continues to find his matter in Irish life ; his choice of it however, and his treatment of it when chosen, are to a greater or less extent imposed on him by alien considerations.

A foreign critic, that Russian we have instanced, knowing that more of our people live outside than within our shores, would naturally imagine that our expatriates find their market in the larger Ireland beyond the seas. But, flatly, they do not. That greater Ireland does not know even their names. Indeed the strange thing is, and how piquantly strange it is, those few of the Irish abroad who keep abreast of the fortunes of Anglo-Irish literature in the world, are those who most likely have severed all except academic connections with Ireland itself. They are not those who hasten home to do their bit when an insurrection is on ; they do not contribute to the funds of any political group in Ireland, and their contributions to Irish cultural establishments are so rare that we can remember only one or two in our lifetime. Such exiles as these are above the battle. They are those who, in the United States, fling the taunt ' professional Irishman ' at those whose efforts in the past have made such vast difference in the political status of Ireland. To all this it will be replied : They have cut off from political Ireland but not from cultural Ireland. The statement seems comprehensive until one reminds oneself that Ireland's culture for them, in almost all cases, consists of little else than this very literature we are considering.

Anglo-Irish literature then, as the phrase is understood, is mostly the product of Irishmen who neither live at home nor write primarily for their own people. Furthermore the criticism by which it is assessed is not Irish, nor even Anglo-Irish. These facts admitted, the foreign critic would recall how powerful are the moulds of a literature, how tyrannously, when once established, they shape out the subsequent individual books although these may come to be written under altered conditions and even in newly-discovered lands. That foreigner would reason thus : Anglo-Irish literature is a homogeneous thing, first fashioned in Ireland for Ireland, pregnant of Irish mind, of the genius of the isle. Those expatriate writers are Irishmen, he would continue, steeped in the traditions of this literature : its idiom is their idiom ; its thoughts their thoughts ; expatriation, it is true, may be having some distorting effect on the moulds, but native moulds are not easily changed, hardly ever shattered : the literature then that those expatriate writers, helped by these moulds, produce, is Anglo-Irish literature.

That foreign critic in reasoning thus would be certain he was right ; we know he would be wrong. He would be taking for granted that this expatriation is a new thing ; that the moulds of the literature were laid before it began ; that there was a time when Anglo-Irish was a normal literature, written at home for the homeland. Of course there never was such a time. The moulds are not native to us for they were never fashioned at the bidding of the people of this land : in their making the intention, whether willing or unwilling makes no difference, was not to canalize some share of Irish consciousness so that that consciousness would the better know itself. The intention was rather to discover some easy way in which the strange workings of that consciousness might entertainingly be exhibited to alien eyes. Expatriation is not of to-day, nor of yesterday. It has been a chronic disease from Goldsmith's time, Steele's time Sheridan's time, Burke's time, Moore's time, Prout's time, Wilde's time, to our own time of Shaw, Joyce and Moore. Expatriation is, therefore, an older feature in this literature than the very moulds of it. The moulds can have been fashioned only by expatriate hands, and such expatriates as we have described : writers who did not labour for their own people. From the beginning then though we may think of this literature as a homogeneous thing, we cannot think of it as an indigenous thing. Its moulds therefore cannot have been fashioned to express the genius of Ireland in the English language. If in later years certain writers tried to do this, as some have tried, the unnatural homogeneity of these moulds proved their greatest enemy, so inflexible they have ever been.

## II.

We know the outlines of the history of this literature. Its earliest moulds cannot be distinguished from those of contemporary English literature. Later, it certainly did develop somewhat different moulds, which can be distinguished. These second-period moulds we may speak of as Colonial moulds. The earliest writers never thought of themselves as cut off from English life or letters ; the Colonial writers felt they were ; they frequently protest that they are as truly English as the English born in India, as those who have gone thither : their writing at all is often an effort to keep in communion with their kind. Their books may be all regarded as an account of this strange country they are condemned to, written not for their brothers and co-mates in exile—not even for them !—but for their kinsfolk in England. Maria Edgeworth's *Castle Rackrent* is the best specimen of this style of literature. No other book did as much in the creation of what was to prove the most favoured of the moulds which subsequent writers were to use. This Colonial literature was written to explain the quaintness of the humankind of this land, especially the native humankind, to another humankind that was not quaint, that was standard, normal. All over the world is not that the note of Colonial literature ? The same note is found everywhere in Kipling's Indian books. From Edgeworth's *Absentee* to *John Bull's Other Island* is a far cry, yet in Shaw's play we have the same theme, with some variations of course. In between, what scores of books have been written in which an Englishman is brought to Ireland and is taken around while a current of comment is poured in his ear, not that he may really understand what he sees, but that he may know that what he sees is only the scum of the milk : he may be a bit of a fool, this Englishman, but still he is normal ; he is not one of a lesser breed ; and it is really his unsuspecting normality that makes it necessary for the guide to hint that things even more strange lurk unknown to him in the background. In this way the writer can also prove his own intimate acquaintanceship with the life of a strange land and a stranger people. Instructed through history, through the poetry written in Irish by the quaint ones in the background, what an exhibition of crass obtuseness that assumption of intimacy now appears to us !

It was natural for the Ascendancy folk of this second period to write in this Colonial manner, for what are all their books but travellers' tales ? It is true that often the traveller was born in the strange land he must write of, but then his father was a traveller if he himself was not, or his grandfather or great-grandfather—and why not take after one's kind ? But it is also true that similar books were written by native-born Catholic Irishmen whose forbears had not come out of England. *The Collegians*, by Gerald Griffin, is an example. In this we have an Englishman to whom the quaintness of the folk is exhibited with the accompanying stream of comment, exactly in the Colonial manner. This normal Englishman is really the symbol of the public for whom the book was written ; and the writer of it, Gerald Griffin, may be taken as the type of the non-Ascendancy writer who under the stress of the literary moulds of his time wrote Colonial literature.

In Ascendancy literature the leading theme from the start has been : the decline and fall of an Ascendancy ' Big House.' Maria Edgeworth started this hare also, and the hunt still goes on. Within the last few years we have had *The Big House of Inver* by Somerville and Ross, and *The Big House* by Lennox Robinson ; and in perhaps every decade of years, from Miss Edgeworth's time to our own, one can discover a book with the self-same theme. Synge, in his simple way, unaware that this was the leading theme in Anglo-Irish literature, thought that he had discovered the theme for himself ; he writes : " . . . . . and if a play-wright chose to go through the Irish country houses he would find material, it is likely, for many gloomy plays that would turn on the dying away of these old families."[1] It is as well he himself never wrote such a play, for he had no feeling for history, and the theme is historical, the recognition of which fact makes the moderns, like Mr. Lennox Robinson, treat it very differently from the older writers, like Maria Edgeworth. Sweet are the uses of adversity ! *Castle Rackrent* falls from generation to generation because the family had lost their virtue, but Mr. Robinson's *Big House* falls because the whole Ascendancy had lost their virtue.

This difference between *Castle Rackrent* and Robinson's *Big House* or Somerville and Ross's *Big House of Inver*— the sense that in telling of the fall of one ' big house ' they are describing the fate of the whole Ascendancy, teaches us that this Ascendancy literature is not impervious to the teaching that comes with the passing years. For all that, *The Big House of Inver* is quite as much written for the English people as *Castle Rackrent* was, more than a hundred years before.

The strain of literature just described forms the mass of Anglo-Irish literature—if it be correct so to describe it. It is all written for their motherland, England, by spiritual

[1] *In Wicklow and West Kerry*, by J. M. Synge.

exiles. Personally many of those writers would deny this description of themselves, but it is their works and not themselves we are to go by. It is not however to be thought that all the books which make up this mass of Colonial literature are all equally colonial. Many of the writers did it more naturally, like Sir Andrew Ague-cheek, and we can readily segregate the more Colonial from the less Colonial books by asking does the book live by English or Irish suffrage ? *Castle Rackrent* for instance lives by English suffrage, but Gerald Griffin's *The Collegians* lives by Irish suffrage. Again, the work of Somerville and Ross lives mostly by English suffrage ; while Carleton's work—written quite obviously under Ascendancy influence—lives by Irish suffrage ; and so one may go through the list.

### III.

The end of a boat is wreckage, says the Irish proverb, and certainly the end of an Ascendancy is downfall. When we meet truly Colonial work written in our own day, like that of Somerville and Ross, we feel ourselves in the presence of a survival : for just as Ireland has won far from the flamboyant political oratory of forty years ago, so too we are winning away from the shameful literary tradition of the Prout, Maginn, Lever, Lover school of writers. For very many years past, Anglo-Irish literature has been sitting between two stools : when the land is under the stress of a national movement the literature makes an effort to seat itself on the truly Anglo-Irish stool,—the writers make an effort to express their own land ; but when it is again at peace, the literature returns to the Colonial stool—an attitude that pays better—with less work besides, for to ' explore ' your own land for the foreigner, as Donn Byrne did, is far lighter work than to express it to itself, as Charles Kickham attempted to do, however clumsily.

Those who know of this literature only through modern specimens of it should recollect that these have all been written in a period of national revival : while writing those specimens the writers were sitting on the Anglo-Irish rather than on the Colonial stool. All the work done for the Abbey Theatre from its beginning to 1922 may be reckoned as Anglo-Irish literature, for, whether good or bad in itself, it made an effort to express Ireland to itself. Naturally the writers of plays that were to be performed in Ireland, in a national theatre moreover, were under *geasa* to keep close to the national consciousness ; and in general all the work done in this period—with some exceptions, the work of Somerville and Ross, for instance—is free from the Colonial strain : much of it is freakish, much of it is written under the domination of English literary fashions, yet one does not feel in it that Ireland is being exploited for the foreigner. But then it was nearly all amateur work, indeed 'prentice work ; and one cannot help noticing that in recent years, the national movement having temporarily collapsed, such of its writers as had reached the professional standard, so to speak, have, quite in the old manner, turned their eyes on the English or American markets. The work, mostly amateur, done for the Abbey Theatre between 1902 and 1922 was for Ireland's self ; it was, *in intention*, genuine Anglo-Irish literature, but more than that one cannot say. We must not be waylaid into thinking that because it shed for the nonce its Colonial character it became genuine Anglo-Irish literature, or that because the world accepts it as Irish literature, it may really turn out to be Anglo-Irish literature, or that because it is neither quite English nor quite Irish it must be Anglo-Irish. Obviously to no Irishman is it as Anglo-Irish as Greek literature is Greek or Russian literature Russian. It may best be described as " something escaped from the anchorage and driving free," a craft that thinks no harm of the kindly port it is registered in—let us be thankful !—but prefers for all that to keep its eyes, more especially in these later years, on the foreign merchants who are to purchase its wares. It may be that it is no more than an exotic branch of English literature.

One cannot expect an outsider to agree that a certain literature is exotic just because he is told as much. The native of the isle who tells him so is aware that it is not enough to say to him : Take up and read ! For how is the outsider to know what is or what is not exotic to the genius of both the Irish and the English peoples ? If indeed he be acquainted with other exotic literatures—that of the old New England school for instance—he may be asked if this literature of ours has not the same airs and graces—the same scorn of native criticism, the same ineptness in dealing with the material round about it, the same leaning towards the fanciful, the same scorn of the homely ? The Irishman looks in the face of his own people, hears them utter themselves with intimacy, knows what is deep in them, what is merely fleeting, has old-time knowledge why they are such and such ; knows finally, in some queer way, his own consciousness, has discovered in his heart some guidance to the matter at issue : aware of himself thus advantaged, as with those reasons which the intellect knows not of, the Irishman feels it in his bones that Ireland has not yet learned how to express its own life through the medium of the English language. If he be a literary Irishman he knows that whatever moulds exist in this literature are not the inevitable result of long years of patient labour by Irish writers to express the life of their own people in a natural way. If he be not a literary man he can but feel that something is wrong. But how bring it home to the outsider that all this is true ?

I recall being in Thurles at a hurling match for the championship of Ireland. There were 30,000 onlookers. They were as typical of this nation as any of the great crowds that assemble of Saturday afternoons in England to witness Association football matches are typical of the English nation. It was while I looked around on that great crowd I first became acutely conscious that as a nation we were without self-expression in literary form. The life of this people I looked upon—there were all sorts of individuals present, from bishops to tramps off the road—was not being explored in a natural way by any except one or two writers of any standing. And even of the one or two, I was not certain, their efforts being from the start so handicapped. It was impossible to feel that one could pose such Anglo-Irish writers as the world knows of against that multitude. To use the American phrase, the writers would not belong. One could not see Yeats, A. E., Stephens, Dunsany, Moore, Robinson, standing out from that gathering as natural and indigenous interpreters of it. On the other hand there seems to be no difficulty in posing Galsworthy, Masefield, Bennett, Wells, against corresponding assemblies in England. Those writers do belong. They give the crowd a new significance : through them we may look with better eyes at the massed people of England. The crowd equally deepens the significance of the written word : what stranger, learned in English literature, recollecting it, would not be glad to find himself in their midst, viewing them, listening to them ? He might surely well forget the footballing.

Some one here may say that literature is not a mirror of the mob mind. But one does not think of such English writers as we have named as mirroring the mob mind, nor of its being mirrored by the writers of an earlier day—Meredith, George Eliot, Dickens, Thackeray. We are not thinking of the crowd as such, but as an assembly of a number of the nation's individual souls. Those English crowds are 100 per cent. English ; and the writers who best express the individual souls that make them up are 100 per cent. English.[1] It was never otherwise, it never will be otherwise. The writers in a normal country are one with what they write of. The life of every other people they gaze upon from without, but the life of their own people they cannot get outside of. That is why they belong. The position they thus occupy in the life they deal with has no resemblance to the position occupied by the world-famous Anglo-Irish writers in the life they are supposed to deal with.

[1] At this point it may be well to recall Rupert Brooke's : *If I should die.—*

IV.

We have said that one or two living writers may be excepted from this general condemnation—for instance, Padraic Colum and T. C. Murray. They have come not from the Ascendancy but from the people. And yet even in the case of these, which is equivalent to saying in the case of all, one may well be doubtful, the difficulties in creating genuine Anglo-Irish literature are so immense. It seems indeed an almost impossible task.

The difficulty is not alone a want of native moulds ; it is rather the want of a foundation upon which to establish them. Everywhere in the mentality of the Irish people are flux and uncertainty. Our national consciousness may be described, in a native phrase, as a quaking sod. It gives no footing. It is not English, nor Irish, nor Anglo-Irish ; as will be understood if one think a while on the thwarting it undergoes in each individual child of the race as he grows into manhood. Though not quite true, let us take it that the Irish-born child is as Irish in his instincts, in his emotions, as the English child is English : the period of education comes on : all that the English child learns buttresses, while it refines, his emotional nature. Practically all the literature he reads focuses for him the mind of his own people ; so also does the instruction he hears. At a later stage if he come to read a foreign language he seizes what he reads in it with an English mind. He has something of his own by which to estimate its value for him.

How different with the Irish child ! No sooner does he begin to use his intellect than what he learns begins to undermine, to weaken, and to harass his emotional nature. For practically all that he reads is English—what he reads in Irish is not yet worth taking account of. It does not therefore focus the mind of his own people, teaching him the better to look about him, to understand both himself and his surroundings. It focuses instead the life of another people. Instead of sharpening his gaze upon his own neighbourhood, his reading distracts it, for he cannot find in these surroundings what his reading has taught him is the matter worth coming upon. His surroundings begin to seem unvital. His education, instead of buttressing and refining his emotional nature, teaches him the rather to despise it, inasmuch as it teaches him not to see the surroundings out of which he is sprung, as they are in themselves, but as compared with alien surroundings : his education provides him with an alien medium through which he is henceforth to look at his native land ! At the least his education sets up a dispute between his intellect and his emotions. Nothing happens in the neighbourhood of an English boy's home that he will not sooner or later find happening, transfigured, in literature. What happens in the neighbourhood of an Irish boy's home—the fair, the hurling match, the land grabbing, the *priesting*, the mission, the Mass—he never comes on in literature, that is, in such literature as he is told to respect and learn. Evidently what happens in his own fields is not stuff for the Muses ! In his riper years he may come to see the crassness of his own upbringing, as, doubtless, T. C. Murray and Padraic Colum see it ; but of course the damage is done : his mind is cast in an unnatural because unnative mould. So does it happen that the Irishman who would write of his own people has to begin by trying to forget what he has learnt.

If it be so, and it cannot be otherwise, with T. C. Murray and Padraic Colum, men sprung from the people, sharing their national memory in all its ramifications, what chance of expressing the people of Ireland have those writers who, sprung from the Ascendancy, have never shared the Irish national memory, and are therefore just as un-Irish as it is possible for them to be ? In the case of writers sprung from the people, what creates the difficulty is the over-whelming prestige of English culture in all Irish scholastic systems, and therefore in Irish life generally. Accepted as the only one possible, that culture, not rooted in their own emotional nature, as a national culture would be, puts their emotional nature out of action, or, at the least, drugs it with a sense of its own impotence. In the case of writers sprung from the Ascendancy their emotional nature differs from that of the Irish people (differs also of course from that of the English people) and such as it is is also doubtless thrown out of gear by the educational mauling it undergoes. They therefore are doubly disadvantaged. To become natural interpreters of the nation they need to share in the people's emotional background; moreover they need to become possessed of a culture based on that emotional subconsciousness. In the case of the writer sprung from the people all that is necessary is a mental equipment fitted to shape the emotional content that is theirs, as well as the nation's, into chaste and enduring form.

v.

If this reasoning is right we now know why that crowd of 30,000 human souls I saw in Thurles—a crowd with a national tradition behind them—are still left unuttered in literature. And we may in the light of such reasoning begin to understand curious traits in the literature as it exists, traits that show it to be exotic, not national, not normal, not natural.

A national literature foretells the nation's future. Eighty years ago, sixty years ago, Prout, Lever, Maginn, Lover, others, were accepted by the English-speaking world as the genuine voice of the Irish nation. One wonders if any foreign critic thought it worth his while to forecast the future of this nation in the light of their pages. How interesting now to come on such a forecast! The Irish peasant, with no national assets in his possession outside his own knowledge that he was the native of the isle, during that period fought for the soil of Ireland, and by his own grit and courage, became possessed of it. Not only does he now possess the soil; he also fills the highest offices in the country, in Church, in State, in Learning—everywhere. This the literature of Lover and his compeers hardly promised. Extinction rather than distinction was what it threatened, laughing, ' with foreign jaws,' as it did so. The future conquest of the soil was part of Irish consciousness : if it were not, the thing could not have come to pass ; and anyway those of us who have read Irish poetry know that it has for many centuries been one of the deepest things in Irish consciousness ; our ' national ' writers however either were not aware of it, or, aware of it, could not or would not give it utterance. Yet this literature, so little at one with the national consciousness, is called variously Irish literature and Anglo-Irish literature ! And no school of criticism has arisen in Ireland to warn us that if this literature in the future is to be more trustworthy, its creators must not go the way Prout and the others travelled ; indeed by laughing ' with foreign jaws ' at the 100 per cent. type of Irishman, such critics as we have urge the young writers on to the selfsame disastrous road. If Maginn and his fellows were absorbed in the Irish scene, had to write of it for native eyes and not for London drawing-rooms, they could not but have felt that already the disintegration of the Ascendancy in Ireland was setting in. The literature they produced is typical of Anglo-Irish literature in the mass. We do not say that now and then that literature does not send forward-struggling beams ; what we assert is that of all living literatures its message has been most often and most utterly belied by what the years have brought to pass. It has always failed to speak the secret things in the nation's soul. Only at rarest moments does it penetrate the superficialities of Irish life ; so that one does not wonder if the foreigner who browses on its ' glamorous ' pages picture us as given over either to a wild whirl of fox-hunting and rioting, or as spell-bound by fairies that troop nightly from our prehistoric ruins, moping out an existence not wholly in this world nor quite beyond it.

## VI.

The paucity of even good, not to say great, fiction in this literature has been frequently noticed. Of that better sort

17

of novel, which is little else than an impassioned study of the reactions of individual souls to their social environment, scarcely a single example is to be had. But from what we have been finding out about this literature, its lack of grip on the emotional background of the people, is not this easily understood ? How could it be otherwise, if, more than any other form in literature, the novel, for its writing require a thorough intimacy with not only the scene itself and the people themselves but with all that gives one little world a distinctive vitality ? The whole topsy-turvy scheme of Irish life makes against this. If we take up the first Anglo-Irish story to hand we can find no Irish homeliness in it : we may discover an attempt at the idyllic—watery gruel ! Homeliness being beyond the knowledge rather than the power of the writers, they take refuge in the freakish, the fanciful, the perverse. Brilliancy often results ; and it is strange, yet significant, that the more utterly expatriate the writer the more brilliantly his pages shine, Sheridan, Prout, Maginn, Wilde, Shaw—those who most summarily dismissed the claims of their own people, being the most brilliant of all. What is the explanation ? " Something escaped from the anchorage and driving free,"—that line already quoted from Whitman may help us. Given an acute mind, given also an upbringing in Ascendancy circles, or adoption into them, or assumption of their ways, with their tradition of insolence, cynicism, recklessness, and hardness, what other note could be looked for from them when they had been received into a people among whom the very word ' home ' is like a holy word—a people who in their native land are anything but insolent, cynical, hard, or reckless ? The brilliancy of such writers is often described as Irish, whereas in reality it may be due to that disparity of intellect and emotion we have already mentioned. Into the English field of emotion, that world of homeliness, they have no entry ; they are the creators of literature in which collaboration can have no part, and Shaw or Wilde attempting to do for England what Ibsen did for Norway or Chekhov for Russia, or what Molière did for France, is really matter for a Shavian comedy.

Mr. Shaw has described himself as the faithful servant of the English people ; is it not a strange thing that servitude to the stranger should eventuate in brilliancy ? Yet is it not an old and a constant theme in literature ?—the jester, just because he is not one of ourselves, is privileged to loosen his tongue—only that the jester in literature has a secret sorrow in the background, as if to preserve the natural roundness of life—heart as well as brain. All those writers were, as much as Mr. Shaw, servants of the English people : one wonders if their desertion of the land that most required their services was not their secret woe ? From Prout's bitter gibing at O'Connell—that great if imperfect figure—one thinks it may have been so ; that his secret sorrow should have expressed itself not in tears but in tauntings of one who did lay his gifts at his country's feet, must not surprise us, since the jester must find an unusual way.

VII.

The three great forces which, working for long in the Irish national being, have made it so different from the English national being, are : (1) The Religious Consciousness of the People ; (2) Irish Nationalism ; and (3) The Land.

Now the mentality of that crowd of 30,000 I looked upon in Thurles was chiefly the result of the interplay of these three forces. To let one's mind, filled with this thought, rest on that crowd, scanning the faces for confirmation of it, and then suddenly to shift one's thought on to the mass of Anglo-Irish literature, is to turn from solid reality to a pale ghost. For, for instance, who can name a novel dealing adequately with their religious consciousness ? Yet this religious consciousness is so vast, so deep, so dramatic, even so terrible a thing, occasionally creating wreckage in its path, tumbling the weak things over, that when one begins to know it, one wonders if it is possible for a writer to deal with any phase whatever of Irish life without trenching upon it. To adopt the convention of Anglo-Irish literature, that is, either to leave it out, or to substitute for it the wraith-like wisps of vanished beliefs that still float in the minds of a tiny percentage of the people, is to cut out the heart of the mystery. So firm is the texture of that consciousness that one may sometimes think that only about Irish life can a really great sex novel be written in these days ; for the subject can have no great attraction for the serious artist except where the moral standards are rigid, and the reactions transcend the lusts and the shiverings of the mortal flesh. (Mr. James Joyce has gone astray—although that very texture we have spoken of nearly succeeded in holding him fast). We may perhaps know that genuine Anglo-Irish literature has come into being when at every hand's turn that religious consciousness breaks in upon it, no matter what the subject, as it does in the Greek plays—comedies as well as tragedies—or as it does in mediæval art, grotesques and all.

As for Irish nationalism, how can normal countries understand it ? If one cannot live in Ireland long enough to have it penetrate one's being, driving one although quite a foreigner to take sides, as has so often happened, the only other way to get to know it is to learn the Irish language and read the poetry in it ; for such is the nature of Irish nationalism that it demands sincerity, intensity, style for its utterance, in other words, poetry. We who have lived in Ireland in recent years, who have seen what we have seen, need no further instruction to believe that prose is no medium to express it in, no more than it was for the Jews in their ancient captivity. Like all forces, it wrecks as well as saves. We here are not concerned with the wisest way of dealing with it ; we would only point out that it is one of the deepest things in Irish life, searching into the souls of men, drawing sanction, as it does, from hundreds of battlefields, slaughterings, famines, exoduses, as well as from hundreds of heroic lives and the piety of verse. Yet in the eyes of the world, taught of what the world calls ' Irish ' literature, that force is a thing for derision, fitted rather for comic than for serious treatment in literature. What a curious message for ' Irish ' literature to deliver to the world—as if a fish-monger should cry out rotten fish ! Topsy-turvy cannot sing, it seems, except in a cracked voice. A stranger, one fancies, could from the pages of Conrad gather a truer idea of the nature of Irish nationalism than from the heaped-up books of this literature the world knows of. One may be sure we are come upon genuine Anglo-Irish literature when, as with the force just spoken of, that spirit of Irish nationalism expresses itself almost in every page, no matter what the nature of the expression may be, direct or indirect, heroic or grotesque, or perverse, but not alien-minded.

Of the Land as a force in Irish life, we may, the better to contrast it with the same force in English life, recall that according to the late Sir William Butler, there have been no peasants in England since Queen Elizabeth's reign. Over-statement or not, to-day in England only 6 per cent. of the people work on the land, whereas Ireland, in a sense, is a peasant-ridden country, 53 per cent. of the people actually working in the fields. It will then be understood that when under the domination of a national movement, certain writers in Ireland began to deal with this force in their novels and plays, they undertook pioneer service to their country. It also will be understood that while from certain Continental schools of literature they learned a little, from England they learned nothing. It was a doubly new experience for writers such as these, first to have to fend for themselves without help from England, secondly to find they had hitched their wagon to a living force. What wonder that those of them who most deeply sank themselves in their subject wrote far above their accustomed pitch ? Darrell Figgis with his *Children of Earth ;* T. C. Murray's *Birthright* and *Autumn Fire ;* Seamus O'Kelly's *Wet Clay ;* Padraic Colum's *Castle Conquer ;* Lysaght's *The Gael* may be taken as evidence of this. The Land then is a huge force in

Irish life. It is not however as universal in it as the other two; one cannot therefore predicate its breaking in upon every page, yet one can understand how when true Anglo-Irish literature comes to be written, if ever, for a long time the Land must lie behind the literature in some such way as the freeing of the serfs lies behind Russian literature—with political rather than social affinities. Only after long years will those political memories drift from the consciousness of the Irish people.

These forces exist in all countries; in Ireland they have however been so hardened and sharpened, given, by centuries of onslaught, such momentum, that only such other countries as have also been or are still enslaved can feel with any fitting comprehension the intensity they have now acquired. For one who has come earnestly to know them, to recognise them in the build, the attitude, the eyes of our men and women—how visibly portrayed they were in those faces in Thurles!—it is impossible for such a one to take seriously such Anglo-Irish literature as exists. So measured against life itself, as it were, it has not begun to be.

### VIII.

We may be reminded that a good critic, the late Rev. Stopford A. Brooke, having examined Anglo-Irish poetry, named the notes of Religion, of Nationality, of the Peasant as chief among them [1] —the very notes we have been naming as having had most to do with making the Thurles crowd into what they appeared and into what they were. Therefore, it seems, it is not right to say that these notes are absent in Anglo-Irish literature.

All Anglo-Irish literature, including what is being written to-day, may be divided into two kinds—the literature of the Ascendancy writer and that of the writer for the Irish people.

[1] *A Treasury of Irish Poetry in the English Tongue.* Introduction by Stopford A. Brooke.

Roughly, the first kind includes all the literature that lives by foreign suffrage ; the second, all that lives by native suffrage. It was in the second class that Stopford Brooke discovered these notes. One is therefore driven to the conclusion that the second class is true Anglo-Irish literature, since in it we find reflected the face of the people of the land. But this sort of Anglo-Irish literature is hardly ever heard of outside Ireland, and this one does not greatly deplore, for it is not intrinsically good. Such of us as know how these native notes are to be come upon in Irish poetry, never without artistry, intensity, sincerity, style, have no desire to find the world at large experiencing them in the poems of Davis, or Charles Kickham, or even Mangan. These and all their fellows Mr. W. B. Yeats might not hesitate to call " bad popular poets," and he would be right. Yet it is these bad popular poets, in spite of their deficiencies, that somehow, in our poverty, carry the message that is in Ireland's heart. The emotional content in them is sterling ; their mental equipment, with its lack of self-criticism, was not, however, strong enough, keen enough, to shape the message into beautiful song. Only seldom is their work not mediocre, and it is never really good. Yet it lives on ; and entirely by Irish suffrage. And this happens because its emotional content, as has been said, is right ; and Ireland—the Ireland that counts—almost entirely educated, up to the present, in the Primary school,—does not see its defects of form. This popular literature probably bears the same relation to the Irish consciousness of our time as the more intense, more sincere, more polished poetry in Irish bears to the Irish consciousness of the eighteenth and previous centuries, when education was of a different brand.

In this submerged underworld of Anglo-Irish literature then, loose in texture, superficial, and mostly unnative in its forms, as it is, it was that the critic discovered those three notes to be of importance. In the world-famous literature the critic may perhaps also discover the same three forces, or rather ghostly echoes from the noisy smithy in which they work; but that they were, and are, the deepest factors in the national consciousness of Ireland he certainly never could discover from its pages.

If one then hold that Anglo-Irish literature has scarcely begun to exist, one may ask : Whether is this unsophisticated popular literature, with its Irish message, or the exotic poetry that Ireland, the Ireland that counts, cares so little for, the better foundation to build upon ? Does it not seem that this simple poetry, close to the ground, clumsily endeavouring to recapture the notes that beat, pulse-like, in the nation's heart, is capable of being refined, of being intensified, of being carven into shapely forms ? Whereas one may well wonder if the all too sophisticated alien-minded poetry of the ' Celtic Revival ' school, dead tired as it is, weary of staring at its own airs and graces in the mirror, is capable of further growth. Says Mr. Yeats very truthfully, almost as if he were thinking of this :

Nothing but stillness can remain when hearts are full
Of their own sweetness, bodies of their own loveliness.

Such hearts and such bodies, one fancies, are not to be tempted to the adventure of further growth, which so often means pain and disfigurement. If one approach ' Celtic Revival ' poetry as an exotic, then one is in a mood to appreciate its subtle rhythms, and its quiet tones ; but if one continue to live within the Irish seas, travelling the roads of the land, then the white-walled houses, the farming life, the hill-top chapel, the memorial cross above some peasant's grave—memorable only because he died for his country— impressing themselves, as the living pieties of life must impress themselves, upon the imagination, growing into it, dominating it, all this poetry becomes after a time little else than an impertinence. It is not possible to imagine it as the foundation of a school of poetry in which those three great forces Religion, Nationalism, the Land, will find intense yet chastened expression.

As with the poetry, so with the prose. *Knocknagow*, one of the few books which have furnished living figures to the

Irish consciousness, as the *Pickwick Papers* has to the English or *Père Goriot* to the French, is of this submerged Anglo-Irish literature. It is a book unknown except to the Irish; and again one is not sorry, for, when all is said, it is only good in parts, and not great anywhere. The emotional content here also is right; the mental equipment, however, that shaped it out was not hardened by culture and discipline. And it may be taken as the type of many other such books, Carleton's—than which it is more popular yet not at all as good—the Banims' and those of others. So that the same question arises : Is the development of this prose literature, in which under-educated Ireland discovers its own image, the way for Anglo-Irish literature in the future, or shall the alien market decide for ever the way of it ?

As regards this bulk of popular poetry and popular prose, there is this further to be said : if a foreign student wish to come on Irish history and on Irish life generally as mirrored in imaginative literature, him one must direct towards it and not towards the Anglo-Irish literature that the world knows of. The years as they arrive do not belie its message, which is enough to approve it as of the Irish consciousness. It is obviously the result of collaboration, always unconscious, between writer and people. And the foreign student will find in it the interplay of those great forces—Religion, Nationality, the Land, expressed, clumsily it is true, yet naturally, and without obligations to alien markets ; whereas in the world-famous sort of Anglo-Irish literature, of which the Irish people know so little, he will discover that some of those forces are scarcely to be felt at all, and that none of them is expressed naturally with any such intensity as is integral in the force itself.

## IX.

Having now looked at the humble literature in English that, unknown to the world, finds shelter and affection in Irish homes ; and looked also at the literature that goes out from Ireland to the literary world, it is time to bring our conclusions together. The underworld literature is infantile ; yet one feels that if ever a school of genuine Anglo-Irish literature emerge, it will grow rather from that literature than from its more famous, very distant relation above in the drawing-room. It is against the insolence of this still Ascendancy minded literature we would argue. Our complaint against it is that the mass of it cannot be held up to Irish life as interpretative of it ; that its writers do not adhere to Irish life, as English writers to English life or French to the life of France. We complain that the three great forces that work their will in the consciousness of the Irish people have found little or no adequate expression in it, that its genius is set against any sympathetic interpretation of them as a trinity of forces which interplay each one with the two others. We complain that it has thrown up no body of criticism adhering to itself, anxious to assess its value and to place its writers.[1] We complain that it does not foretell our destiny, that it is, contrariwise, surprised with what the years bring to pass. We complain that in it is to be observed a disparity between the emotional and the intellectual background of the writers ; that such writers of it as were, like Griffin and Prout, initiates of Irish consciousness, using Ascendancy moulds, went astray ; and that those others, not initiates by birth, took no trouble to become so, nor made any use of such intellectual equipment as they possessed, sometimes admirable in itself, for the high purposes of art— the shaping out into chaste and enduring form of a genuine emotional content, personal to themselves but conscionable to the nation. Finally we complain that all those writers would have written quite differently if extramural influences, such as the proximity of the English literary market and the tradition of expatriation, had not misled them from the start. Whether these extramural forces can be withstood as long as England and Ireland speak the same language is another question.

1 There are really only a few books on the matter—and only one of them really helpful : *Ireland's Literary Renaissance* by E. A. Boyd.

## X.

The traits of this literature have been so seldom examined, are so little understood, that without some such study as this just made, we are not aware that Synge, as a portent in its annals, could be treated of. Those to whom his work is already known, begin, perhaps, to see why we may quite justly speak of him as a portent. Here, by one stroke, to show how he stands apart from all his fellow Ascendancy writers, it is but necessary to state, that he, an Ascendancy man, went into the huts of the people and lived with them.

# CHAPTER II.

## THE MAN

### I.

JOHN Millington Synge was born on 16th April, 1871, at Newtown Little, near Rathfarnham, a village in the outer suburbs of Dublin.

His father, John Hatch Synge, was by profession a barrister-at-law, and is described as " a modest, thoughtful man who preferred the quiet of home life to any outside amusement." [1] He was not altogether barrister ; he had inherited some landed property in Co. Galway, which brought him an annual rental ; and in those years a barrister who had landed property behind him differed from one who was merely barrister.

John M. Synge's mother was the daughter of Rev. Robert Traill, Rector of Schull, in Co. Cork. The famine of 1847 fell more heavily on that district than on any other part of Ireland, and the Rector died of a fever contracted while relieving the poor. As for Synge's people on the father's side, it was customary with such of them as took a profession to be ordained in the Established Church. John M. Synge therefore came from Protestant Church of Ireland families on both sides. The Synges were an old Wicklow family which had given a long line of bishops and archbishops to the Ascendancy party. They had been therefore several hundreds of years in Ireland if not of Ireland. The great-grandfather of the dramatist sat in the last "independent " Parliament of Ireland, and voted against the Union ; it redounds to his credit but in no way proves that the Synges

---

1 *John Millington Synge*, by Maurice Bourgeois.

28

were Irish, for the Parliament he would have saved was itself in no way Irish. It was only Ascendancy.

John Hatch Synge, the dramatist's father, died in 1872. John M. Synge, not yet two years old, can therefore never have known his father. The family then moved to Orwell Park, Rathgar, which is in the inner suburbs of Dublin. At Rathgar the boy grew up, living there until he was nineteen.

He received, we are told, " a somewhat desultory education, at which in after life he would sneer with a violent sardonic scorn." [1] He attended private classes in Dublin and afterwards in Bray. At fourteen he was taken from school, his health not being good, and set to read at home with a private tutor till he was ready for college. He entered Trinity College, Dublin, in June, 1888, as a pensioner; his tutor there was his mother's first cousin, Dr. Anthony Traill. At Trinity, in 1892, he obtained prizes in Irish and Hebrew—the choice of subjects suggests that he too, following the family tradition, had thoughts of going into the ministry of the Church of Ireland; and in Michaelmas term of the same year he obtained his B.A. After June, 1893, his name is found no longer on the College books. At this time his chief interest was in music. He had taught himself the flute, and become expert on the violin and piano. But he had other interests as well, natural history being one of them. While still in his teens he became a member of the Dublin Naturalists' Field Club, and, even before that, loved to take long and lonely rambles in the country, observing wild life and collecting such heterogeneous treasures from ditch and branch as only a boy's eyes can spy out. In languages too he was already interested as also in literature; he had got even as far as relieving his feelings in plays and verse. Neither at this time however, nor for years afterwards, was literature the chief passion of his life; his art was music, he thought, and it was for the further study of it he set out for Germany as soon as he was free to do so.

[1] *John Millington Synge*, by Maurice Bourgeois.

He may not have known it, but his ' new life ' began with his leaving of Ireland. He stayed first at Darmstadt and Coblentz and later on at Würzburg. It is not clear whether he aimed at becoming a composer or executant of music, or both. The violin chiefly occupied him, but he also studied composition and harmony. By 1894 he had made up his mind against becoming a professional musician. He told one of his nephews that he could not go near the Germans in composing, and that he was too nervous to perform in public. M. Maurice Bourgeois records in his very useful book that Dr. Michel Elmassian, who knew Synge in Paris, stated that he gave up music because he had been unsuccessful at a competition in original composition ; he had failed to develop a given theme.

His sojourns in Europe were mostly in Germany and France, but he spent from February to May, 1896, in Italy, at Florence and Rome. His allegiance had been gradually shifting, it appears, from music to literature, and in Paris the desire to write revived in him. He thought of becoming in English an interpreter of French life and literature.

We know but little of those wanderings of his on the Continent. Even those who afterwards became very friendly with him, such as Mr. John Masefield and Mr. Jack B. Yeats, can recall that he communicated but little to them of those European years. " He was silent about all that," says Mr. Masefield, but it is right for us to recollect that about everything else as well that had any bearing on his own life he was equally silent. He was a more than usually reticent man. During those years it was noticed at home that he had become unorthodox in religion. He once said to a friend : " It is very amusing to me coming back to Ireland to find myself looked upon as a Pariah because I don't go to church and am not orthodox, while in Paris amongst the students I am looked upon as a saint, simply because I don't do the things they do, and many come to me as a sort of

Father Confessor and wish they could be like me." [1]   At this time he was about twenty-six.   In Paris he met a type of Irishman and Irishwoman he would probably never have met with had he stayed at home or in England—the Irish revolutionary, the extreme nationalist, of which type Paris had had, ever since the days of Wolfe Tone, its fair number.

It was in Paris, in March, 1898, that Mr. W. B. Yeats advised him to give up writing for English papers, and to take himself off to the Aran Islands in Galway Bay. Acting on this advice he left France in May, 1898, and came to Aranmore.   From this on—he had still eleven years to live— he spent much of each year in Ireland, either in Dublin, when his plays were being rehearsed, or in the Aran Islands, or in Kerry, or Wicklow or Connemara, or the Blasket Islands, which are off the Kerry coast.   In between, he went back to Paris, less and less often however as the years went on. He gave up his lodgings in Paris towards the end of 1902, and on his way home spent some months in London.   His first play, *In the Shadow of the Glen*, was produced in 1903, *Riders to the Sea* in 1904, *The Well of the Saints* in 1905, and *The Playboy of the Western World* in 1907.   He suffered much from ill-health in 1908 and in March, 1909, he died in a Dublin hospital.

### III.

We have now divided his life, short though it was, into a number of chapters—his youth in Dublin, his wanderings in Europe, his discovery of Ireland—for that is what it was— his activities as dramatist, his death ; and by looking more closely at these chapters in turn we may find ourselves gradually winning to some intimacy of feeling with the spirit behind the plays.

He was the youngest of the family.   It was a large family. Even when, quite young, two brothers and one sister had died, he had still three brothers left him and one sister.   It

[1] " C. H. H." in " Irish Statesman," 5 July, 1924.

is accepted that the eldest or the youngest in a family is most likely to be endowed with genius. When it shows itself in the eldest, one thinks it has been induced in him by careful training ; he has been petted into self-realization. If it break out in the youngest the reason often is that left very much to himself he comes upon strange realms, rather within than without his own mind, which, he discovers for himself, he can people with creatures more vital than the casual beings he strikes against upon the earth. Who can guess how much of the genius of the world is due to that division that comes so naturally to be made between the youngest and the other child members of a large family ? To those other members he is so often handed over, and they so often find him in the way : his young feet are neither swift nor strong enough for theirs, and his spirit is not daring Of course there is no intentional neglect ; if there is callousness it is unconscious ; and in the case of John M. Synge one certainly finds no hint of division between himself and the others ; while between himself and his mother—his father, as we have seen, died when the boy was not quite two years old—the most tender affection existed until her death, which predated his own only by a few months. Yet one fancies that that reticence, that silence in company which so marked him out in after years, may have had its origin in the almost unguessed-at loneliness in which so often the youngest member of a family grows up.

He was not only the youngest, he was also delicate. " We have reason to believe," says M. Maurice Bourgeois, " that the influence of home never greatly told on him ; indeed, as a lad, Synge was strangely reserved and even unboyish to a certain extent ; he shunned rather than desired companionship ; he would hardly take part in the games of his age, and much preferred open-air exercise and solitary rambles in his beloved Dublin mountains to indoor life." ' He shunned rather than desired companionship.' But is it not those very boys who most of all desire companionship that seem most of all unable to achieve it ? Young Synge found companionship for himself in the wild; in plant life and animal life and in the formation of the rocks. He was fortunate in having so vast and varied a hinterland as lies within reach almost on every side of Dublin; while his holidays were spent in Wicklow, a garden of delights. He surely was such a boy as might easily come to be haunted by its cataracts and wooded glens.

His boyhood then was wayward, self-led, not put upon, inward, not alert, except to such phenomena as had stirred his affections. That solitude which in Goethe's thought fosters genius was his, and wisely Jacob Böhme said: " Whoso lives quietly in his own will, like a child in the womb, and lets himself be led and guided by that inner principle from which he is sprung, is the noblest and richest on earth."

Later on he found in music another world to which he could retreat. This study he fortunately kept up during his College days. His teachers were good, and his progress must have been marked since he thought of finding his career in it. If it were this idea that sent him to the Continent and not to England, we may hold that it was music which unwittingly lured his feet into his own especial realm.

One is surprised to find him, in the 'nineties, studying Irish in Trinity College. Our surprise might not be so great if we knew exactly why: College regulations, premiums, study courses, if only one were familiar with them, might explain it. In Trinity, Irish at that time was of course studied as a dead language; and indeed it was little better with it anywhere else. The great awakening that was to make later on such difference to Synge himself had not yet come. Yet dead and all as that study was in Trinity in those days, it may have had its share in first inclining his mind towards the European scheme of things, languages and all. It has done so with many others since.

About those University years of his we have not very much information; we know however that he came to dislike Trinity as soon as he became nationalist. While a student there he seems to have worked diligently.

c

One gladly notes that he exhibited none of that devastating precocity which repels one in those who in their teens make up their minds to write masterpieces before they are five-and-twenty. And the child was father to the man : his whole life long he despised cleverness. Would that his mantle had fallen on a school of writers that since his death has arisen in Dublin !

IV.

Done with the University, he set out for Europe. M. Bourgeois hints at " an unfortunate and mysterious love affair " as one of the motives for his departure ; he however adds : " In so doing Synge was also following the tradition of literary absenteeism which has set in with most of the modern Irish writers—Oscar Wilde, Mr. G. B. Shaw, Mr. George Moore, Mr. W. B. Yeats." But surely Synge's case was different. Most of those writers and all our other literary absentees were simply so many workmen making towards the labour mart ; that mart was in London and thither they went and settled. The love affair apart, one thinks that it was music and not literature hastened Synge's feet from his native Dublin. It cannot have been literature. That would surely have landed him in London, and even if, landed there, he did unconventionally still hanker after Europe, he would have received such instruction as to what was right and proper in Continental literary circles, and who were and who were not to be consorted with there, and what salons and theatres and studios were significant, that the free spirit which did actually set out for Europe would have been bewitched and bewinkered before it got to the Continent at all. His subsequent experience then would have been o European literary circles, and not of European life. That misfortune he escaped, and we may thank his love of music for it. In the years to come, nothing else was to befall him so significant as this skipping over London.

There was at least one other Ascendancy Irishman who skipped over London in this way on his passage to Europe. That was Oliver Goldsmith. He, it is true, did not get to Europe without lingering for some time in Edinburgh, but Edinburgh is not London, and in those days was ·far more itself than it is now. The effect on Goldsmith's work of his coming on London only after long and haphazard wanderings in Europe, we have never seen treated with even ordinary insight. Has anyone suggested that it may account for his standing apart, as he does in his work, from the others of his day ? He is not an Irish writer, he is not even an Anglo-Irish writer, but the recollections of his youth in Ireland succeeded in impregnating the work of his ripe manhood with that element of homeliness which is the quality that distinguishes it from that of his contemporaries ; and this functioning in his later days of his earliest perceptions would never have happened, we hold, only for his continental experiences ; for it was these that sanctioned in his mind the homely phenomena of his youthful surroundings, sanctioned them as normal and sterling and neither unique nor freakish. In nature Goldsmith differed much from Synge yet he also had much in common with him. Both were emotional rather than intellectual ; and to the fact that their emotional equipment, so to speak, was not put out of action may be attributed all that we have enduringly from their pens. If *their* emotional equipment had been destroyed, they would have had nothing left. When that fate overtook others of the Ascendancy Irish, from Sheridan to Shaw, they either fell back on intellectual brilliancy or perished in the void. Their work therefore, and that of all their kind, as one may understand, lacking those emotional overtones which are so precious in literature, which are indeed the very touch of nature, have something of a dry brittleness in them. One reads them in a sort of fear, uncertain that inhuman laughter may not at any time assault our ears. It was contact with Europe kept open the channels through which both Synge and Goldsmith conveyed to us the beatings of their impulsive hearts. In Goldsmith's case, as has been said, it permitted him to use up the memories of his youthful Irish days. In Synge's case it acted differently, for he had not had the good fortune to be born and reared in rural Ireland—land of homeliness and freedom—and so could not draw, in the same way, on his boyish recollections. Yet that which contact with Europe did for him may have been greater : to a large degree it purged his eyes of Ascendancy prejudices ; it taught him that rural Ireland, strange and unruly land as it was, derided, despised, impoverished, unkempt, ignorant, was not, for all that, abnormal, was instead, a natural sort of place, with many features in it that compensated for the regulated comfortableness of English life, the ideal of all his class. There was then no reason for thinking that hearts that beat in the Irish way were not as sterling as those other hearts that beat in another way. It is not that there are not many differences between Irish life and European life, but these differences are not unexpected in places so far apart, places speaking different languages and living under different suns. What stultifies the Protestant Ascendancy man who for the first time leaves Ireland for England is that the two schemes of life should be at once so similar and dissimilar. He has been always taught that one was the norm ; and on acquaintance he confesses that such indeed it is for him. What can *he* do with his youthful perceptions of life ? He had better forget them ! What wonder then if people like Mr. St. John Ervine become so much more British than the British themselves ? [1]

He who goes to Europe is as conscious of change ; but, as

[1] Mr. St. John Ervine, commenting in a letter to the " Times," 8 Sept., 1930, on " The puzzling fact that any Briton who defends his country in the United States is stigmatised as a propagandist," writes : " May I express my belief that the effort to avoid ' irritating ' Americans by defending our country when it is attacked is being overdone ? Frankly, I do not care whether I irritate Americans or any other people by stating what I believe to be the truth about my country. Heaven forbid that we should seem always to be apologising for ourselves, but heaven forbid, too, that we should stand tamely by while we are aspersed or misrepresented, on the ground that if we dare to defend ourselves or to correct misstatements we shall upset people."

hinted, he expects it ; and then if he travel off the beaten track in Europe he begins to discover, beneath the great differences, fundamental resemblances, which fact sets him thinking in a new way on Irish history. Not Ireland itself, under its alien Ascendancy, has been more war-ravaged than parts of Europe : indeed there is hardly a spot of European ground that has not in this regard more resemblance to Ireland than to England—England fattening and refattening its haunts of ancient peace, century after century, while its soldiers campaigned abroad. We recollect that in the early stages of the Great War a writer in an English review mentioned how struck he was with the resemblance he noted between the small towns and villages of Poland and those of Ireland : he did not, however, bethink himself of the untoward circumstances that had brought the similarity about.

In Europe, then, the Ascendancy man may come on such instruction as enables him to read the map of Ireland anew. If that map show unkemptness in the landscape, that unkemptness is not without cause, nor does it prove the people freakish or inept ; for those other countries whose stories are similar are not different. There is also, of course, the vast teaching he may come upon in the Catholic portions of Europe. He may note many differences between European and Irish Catholicism. The probability is, of course, that he has never been in an Irish Catholic church in his life, but however great the differences he must at least be led to question which of the two religions he knows of in Ireland is the more European. If he plunge, as Synge did, not only into the literature, the art, the music, but also into the life of the common people in such countries, his instruction will of course be bettered immensely. It is unthinkable therefore that an Ascendancy man after coming thus in liberal contact with European life would not come back to a reading of Irish life with clearer vision. Yet we find M. Bourgeois writing this extraordinary sentence : " His (Synge's) European learning did not hamper his perceptions of Aran life, or of

Irish life at large." [1] But M. Bourgeois, though learned in Ireland and its ways, is for all that a foreigner, and so is to be forgiven. Of course it was Synge's European learning enabled him to look at Irish life without the prejudices of the Ascendancy class coming in the way. For Goldsmith his European learning did no more than make available for literary traffic, if one may say so, his memories of such intimations of immortality as fell upon him in Irish valleys and beneath Irish rooftrees. He never came back to those childhood scenes, nor did he ever dream of writing of them for an Irish public : for all that, these recollections of his youth are the native salt that keeps his work fresher and saner than that of any of his contemporaries—more modern too, for Europe in teaching him the value of the homely in literature had democratised him far beyond the uses of his day in England. But Europe in helping to remove the prejudices from the vision of John Synge did really more for him. These prejudices removed, he should be clear-sighted then ? Yes, but from clear-sightedness to warm affection is a far cry. The scientist's eye is very different from the lover's. It was Europe cleared his eyes of the fogs of prejudice, not entirely of course. It was Nationalism however that lit the flame of love within them ; and the second change could never have taken place only for the first.

The ingrained prejudices of the Ascendancy mind are so hard, so self-centred, so alien to the genius of Ireland, that no Ascendancy writer has ever succeeded in handling in literature the raw material of Irish life as, say, a sculptor handles his clay. From old intimacy the sculptor's thumb assumes a quickened sensibility as the clay heats upon it ; the clay seems to master him ; it leads him on ; this he is to do, and not that. But what if he despise the clay ? If, taught of the centuries, he fear its contact, instinctively withdraw from it as one does from a stuff that is not only slimy but treacherous ? No Ascendancy writer has ever succeeded in creating a living picture of Irish life : *Castle Rackrent*—

[1] *John Millington Synge*, by Maurice Bourgeois.

which, to repeat, is the best thing they have done—is of
course a picture of the English in Ireland. The life of Ireland,
which is the life that counts, the national life, is not for them ;
it is as deeply hidden from them as the life of India is from
the English Ascendancy there. An Ascendancy is an
Ascendancy, and has to pay the price. We recall to vision
an estate round which one of those Ascendancy families had
erected a wall ten or twelve feet high and fully seven miles
in length. As I read Ascendancy literature, such walls—
and they are everywhere in the Irish landscape—throw their
shadows across the pages. Many an Ascendancy writer must
have wished to present, under the form of art, the teeming
life he saw about him, many must have believed they had
done so. But where now are their novels or plays ? No one
casts the failure in their face ; it was not from any want of
heart or goodness or intelligence or scholarship or craft they
individually failed ; it was that the system into which they
were born made it impossible for them to succeed. Their
hands were gloved with so thickly protective a covering
that the clay would not adhere to their thumbs ; clay and
thumb were disparate. An alien Ascendancy the artist cannot
choose but loathe, it has, whether Asiatic or Roman or
Spanish or British, always been so streaked with the vulgarity
of insensibility. Such an Ascendancy is *l'étatisme*—the
coldest of all cold monsters—freed of all the kindly influences
of tradition, set loose to prey not on its own people, as it even
will, but on its enemy—*l'étatisme* therefore at its most callous,
because at its most fearful and frenzied. Its spiritual growth,
one may say, is from insolence to insolence. In the end it
produces extreme types like Sir Henry Wilson, at whom,
when they unwisely declare themselves, the world wonders.

Again, wherever there is an alien Ascendancy there is
topsy-turvydom. To deny this is the lie agreed upon in the
Ascendancy mind. When they create a literature, as in
Ireland, that lie agreed upon is the foundation of that
literature. Indeed when in spite of itself, Ascendancy
literature begins to question its own traditional assumptions—

as Standish O'Grady did in our case—the days of that Ascendancy are numbered. Yet of course the lie has been long abroad in the world, is so sanctioned by years, so adopted as sterling truth, that one almost despairs of undoing it. In that is the difficulty of presenting the Irish case ! It cannot but be taken amiss, and for two reasons. The topsy-turvydom that obtains in an Ascendancy-ridden country cannot be conceived of in normal countries that live their own life. Secondly, in the literature which the Ascendancy has for years or centuries been creating, the topsy-turvydom is not adverted to. The outsider, therefore, unless he read between the lines of this literature, is without the clue that would help him to test the whole scheme of things. The reformer who begins by saying that mentally Ireland is topsy-turvy is not listened to ; he is written down a crank, an odd-man-out, by outsiders who actually quote Ascendancy literature against him ! By the Ascendancy at home, and all their hangers on, he is made to feel that he does not play the game ; which of course is a quite correct description of him.

The moment one has the clue he will find at every turn evidence of the mental upset ; he will find it in the Dublin drawing room, in the Catholic college, in the press, in the theatre, everywhere. Take for instance the words so sane a critic as Mr. E. A. Boyd writes of John Todhunter : " He did not—he could not—wholly de-Anglicise himself, but at all events he succeeded for a time in seeing Ireland with the eyes of an Irishman." [1] One can easily imagine the casual reader passing on without adverting to the implication in these words that the whole working mentality of Ireland must be upset. Here is an account of a very decent, intelligent, Irish-born, Irish-reared, Irish-educated gentleman—if Trinity College, Dublin, be reckoned as in Ireland,[2]—who, under

---

[1] *Ireland's Literary Renaissance*, by Ernest A. Boyd.

[2] Here is the History and Geography paper for the Entrance Examination in Arts set by Trinity College in April, 1929. (A) What was Domesday Book ? What do you know about Simon de Montfort ? In what circumstances did Henry VIII become *King* of Ireland ? Give an account of Monmouth's rebellion ? Describe the movement which led to the Reform Bill of 1832. What was the Ballot Act ? (B) What is the commercial importance of the

the stress of a national movement, did for a time succeed in seeing his own country actually with his own eyes ! Swift could not have thought of a more alluring theme for an extra chapter to Gulliver. Of course John Todhunter did not long remain at normal, the strain was too great ; he went back, ' naturally,' to the abnormal and was, we are to presume, once more at peace.

Or take the same critic's telling of Standish O'Grady's awakening : " It so happened that, about the year 1872, a young student of Dublin University (*i.e.* Trinity College) was obliged to spend a wet day indoors at a country house where he was visiting. While exploring the book-shelves he came upon the three volumes of O'Halloran's History of Ireland, where he made the discovery that his country had a great past—an interesting, but awkward fact, which had been well hidden from him, in accordance with the current precepts of Irish Protestant education." Is it any wonder that such Irish Protestants as come over to the nationalist side, as discover that Ireland was and is a nation, feel all as much bitterness towards their Alma Mater as Synge ? Or take Mr. W. B. Yeats's statement, that a time comes to every Irish writer when he has to make up his mind either to express Ireland or to exploit it. It needs only to be pointed out that such a time never arrives for the English, the French or the German writer, or indeed the writers of any normal country.

Once our eyes are opened to this we cannot help but notice now with surprise, now with indignation, then with scorn or with mere helpless laughter, the topsy-turvy that is the ripe creation of centuries of Ascendancy rule and Ascendancy thinking. And all that should help us to right the wrong is so likely to be against us :

> Et l'obscur ennemi qui nous ronge le coeur
> Du sang que nous perdons croît et se fortifie !

Panama Canal ? What are the characteristics of the Baltic Sea ? What do you know about the great cattle-and-meat-exporting countries of the world ? What country exports the largest number of live cattle ? Where are Detroit, Minneapolis, Lexington, Oran, Nara, Amritsar, Lemberg, Stranraer ? Mention points of interest in connection with any of them.

What a curious study then must the literature of such a country always be !

All this is to be dwelt upon if Synge's significance in Anglo-Irish letters is to be understood. We do not say that Synge came to see the problem as it has here been stated. What we do say is that Europe, removing from him many of the Ascendancy prejudices born with him, left him open to the teachings of nationalism. How Europe might have done so has been indicated. His studies in languages gave him a feeling for the local as opposed to the cosmopolitan. This feeling is of all those he developed the most noticeable ; it breaks out everywhere in his essays ; and, after all, what is nationalism but the force that defends the local—the local custom, rich with tradition, as against the cosmopolitan, traditionless, and therefore vulgar ? He may never have identified himself with the " wild Irishmen " of Paris ; he cannot, however, have failed to see a reason in their madness far beyond what his own people in Ireland would ever have guessed at. He may never have come to the belief that the very force, nationalism, must itself be fostered, if in turn that force is to foster the local custom ; just as he may never have attained to the faith that Ireland can ever again become an Irish-speaking country. There are however many stages between one who blindly denies that there is or that there can be an Irish custom in Ireland, and one who is ready to practise many inhibitions, and to risk many ostracisms in order that the over-borne native custom may more strongly challenge its oppressor. In nationalism there are many currents, and one may be conscious of one, and favourable towards its impulse, without giving much attention to the others ; and so it was with Synge. One may behold the topsy-turvydom in local instances, without seeing it as the very ' life ' of the whole Ascendancy building ! One may gird at vulgarians without connecting them with old unhappy far-off things.

## V.

But it may be well to establish, once for all, that Synge did become a nationalist, even if he never made himself familiar with all the tenets of that faith. Of the books written on him immediately after his death most took the matter for granted, while others made no mention of his nationalism at all. None of the books, whether mentioning it or not, stressed it as of any particular consequence, none of them took the view that it was his conversion to nationalism made the difference in what he wrote before and after his visits to the Aran Islands. If we hold that that great difference is due to his conversion it is necessary to show that he was converted. Besides, in recent years when, owing to many causes, nationalism has been under a cloud in Ireland, we find it hinted that he was never a nationalist at all, that he did not believe in the Gaelic League idea, that in fact there was no difference between him and other contemporary Ascendancy writers in this matter.

To show this Mr. John Masefield has been quoted : " He would have watched a political or religious riot with gravity, with pleasure in the spectacle and malice for the folly—he would have taken no side and felt no emotion." Mr. Masefield is an Englishman, and certainly one cannot imagine Synge looking on at any political riot that could have taken place in England when these words were written—before the Great War—with anything but amusement. When however he beheld the ' forces of Law and Order ' coming to carry out some eviction in the Aran Islands—and all evictions in Ireland in these days were more or less bound up with politics—he looked on with anything but amusement : " When the anchor had been thrown it gave me a strange throb of pain to see the boats being lowered, and the sunshine gleaming on the rifles and helmets of the constabulary who crowded into them." [1] But the description of the whole incident had better be read if one would know how far beyond mere humanitarianism his anger had almost carried him.

[1] *The Aran Islands.*

Colonel Arthur Lynch, who was one of the Irish revolutionaries Synge met with in Paris, writes : " Synge was, I believe, only mildly Nationalist. I cannot speak with certainty on this point, for although he was a visitor at our house, I seem to have no recollection of having ever discussed politics with him, and it is from Mrs. Lynch that I have had the suggestion that Synge was critical rather in respect to our means of action than to our ultimate aim." [1] This point—that Synge did not hold with extremism in politics— is stressed by various writers. A friend of Synge's writes of those Irish meetings he attended in Paris : " He spoke of having met Miss Maud Gonne at Irish meetings, and that she looked like a tragedy queen, and when she spoke of the wrongs of Ireland she was like one possessed. He was interested in those meetings, but when he found that they were prepared to go any length to gain their ends, he felt he must drop out. He was not an extremist, though he told me he was immensely proud that his grand-father was one of the " Twelve Righteous Men," having refused a peerage at the time of the Union." [2] Mr. W. B. Yeats too mentions that Synge drew aside when he found that the Irish in Paris were willing to create trouble between England and certain countries in Europe, and that he believed England would not release Ireland until she could do so with safety.[3]

Now those passages prove no more than that Synge was not an extreme political nationalist. Our own idea of him is that one who seeks to find political nationalism in him is on the wrong scent ; he was not given to politics ; he was only as political as the ordinary citizen who is far more interested in other matters. What we are to understand by nationalism in his case is cultural nationalism—a holding by that inner core of custom of which political nationalism is the shield and defence. At this very time, as we shall show later on, Ireland was in one of her periodic reactions against

[1] Letter from Col. A. Lynch to *Irish Statesman*, October 20th, 1928.
[2] C. H. H. : *John Synge As I Knew Him* in *Irish Statesman*, July 5th, 1924.
[3] *Autobiographies*, by W. B. Yeats.

politics and politicians ; it was the period of the Parnell split ; it was the period when the Gaelic League was catching hold of the young vital mind of the country, was teaching it that politics and nationalism must not be confounded— with the result that practically all who hearkened to its appeal became not alone non-political but anti-political, for they held that the politicians, by neglecting such national pieties as the Language, were simply killing the soul of the country. Anybody who lived in Gaelic League circles in those years needs no instruction as to what kind of nationalist Synge was, for the land was full of such as he became. They were all young, they were all Language men, and they were all quite certain that they had the right end of the stick in their grasp ; the thing was to build up the Irish nation on its ancient Gaelic foundations. They called themselves nation-builders, not state-builders.

It may however help us if we glance at a few foreign opinions on Synge's nationalism. M. Anatole le Braz, the Breton folk-lorist and writer, met Synge in Dublin in April, 1905, and made some notes on him in his diary ; among these we find : [1] " L'homme n'a pas cette morgue enfantine qui m'a frappé chez beaucoup de ses compatriotes, aucune 'pitrerie' non plus, mais un grand sérieux, une foi profonde dans la vitalité du mouvement irlandais, un enthousiasme contenu qui, parfois, illumine le regard, affermit la voix, le sentiment aussi, général chez ses congénérés, que ce qui s'accomplit en ce moment en Irlande est un phénomène historique unique au monde et dont les fastes des autres nations ne contiennent pas d'exemple." " In the Connemara papers," writes M. Bourgeois, " he (Synge) avowedly sub- scribes himself a Home Ruler, . . . . Still he never was . . . . politically inclined." [2] And further on M. Bourgeois tells us of an inscription written by Mr. J. B. Yeats in the margin of a copy of *The Playboy* :—" an ardent Home Ruler and Nationalist . . . . yet so little pugnacious that he

[1] Quoted in *John Millington Synge* by Maurice Bourgeois (p. 65).
[2] Papers written by Synge on a tour in Connemara.

never declared his opinions unless under some sort of compulsion. A resolute peaceful man." [1] But the statement that is most emphatic and indeed most authoritative is that of Mr. Stephen Mac Kenna—the translator of Plotinus—who was one of Synge's closest friends : "As regards political interest, I would die for the theory that Synge was most intensely Nationalist ; he habitually spoke with rage and bitter baleful eyes of the English in Ireland, though he was proud of his own remote Englishry ; I take it he wanted as dearly as he wanted anything, to see Ireland quite free ; but one thing kept him quiet—he hated publicity, co-operation and lies. He refused to support the Gaelic League because one pamphlet it issued contained the statement (I indicate roughly) that to know modern Irish was to be in possession of the ancient Saga." [2]

This is conclusive ; and the point about his breach with the Gaelic League is instructive also on his type of mind. Synge was too inward, too individualistic, to be of use to any movement ; he would always have found points on which he could not agree ; but from all the statements gathered here, it is clear that, although not a politically-minded man, he had become even more politically national than might have been expected. Is not this statement also significant : " Once, when in later years, anxious about the educational effect of our movement, I proposed adding to the Abbey Company a second Company to play international drama, Synge, who had not hitherto opposed me, thought the matter so important that he did so in a formal letter." [3] And we also know that he indoctrinated his nephews with his own new faith.

But indeed to anyone who reads his book on the Aran Islands with understanding such gathering of opinions as has been here done is not necessary. For it is the book of not alone a Nationalist but a patriot. Does anyone think he could

---

[1] *John Millington Synge*, by Maurice Bourgeois.
[2] Stephen MacKenna, in a letter to the *Irish Statesman*, 3rd Nov., 1928.
[3] *Essays*, by W. B. Yeats.

possibly have written such a book about any other country in the world ? Mr. Padraic Colum, who knew him personally, who at the same time has an intimate knowledge of all things Irish, such as Synge could never have attained to, writes very justly of him when he says : " It might be said of him that at the very start of the Irish Theatre he brought us a way of looking at life that belongs essentially to the Gaelic tradition. His plays were denounced as being alien to Irish life and to the Irish mind. Those who denounced them in these terms were wrong, and they were wrong because they knew nothing about the Gaelic tradition as it has been expressed in poetry." [1] In the same book he further writes of him : " John Synge's work augments the spirit, and it augments it by discovering and revealing to us the national virtue. He was fortunate in that he found on these roads men and women, who, however disreputable, had in them something of the national virtue ; who had something of the same outlook on life as he had, and who had a speech through which elemental humour and poetry could once more be expressed." Of what other Ascendancy writer could such words be written, if not of Dr. Douglas Hyde, who of course had become a convert to nationalism in his very boyhood. Perhaps one may think Mr. Colum's statement too comprehensive, that he might have contented himself with saying that in his work Synge discovers and reveals to us some share of the national virtue, but then no writer is ever privileged to do more than that. The national virtue is a kingdom of many mansions, and though some national writers may be freer of the kingdom than others, none of them can ever succeed in interpreting to us more than a few of the constituent mansions. With that we must be satisfied.

## VI.

This individual and that other may have had something to do with Synge's conversion to nationalism ; if so they

[1] *The Road Round Ireland*, by Padraic Colum.

were but so many gospellers of the new revelation that was in their native land. The only minds in the country that were not touched by the new learning were either those of the very aged or minds inveterately political, the Irish Parliamentary Party on the one hand, and the opposed minds of Ulster on the other. All others, except the utterly frivolous, it is safe to say, came to a greater or less degree under the spell of Irish Ireland in the years from 1898 say, to 1914.

Ireland is a passionate country : like the face of a passionate man it is either dull and expressionless or else ablaze with vision. That in itself, of course, is the effect of long years of spasmodic revolt ; it is part of the general topsy-turvydom. When Ireland is quiescent the custom that lies upon it, " heavy as frost and deep almost as life," is not its own custom, it is England's ; so that Ireland has always been most provincial when most peaceful. To dissipate, even momentarily, that English custom, an extraordinary rise in temperature is necessary. In the throes of revolution, from 1918 to 1923, more books were written and published, more pictures were painted, more schemes of all kinds started into growth, than in any previous or subsequent period of the same length. Life is life. But alas, in those moments of vision,—comparatively speaking, they are seldom more than moments—the amount of actual art work created is only relatively large, and its quality only relatively good, for the necessary mental equipment is not at hand ; the slow upbuilding of a native art tradition has not taken place ; scholarship has not been fulfilling its duty during the long preceding hours of gloom, has neither been examining the national literary moulds, for instance, nor assessing whatever art work is natively our own ; has failed therefore to play its part in clarifying, strengthening, and equipping the national mind. Ireland had no existence, for instance, for Professor Dowden, who, in the dull years before the Gaelic League arose to wrestle with the English custom, was so busy with his Shelley and his Shakespeare. If he had looked at either from an Irish point of view, as, willy-nilly, a German would from a German point of view, or a Frenchman from a French point of view, then he might have made some little preparation towards Ireland's better self-expression when the stormy moment of vision was once again come round, for so working he would have been strengthening the Irish custom and keeping the moulds clean. Ireland was not helped by such scholars as he ; nor was it much helped by its politicians. They, from O'Connell to Parnell, were not nation-builders in the sense that a nation is simply a multiple custom ; though of course it is true that each partial victory they won did make it possible for what still remained of the national custom to defend itself with more confidence than before. The fact is we contented ourselves with politicians when our need was creative statesmen. They would not have lacked a sense of proportion ; they would have seen that it was the entrenched English custom that all the time was more than anything else stultifying and smothering the national virtue, not only making it impossible for it to express itself in national pieties and works of art, but depriving it even of the very desire to express itself at all. What was wanted was a succession of such men as Thomas Davis who saw that many other agencies as well as politics should be brought to bear upon our case if the Irish custom was to be levelled up mentally and socially to the English custom as we know it in Ireland, was to challenge it, and to pluck from it first its insolence and then its stability.

Now Synge's great good fortune was that with his mind opened up by contact with many peoples and many cultures, he happened on Ireland at a time when Davis's spirit was abroad in the land : the Irish custom was being brought in from the enshrouding hills, where it had lain forgotten and enfeebled by neglect, was being newly assessed, interpreted, ministered to, affectioned. Its ministrants, its chivalry, were the youth of the nation who had grown up while their elders were, consequent on the Parnell debacle, bitterly at one another's throats.

D

The best-founded national movement that had overtaken Ireland since 1685 was in its first vigour when Synge, at the bidding of Mr. W. B. Yeats, came home from Paris. Already in 1892 the Irish National Literary Society had been established. Seven years afterwards this society gave birth to the Irish National Literary Theatre which in course of time became the institution we know as The Abbey Theatre. But the institution that most significantly manifested the pressure of the time was, of course, the Gaelic League. Once for all, that body made clear to every vital mind in the country the fact that we were engaged in a struggle between two customs—the Irish and the English. It instructed us as to what nationality really was ; that it was a matter of culture rather than politics. Whether it believed it or not it taught us the modern doctrine that race is rather the effect of culture than culture the effect of race. It taught us that politics could and should provide and maintain those channels through which nationality utters its message—important task, yet meaningless unless there is a message to be uttered. The Gaelic League was non-political, absurdly so in such a land. If we remember right, a branch of the Gaelic League in Cork that desired to call itself the Robert Emmet branch was not allowed by headquarters to do so ! And the League officially was not more non-political than the individual members of it ; they were not only non-political, they were anti-political, for they held that the politicians had lost the sense of direction and were leading the nation to perdition. Yet, as everybody knows, it was this same League that came out in Rebellion in 1916—this League of bookworms and students at whom the politicians were wont to jeer.

National movements are a necessary evil in every land where an alien Ascendancy has driven the national virtue into the distant glens. They are impulses towards the normal. In Ireland whenever such a movement once more undertakes the task of pitting the native custom against the foreign, we discover once more how rich and varied that native custom is, or was, while intact. If one of the Gaelic

League's most gifted children spoke of it as the most august tradition in western Europe his enthusiasm is not to be scorned, for who will name a greater ? In those years the Gaelic hinterland was little by little being opened up to our astonished eyes ; and now after more than thirty years we know that we are still engaged in only clearing the ground. If we who were Irish and not Ascendancy were surprised by the vision of this Gaelic hinterland of ours, with its immemorial mythology and literature, so rare, so native, so intrinsically beautiful, the revelation cannot but have been astounding to those few Ascendancy folk who had had the courage to turn their backs on the idols of their market-place and give heed to it.

The intensity of that revival may be tested in this way. We can take George Birmingham's latest novels and compare them with such books as *Northern Iron*, or *The Seething Pot* which he wrote while he was a member of the Gaelic League. Or we may take some of Mr. Lennox Robinson's latest ' international ' plays and set them against his early plays or his short novel, *A Young Man from the South*—which is indeed the story of a young Protestant who comes into contact with the national tradition ; or we may compare Mr. St. John Ervine's latest plays with those he wrote when Ireland was the only country he knew ; or such books as the late Darrell Figgis wrote in England before he had come under the spell of the Revival, with *Children of Earth*, which he wrote in Ireland under its influence. In the last-mentioned example there seems a positive access of genius ; in all the previous examples we feel that the writers have now become mere craftsmen who are earning their living by writing. The light in their hearts is quenched. None of those mentioned was a Catholic ; yet all their ' revival ' books show a genuine desire to explore rather than exploit the life of their own country. Considering the way the life of their country had been scanted by its writers, that of course was their duty ; on that duty they have since turned their backs ; whether in deserting their country for the whole English-speaking world their pens have assumed new powers of expression or even retained the old, one is not at all certain. One fears that a future critic will write of each of them as Mr. E. A. Boyd has written of John Todhunter : " at all events he succeeded for a time in seeing Ireland with the eyes of an Irishman." He who will make such comparisons as are here suggested will have some understanding of the nature of the revival that was then in the land.

This was the period in which John M. Synge wrote his works. Even had we no evidence from himself or from his friends as to his conversion to nationalism, we could almost with certainty deduce it from what we know of the condition of the land to which, aged, say, twenty-seven, he returned. If all or practically all the writers of his time were travelling in a certain direction, it is not presumptuous to suppose that he also came under the same influences. To know, as we know, that he was the only one of them who took the trouble to learn Irish so well that he could freely converse in it with native speakers, to know also that he was the only one of them who took the trouble to make himself familiar with the details of the peasants' lives, is to know how much farther he went in his nationalism than the others.

## VII.

Now conversion to nationalism in Ireland is a very different thing from conversion to nationalism elsewhere. An Irishman wonders what meaning that phrase can have for the natives of normal countries. He suspects it cannot possibly have the meaning for them that it has for him. In the first place there is no such thing as nationalism *qua* nationalism : there are, however, such things as Irish nationalism, English nationalism, French nationalism, and so on. Each is a force similar to the others, but each has its own peculiar sanctions, its own native emotional content, its own historic momentum. To form any idea of the momentum of such a force one must needs know the obstacles that have been opposed to it, the blows struck against it, the hate it has engendered in others To feel its emotional content one must reckon its lovers, and the songs they made for it with dying lips. For its sanctions one must search for its origins : does it take its rise in some Agreement, Concordat, Treaty, of which we can name the time and place ? Or are we conscious that its origins will never be known, that we come upon it as upon some natural thing—a torrent flowing headlong from the hidden recesses of crowded mountain ranges that never can be explored ? Such a force therefore is not to be reckoned according to the extent of territory after which it is named ; it is of course a quasi-spiritual essence.

Now, the conversion of one of Synge's type to Irish nationalism means really the winning over of one who would in the natural way of things hate everything really Gaelic so bitterly as to be ready and eager to debauch the national tradition, the very pulse of which is the desire for freedom, wherever and whenever opportunity offered. For Synge would certainly have had affinities with that class of which Standish O'Grady—himself one of them—wrote such bitter words : "At Ireland and all things Irish you girded till, like the doomed suitors, you are forced to laugh with foreign jaws as this beggar nation, ragged and mendicant, whose substance you devoured and whose house dishonoured, springs like the revealed demi-god of yore upon the threshold and twangs the new-strung bow." [1]

We do not know how Englishmen, Frenchmen, or Germans can intimately understand such words : they lack the local instance. No Englishman knows what it is to be so actively anti-English as to be ready to debauch the national tradition that others too may be brought to disrespect it. He may deem himself a citizen of the world ; even so, he is not more set against English nationalism than against any other. He can never understand how provincial, how protestant a creed

[1] *Ireland and the Hour : To the Landlords of Ireland*, etc., by Standish O'Grady.

the Ascendancy folk in Ireland developed in themselves after the Union.

Enough has perhaps been said to give the outsider to understand that conversion to nationalism in the case of an Ascendancy man in Ireland means far more than the giving up of one set of opinions for another. It becomes a change more of heart than of head. It is a rebirth. A nation with its memories is a fount of inspiration ; to come to drink of the waters of that fountain is an experience little less than mystical. We do not say that any outsider, such as Synge was, ever succeeds in coming into perfect communion with the race mind : this he suspected himself ; it was a trouble to him. We do say, however, that Synge came at moments into surprisingly intimate communion with it ; of this his play *Riders to the Sea* makes us certain.

VIII.

It may be thought that we are lingering too long on this conversion. It was, however, the most significant event that ever befell him ; only for it his literary remains would not only be quite different but would be quite without distinction. And we have lingered on it also for the reason that our thought in writing on him at all embraces those others who went the same road a little way and then turned aside, as also those others, now setting out on their labours, to whose turn it will surely come, it cannot but come, to choose between the same two roads.

In his conversion to nationalism, his own personality came into play. That personality had much to do with deter-mining into which of the mansions of Irish nationality his feet should stray. In Mr. Lennox Robinson's sprightly story *A Young Man from the South*, the young Protestant who undergoes such conversion learns to write successful plays for the Abbey Theatre, but also, and quite naturally, as anyone who knows Ireland will admit, plunges into the storm winds of Irish politics. It might so have happened with Synge if he had not been the man he was.

Picture him : the boy, one of a large family, left, one thinks, much to himself, not robust enough to join in the usual games—and how much that means in the development of a boy's character !—driven in upon himself, finding solace in nature and the wild,—companionship that does not betray. He takes to music also, the most social of the arts, yet it was for himself and not for others he was accustomed to play ; nor does his time in Trinity College help him to overcome his shyness in company, his desire to sit silent and unnoticed. One feels that no sooner was the long vacation at hand than he resumed the lonely-wandering boy in the Wicklow hills. He was emotional, instinct-led ; and sought affection not from his intellectual equals but from others like himself, hearts fundamentally simple.

The stranger, however much he scorns or rails, cannot wound such a one, but the friend, with but a questioning glance, can pierce his heart as with a sword. Always therefore desiring affection yet always afraid of it, such a one wanders with his dog and mumbles snatches of lyric poetry to himself as he makes across the hills. All softness in a certain sense, yet untameable also, and through his aloofness and his power of seeing the comedy in men and things, gaining the name of hardness ; yet whoever knew a person really hard in character to be susceptible to loneliness ? No, if Synge was such as we imagine, it is not the politics, naturally part and parcel of Irish nationality, that would coax him to its service ; rather is it the folk, the Gaelic-speaking peasantry, with their immemorial lore, their aloofness from the modern world, their simple life ; for going to them would be for him a way of extending the passions that warmed his breast in boyhood. In the country of the Irish-speaking folk, apart from the modern world, out in the sea, hidden like Moy Mell in an ' incomparable mist,' was a hinterland more strange than any he could remember having dreamt of while young. It was a hinterland not only in space but in time. And it would be his own : who else had interpreted this folk ? He would do for them what Loti had done for the Bretons. In some such spirit, probably, he went to the Aran Islands. He remained long enough to be troubled with the thought that he could never become more to the islanders than a stranger. This trouble he openly cries out again and again. It is the ' cry over the abyss ', the forlorn wail of the tribeless. Because he raised it, he differed from his fellow Ascendancy men.

It was the living tradition in the possession of the Aran people that most impressed him. He was unbookish by nature. He was a man of the open air and the roads, learning much from the vernal woods. He knew literary Irish : we find him reviewing Keating's poems, not an easy book ; he probably had some fair knowledge of Old Irish, could, with the help of a translation, read the ancient stories ; but though from those old stories and from Keating's poems to the folk tradition is a far cry, yet it is to the living tradition he gives his whole heart. Dr. Douglas Hyde's *Love Songs of Connacht*, which is little more than the living tradition set down in print, was ever in his hands : it influenced him as much in one way as Loti in another. Of the older literature one finds traces, naturally, in his *Deirdre of the Sorrows*—its bleakness, its spirit of denudation, but then what is his version of Deirdre, taking it as a whole, but a transliteration, so to speak, from literature to folk-lore ? That is how it feels if one come to it fresh from a reading of the saga in the Irish. The fact is that even in literature he wished to have about him only such unsophisticated hearts as he would willingly make speech with on a country road.

His going to the islands in the spirit he did fell in with the deepest traits in his own personality ; it also fell in with the spirit that was then in the land. That was a Gaelic spirit. It was, as we know, Mr. Yeats who sent him to the islands, yet, wonderful to tell, it is Mr. Yeats himself who has given us the craziest interpretation of that pilgrimage. " It was, as I believe, to seek that old Ireland which took its mould from the duellists and scholars of the eighteenth century and from generations older still, that Synge returned again and again to Aran, to Kerry, and to the wild Blaskets." The interpretation is so characteristically wrong that one shrinks from adding a word. The Gaelic tradition *moulded* by the bucks of the eighteenth century ! One is sorry that Synge himself did not live to read the words.

## IX.

But one may wish to look at the man as he appeared to other men. "He was then about twenty-six," says one who knew him before he had become a playwright, "a strongly-built man with a rather thick neck and large head, a wonderful face with great luminous sad eyes, and though he was tanned from being constantly out of doors, there was a sort of pallor on his face that gave it a look of delicacy belying his figure, which was that of a hardy mountaineer." [1]

Commenting on this description Mr. Padraic Colum writes : "I first met him when he was seven years older. His face was grey ; he had kindly hazel eyes, and he wore with his moustache a little chin tuft ; his brow went up steeply, and he had strong hair that was neither black nor brown. In a way he was like Fritz Kreisler—less couth, less vivacious, wearing rougher clothes, but still as like as a brother might be who had gone, not on to the platform, but into the study." [2] Farther on Mr. Colum tells us "he kept neither aloof nor apart, but in a city of people who talked eagerly, he, with that modelled head of his held so well up, and with his air of a foreign student, was noticeably quiet and unassuming. He was not like any poet I have known."

Colonel Lynch, who, as we have said, knew him in his Paris surroundings, writes of him : "With his huge frame, and

[1] C. H. H. in *The Irish Statesman*, July 5th, 1924.
[2] *The Road Round Ireland*, by Padraic Colum.

enormous head, he seemed hardly to belong to the somewhat decadent world of these latter days, and in recognition of this fact he had a modest and even gentle and pleading air." [1]

" The head was large and massive," writes another, " with long, dark—rather brown than black, almost auburn— tossing hair. Synge looked much older than his age. The swarthy complexion of his grave, deeply-lined face, with delicacy and pain written over its expression, and a force of iron will peeping out through the hazel-grey eyes, seemed to ' put on ' years to his appearance. The cheeks were drawn and seamed, the jaws square-set. The bushy moustache partly concealed the wide mouth, on which there was a great play of humour. The chin was clean-shaven, but for a little tuft of hair, smaller than a goatee, and answering rather to the description of what is known as a " smeg " (" smeggeen," " smiggin ") in Anglo-Irish. The voice was hoarse and quick and often difficult to catch, with hardly any mellifluous Irish brogue in it." [2] And M. Bourgeois further records that Mr. G. Bernard Shaw once said to him that ' Synge had a face like a blacking brush ; ' while Thomas Mac Donagh tells us he bore a strong resemblance to certain portraits of Oliver Cromwell.

Perhaps the most living portrait of him is found in the notes M. Anatole le Braz wrote in his diary : " La figure de Synge est typique : une tête longue, un peu carrée, aux traits tourmentés et, par moments, quasi douloureux, pas belle, mais singulièrement expressive. La moustache châtaine voile à demi les lèvres épaisses ; une manière de goître enfle le côté droit du cou. Il se montre d'une courtoisie charmante, pleine d'aménité, de douceur, légèrement timide. L'intelligence est ouverte, accueillante." [3] " He was," says Mr. Yeats, " a solitary, undemonstrative man, never asking pity, nor complaining, nor seeking sympathy but in this book's momentary cries : all folded up in brooding intellect, knowing

---

1 Letter to *Irish Statesman*, 20th October, 1928.
2 *John Millington Synge*, by Maurice Bourgeois.
3 *John Millington Synge*, by Maurice Bourgeois.

nothing of new books and newspapers, reading the great masters alone." [1]

"A silent, an aloof, a listening man ! Listening to and watching all that which had never been completely his, and from which he should soon be parted. He would stand on a headland that jutted steeply on the sea, and he would look and look and look at the sparkling waters below. He would look at a meadow, a sunset, a man, as though he must satiate his eyes with their wonder, and, if it could be, saturate his very being with all that he should not carry with him." [2] With this last description we ought all surely to be content : it is the man.

## X.

Then one should like to see this silent, brooding, emotional creature in the surroundings through which he passed on his way to the grave.

Of his wanderings in the woods and on the hills of Wicklow as a boy intent on moths and beetles,—intent on all things both great and small—" he knew the note and plumage of every bird and when and where they were to be found "— we must make our own picture. One thinks that it was only when he reached manhood that he began to look at the vagrants, so numerous according to his own statement in that county, with as alert an eye as he had previously given to the irrational beings of the same habitat.

"His true schooling " says Mr. James Stephens, with complete understanding, " was up in the mountain and out on the bog ; it came from the shy but vital life that moves in solitudes. His professors were the mountainy men and women, themselves almost as humble in station, almost as sundered from change, almost as bereft of ambition, but as

1 From Preface to first edition of John M. Synge's *Poems and Translations*.
2 *I Remember J. M. Synge*, a talk broadcast by James Stephens from London, 15th March, 1928.

vital, persistent, self-centred as was the lowly animal life that throve about them." [1]

Neither have we any definite account of him as a student in college, from which circumstance we may take it that he was not one to attract attention to himself, either by natural brilliancy, or natural or put-on freakishness. And of his subsequent wanderings in Germany, before he made his home in Paris, all that M. Bourgeois can say is : " He was the guest of some ladies living on the banks of the Rhine, and is said to have led a free, unconventional life in those days, listening to stories in the Harz and the Bavarian woods, making friends with servants and poor people, and more than once sleeping out under a hedge or in a farm or hay loft." [2] One likes to know of his attraction towards servants and poor people, it is so characteristic of the man who after-wards lived gratefully in the huts of the poor in the Aran Islands. C. H. H., in her recollection of him, says : " He told us a good deal of his visit to Germany, and was, I remember, collecting roots of ferns to send to some people there who had been kind to him." [3] Of that ' good deal ' one wishes that C. H. H. had reported even a little. To her, however, we must be thankful for her notes of him at this time. Of Synge and his brother she writes : "As a rule during the day we saw little of the two young men, who used to go off early with a few sandwiches to fish in the little mountain tarns or walk the hills which were then covered with heather or gorse, but in the evenings John Synge used to join us. . . . . That was the time for talk, and John Synge used to expand and discuss Art and Poetry. I remember him saying to me he preferred Wordsworth to any other English poet ; he said he was more at one with Nature. . . . He said there was a purity and simplicity about Wordsworth's poetry that appealed to him strongly. Then he talked about Art and told me he loved Corot's work,

[1] *I Remember J. M. Synge*, a talk broadcast by James Stephens from London, 15th March, 1928, and printed in *Radio Times*, 23rd March, 1928.
[2] *John Millington Synge*, by Maurice Bourgeois.
[3] *Irish Statesman*, 5th July, 1924.

and later one day in Dublin, he took me to see a little gem of his, which was in a loan collection. . . . Sometimes while we were sketching out in the woods near Castle Kevin we would hear him playing his violin like some fairy fiddler, and one afternoon in the drawingroom he played for me a lovely wild melody of his own. . . . . Sometimes we went to the National Gallery or some picture exhibition ; sometimes to sit for an hour in St. Patrick's Cathedral and just drink in the beauty of the dear old place." Here surely we have the picture of a young poet, and here perhaps is the place to cry out our thanks that that young poet in some strange way, while perfecting his craft, had not only skipped over London but skipped over Dublin as well—that is, the literary set in Dublin he would most likely have fallen in with, with their crazy hunt after cleverness and cynicism, and their aloofness from the profound and common interests of life. When he did come on them later, he had his own ideas to steer by. At this time Synge, one thinks, had not yet become nationalist. Later on in the same notes the writer speaks of hearing from him in later years of his contact with the extremists of Paris. This passage we have quoted. Still farther on we have : "At this time he was writing a good deal, and shortly afterwards went to the Aran Islands. After that I only saw him a few times. Once after his return from Aran he said : ' Oh, I wish you could go there, you would love the Island people.' "

After Germany he settled down more or less in Paris ; and of his way of living in that city we have been given many interesting glimpses. There he lived now at one address, now at another, always very cheaply. " He lighted his own fire and cooked his breakfast—two eggs, which he boiled in a paper-bag long before paper-bag cookery had any official existence. When he could not afford Duval or Polidor for lunch, he would buy York ham or *veau piqué* at a *charcuterie* in the Rue Vavin. He went but rarely to *tavernes à prix fixe*, which he found utterly repugnant, and often warned his friends against the practice of shilling meals. He drank thin tea in bowls and smoked *caporal*, rolling his own cigarettes and always using a cigarette-holder. In the evening, but never later than ten, he would discuss the whole universe with friends over a glass of hot punch ; for, though he had but little conversational powers, he was an excellent debater ; or (when he could afford to permit himself luxuries) he went fairly frequently to concerts, cafés and theatres." [1] We know that here also he visited Notre Dame, looking on at the ceremonies, was a frequent visitor to the picture galleries, sought out those quieter portions of the city not known to tourists, and generally laid himself out to absorb the life of the place as afterwards he was to absorb the life of the Aran Islands. Yet how great a difference in the results : the heart as a lantern is so different from the mind.

It was while living at the Hôtel Corneille—a place much frequented by Irishmen—that Mr. Yeats said to him : " Give up Paris ; you will never create anything by reading Racine, and Arthur Symons will always be a better critic of French literature. Go to the Aran Islands. Live there as if you were one of the people themselves ; express a life that has never found expression." [2]

Of Synge's stay on the islands as of his previous and subsequent wanderings in Kerry and Wicklow we have his own accounts. These are invaluable ; one thinks his book on the Aran Islands has not been estimated at its proper value ; since however we shall be examining it later on we need not delay here on any one of its many and very beautiful vignettes. What we regret is that we have no record of any worth from the islanders on the strange, silent fiddler who had come to their shores. ' Of any worth,' for records we have, none of them written, however, until the first performance of *The Playboy* had caused ' riots ' in Dublin and Synge had been proclaimed from the housetops as the worst maligner of the Irish people that had yet arisen. The

---

[1] *John Millington Synge*, by Maurice Bourgeois.
[2] Preface to the First Edition of *The Well of the Saints*. (*Essays*, by W. B. Yeats).

statements gathered under such conditions from simple people are of course of no value.

Before he had ceased to visit the islands he had entered very heartily into theatre work in Dublin. He was one of the first Directors of the Abbey Theatre, which opened its doors on December 27th, 1904. In collaboration with Mr. W. G. Fay he rehearsed and produced the plays. "He was a careful producer," we are told, "and before his plays saw the light of publicity he would know all the effects he wanted, and how each word he had written should be recited. In fact, he generally had the text off by heart, and repeated the sentences aloud over and over again till he got the turn of phrase he wished for, and the word-music right."[1] At this period he was probably happier than he had been ever before. Though arduous, what work is pleasanter than producing plays, however meagre the equipment, when the actors themselves are alive and not merely paid hands? Besides he was conscious of his own genius, he was still young enough to feel that he was to do what had never yet been done ; he was moreover alive to the great awakening that was in the land, not only alive to it, but felt that in it he counted for something. Then began the tragedy whose nature lay so far outside the dramaturgy he had fashioned for himself—the tragedy of conscious growth of strength in the mind congruent with failure of power in the body. Some cancerous disease had attacked him. He went into the Elpis Private Hospital. He came out of it in May, 1908, thinking that an operation had been performed, whereas the doctors had merely closed up the wound when they saw the disease had gone too far for them. It was probably now that Mr. Padraic Colum saw him for the last time, as he says, " He was going out to Kingstown and I walked with him to Westland Row Station and sat with him for a while on the platform. He had been in hospital ; his face was hollow, and although he spoke quietly there was great intensity in his speech. He was working on *Deirdre of the Sorrows*, and

[1] *John Millington Synge*, by Maurice Bourgeois.

he had, in spite of his illness, got down to the third act. He began to tell me about this act : there would be an open grave on the stage : I spoke doubtfully of the impression that this would make—would it not be a too obvious heightening of the tragic feeling ? But he said that he had been close to death, and that the grave was a reality to him, and it was the reality in the tragedy he was writing." Convalescent, as he thought, he went to Germany. While there his mother, to whom he was greatly attached, died at home in Glenageary. Soon he was back in hospital again. He was gentle and liked by all. He destroyed many letters and poems the day before he died. That same day he had himself shifted to another room, wherefrom he hoped to catch a glimpse of the Dublin mountains of his boyhood rambles. He found this was not possible and was greatly distressed. He died next morning at 5 o'clock. It was March 24th, 1909. He was buried in Mount Jerome cemetery, Harold's Cross, Dublin. ' Illustrem vatem parvula terra tegit ! ' Donncadh Ruadh cried out when he saw his friend Tadhg Gaedhealach laid in the grave.

# CHAPTER III.

## THE WRITER

ALL that Synge left us in the way of criticism—if we omit his stray articles and reviews—is contained in three short prefaces, six pages crammed so close with matter that they elucidate his entire creative work. Taken together those three prefaces make a clear exposition of his ideals in literature. Two of them we find in his book of plays, the third in his book of poems. Since, however, for him, drama was entirely a matter of literature—he would not have admitted that a playwright might lack the sense of literature yet write, or at least contrive, very effective dramatic works— the prefaces to the plays may be taken together with that to the poems, if we wish to learn from himself how he looked at the writer's craft.

Each of these prefaces is a defence of the work which it opens. *The Playboy* preface is dated January 21st, 1907; *The Tinker's Wedding* preface, December 2nd, 1907; and the preface to the *Poems*, December, 1908. Written all within two years they naturally do not contradict one another; and his whole literary life, including those two years, covering only about seven years, his practice on the whole agrees well with his preaching. Essays, plays, poems, and prefaces are all the outcome of one short period.

### I.

In the preface to *The Playboy* he defends chiefly the use of rich and copious language. In countries, he says, " where the imagination of the people, and the language they use, is rich and living, it is possible for a writer to be rich and copious in his words, and at the same time to give the reality, which is the root of all poetry, in a comprehensive and natural form." He complains that we now find richness only in sonnets or prose poems, " or in one or two elaborate books that are far away from the profound and common interests of life." Mallarmé and Huysmans produce such literature as this, but the writers who deal with the reality of life, Ibsen and Zola, confine themselves to the use of joyless and pallid words. In noting such facts he is really inquiring whether one cannot have both reality and richness in the same book. In the theatre, he states, one *must* have both. " On the stage one must have reality, and one must have joy." In Ireland—where we have still " a popular imagination that is fiery, and magnificent, and tender,"—the dramatist has a better chance of wedding reality with richness than dramatists in other places " where the spring-time of the local life has been forgotten, and the harvest is a memory only, and the straw has been turned into bricks." This relationship between the drama and life as lived in a particular time and place, he expresses elsewhere in the same preface in the words : "All art is a collaboration," and when he tells us how he picked up phrases for his drama *The Shadow of the Glen* from some servant girls he used to overhear through a chink in the floor, he makes us aware of what he means by collaboration.

In the next preface, that to *The Tinker's Wedding*, he tells us that the drama is serious in so far as it gives the nourishment on which our imaginations live. Here he protests against the idea that only those plays which deal with social problems—such plays as Ibsen had written—were serious plays. " The drama, like the symphony," he says, " does not teach or prove anything." He defends humour as one of those things which nourish the imagination.

In the third preface, that to the *Poems*, he complains that while poetic diction is condemned by everyone, poetic material, using poetic in the same special sense, is condemned by no one. " The poetry of exaltation will be always the highest ; but when men lose their poetic feeling for ordinary life, and cannot write poetry of ordinary things, their exalted poetry is likely to lose its strength of exaltation, in the way men cease to build beautiful churches when they have lost happiness in building shops." Farther on : " In these days poetry is usually a flower of evil or good ; but it is the timber of poetry that wears most surely, and there is no timber that has not strong roots among the clay and worms." . . . " It may also be said that before verse can be human again it must learn to be brutal." What he meant by human verse we deduce from a previous paragraph where he states that much of Coleridge and Shelley is inhuman.

## II.

What is to be said of the trustworthiness of those ideas of his ?

His idea of what was fitting language for the dramatist we shall not discuss just now. That put aside, we may dare to restate his creed in some such way as this : The thing is to create a work of art that will nourish the imagination, such a work as one will go to with a foretaste of excitement and joy, the feeling opposite to that we take with us to a bout of preaching. The work must produce a sense of exaltation. This however it cannot do unless it deals with the profound and common interests of life. It must be rooted in reality.

More shortly still, his idea of literature was : an imaginative treatment of the profound and common interests of life so that exaltation might result.

This view, when he expressed it, contained a double protest. It protested against the current idea that only problem plays were serious plays ; as also against the divorce of poetry, including the poetic drama, from the ordinary life of men and women. In other words he sided neither with the theories of Mr. Yeats nor with those which Mr. Edward Martyn shared with Mr. George Moore. Those three men were at the time putting their hands to the movement that has since crystallised into the Abbey Theatre. The future theatre, would, in Mr. Yeats's thought, look for its material in national legend ; a huge wealth of Celtic mythology and folklore was at hand, quarries unworked, almost inexhaustible. With his gift of being wrong whenever he looked into Ireland's future, Mr. Yeats wrote : " Our plays will be for the most part remote, spiritual, and ideal." [1] Mr. George Moore and Mr. Edward Martyn indulged a different dream. Social and psychological plays dealing with Irish life they hoped to see the future dramatists attempting. Mr. Moore had already written *The Strike at Arlingford*, and Mr. Martyn *The Heather Field*. Of those two opposed tendencies—the poetic drama, the social drama—in the movement, Synge was thinking when he wrote his prefaces.

They do no more than reinforce the protest in his plays. His *Deirdre of the Sorrows* is a protest against both A.E's and Yeats's plays of the same name ; and his *Playboy of the Western World* rather outrageously protests against Martyn's dramatic visions of the Irish countryside. The poetic dramas of A.E. and Yeats he would bring close to earth ; the conscientious social plays of Martyn he would make joyous with imagination.

This double protest of his we can bring under one heading : he could not stand what he thought of as artificial literature. And his use of the word artificial would not be a mincing use. Wilde's social plays are worlds away from Ibsen's, yet Synge, one feels, would have had no more liking for *Lady Windermere's Fan* than for *Ghosts*. One he would hold to be impossibly aloof from the profound and common interests of life ; the other, lacking all poetry, could provide no nourishment for the imagination. A serious dramatist would not have written either. At the time he wrote his prefaces, Ibsen was being opposed in many quarters. Synge's opposition stood apart from that generally made : it was his style of writing he condemned : it was his matter the others blamed him for.

One wonders if he would have put A. de Musset's comedies under ban ? In them there is the depth of true poetry, yet little of its warmth ; and casually looked at, with their

1 *Ideas of Good and Evil*, by W. B. Yeats.

*nocturne*-like feeling, how artificial they appear—the low tones, the careful phrasing, the rather formal antics, the lack of wholesome laughter. Yet it is not easy to decide how Synge would have taken them, for they are rich in passages he could hardly forbear from liking : " Hélas ! tout ce que les hommes se disent entre eux se ressemble ; les idées qu'ils échangent sont presque toujours les mêmes dans toutes leurs conversations ; mais, dans l'intérieur de toutes ces machines isolées, quels replis, quels compartiments secrets ! C'est tout un monde que chacun porte en lui ! un monde ignoré qui naît et qui meurt en silence ! Quelles solitudes que tous ces corps humains ! " [1] One thinks he could hardly have read this without at least wishing to translate it into his own idiom. Professor Mair finds some share of ' innocency ' in Synge's characters ; and in many of Musset's characters one discovers the same quality expressing itself however with so different a tongue : in both cases of course it is not true innocency at all, as becomes clear when we recall to our minds the tale of Aucassin and Nicolette or the pictures or sculptures of the Middle Ages. This feeling in both Synge and Musset arises from their own personal desire to turn the back on the commonplace round about them. Yet in spite of this strain, common both to Musset and himself, one still thinks he would have thought *Fantasio* and its companion plays too far removed from the profound and common interests of life to be true art. So too with Maeterlinck : that strange atmosphere which those half-breathed ' No's ' and ' Yes's ' and 'Ah's ' and ' When's ' in his plays induce in us would not compensate Synge for the very watery blood that courses through the veins of those who utter them. Would he have admitted that the Belgian dramatist should be allowed to reduce language to its simplest elements for the sake of atmosphere, if he himself, for the sake of spirit, were allowed to swell it up with gaudy nouns and adjectives ? How easy it is to say a style is artificial—when it is not our own style. Artificial or

[1] *Fantasio.* Act i.

not, one thinks that both Musset and Maeterlinck have something of the true timber of poetry in them ; and, after all, artificial is a brickbat that has been flung at Synge himself.

For a start, then, we may think of Synge as one who cared neither for the poetic drama that Mr. Yeats would have encouraged, nor the social drama that Mr. Martyn looked for ; but neither would he have relished, one thinks, either Musset or Maeterlinck, not to mention Wilde.

### III.

It is however to the intrinsic value of Synge's ideas rather than to the protest they once carried that we should give our consideration.

To conclude, as he did, that the drama was serious inasmuch as it provided nourishment for the imagination, that if it greatly nourished it it was greatly serious—was that a helpful thought for himself ?　All conclusions fervently come to, all resolves, help us forward, at least for the time being : they are a draught of refreshment, a light to our feet ; but the energy they awaken in us may be so short-lived, and the light so false.　Was this theory of his one to urge him to more earnest exploration of life ?　Was it one to deepen the breath, to steady the nerve, so that the whole of life might be surveyed ?　Or was it rather one likely to induce a certain recklessness, or shall we say, wilfulness, into his outlook ? And might it not mean much self-limitation ?　It is clear that such a theory must influence in all directions the working dramatist—in his search for material, in his delimitation of it when found, in his handling of it ; in, indeed, his whole outlook both on art and life.　One thinks it would leave whole realms of human character dull, almost abhorrent, to him ; while, one also thinks, it must urge him to direct his creative energies towards the stimulation of one faculty in his audience, instead of towards the harmonising in a higher plane of all of them.

We can pamper one faculty at a time ; but even while we do so, it is not possible ever to forget the others : they struggle and growl by fits ; and that writer who raises from the depths of the ordinary workaday humanity in us, his public, a wallowing spirit on the one hand and a protesting spirit on the other seems wanting in open-eyed sanity. All artists possessed of strong creative power are of course tempted towards the imaginative view of life and art ; yet to yield to such temptation is for them to create art work not only narrow in its range but peculiar. The dramatist vacates his throne when he asks us to bring with us to his theatre only one faculty, not all. We cannot do so even if we would. But the great dramatist does not ask us to do so. Sitting before *Oedipus the King* or *King Lear,* or *Tartuffe,* plays that in their imaginative reach would surely satisfy Synge himself, are we asked to make no judgements whatever ? And judgements issue from the reason, not from the imagination. Are we asked to think that the moment our minds begin to refer phrases or incidents or appearances in the play to real life, to things actually heard, witnessed, experienced, judging them in the light of the play, judging the play by them, our minds are gone awry, become absent-minded as it were ? When the piece of art has worked its spell upon us, is inciting us to make such judgements, to attempt new evaluations, is it the dramatist's part to whisper us that his tale is after all out of *The Arabian Nights* and that our terror-inspired, pity-inspired, eagerness is vain and must be clubbed down ? Surely no ; for if not a dramatist, it was at least a great poet who held that it was at such moments we saw into the life of things. Is æsthetic pleasure preliminary to seeing into the life of things or is seeing into the life of things preliminary to æsthetic pleasure ? or if in the midst of our æsthetic trance we begin to see into the life of things has our pleasure become impure ? Or is it that we are to see into the life of things without knowing it ? Or again is seeing merely seeing and not judging or revaluing ? Can we see with all our powers yet judge not ? Or is the

dramatist not to foreknow that this miracle may happen ?
Or is he to take care that he does not lend himself to its
happening ?　And is he to hold that if the subject he selects
is, from its own deep-hearted nature, likely to lead to this
willy-nilly judging and revaluing, such subject he must put
aside and choose other matter, such matter as we find in
*The Tinker's Wedding,* in the preface to which it is we find
this statement we are considering ?

But a little farther on in the same preface Synge, as if to
clinch the argument, states that the drama like the symphony
does not teach or prove anything.　It is true that in this
connection there is no difference between the drama and the
symphony.　If by teaching we mean adding to the stock of
our acquired knowledge, the drama certainly no more teaches
than the symphony.　But what if we take teaching to include
the inciting of desire to make new judgements, and, furthermore, the ability to make them, however that ability is
attained to (it may be by throwing whole libraries of information suddenly to the winds) ?　Surely a movement or
even a cadence in a symphony may operate as powerfully on
our spirits as a sunset touch, a fancy from a flower-bell or a
chorus-ending from Euripides ?　For us to be so translated
as even for a moment to be able to see into the life of things,
is surely to be improved ; that is, instructed, and not any
longer what we have been.　The object of all teaching is
improvement, and great art, willy-nilly, achieves that object.
What the dramatist or musician has to remember is that
great art cannot help teaching, and that for him wilfully to
prevent his own work of art from doing so is to practise
abortion or to present a maimed child to the world, however
wildly hilarious that child may be.

The drama or symphony cannot be certified as didactic
simply because it improves us.　The nature of the improvement is what decides the question.　If the improvement is
partial, is an increase in our stock of information, even such
information as directly influences human conduct, or an
increase of strength in our will-power, the work is didactic.

For an increase in our stock of any particular branch of knowledge may possibly hinder our looking into the life of things, such increase leading, it may be, to pedantry or even to the formation of an *idée fixe*—which, of all weaknesses, are those that real art would most dearly win us from : while an undue stimulation of our will-power may result in selfishness, which also may of course very effectively prevent us from looking with open eyes into the life of things. But when the improvement, however little, is shared in by all our faculties, is therefore an improvement of the whole spirit, a harmonious stimulation of all our powers, the winning to a new plane, the formation of a new set of values, then the symphony or drama that has caused the improvement is genuine art.

In this way both symphony and drama may be said to teach ; they accomplish in the grand and perfect manner what all instruction aims at : they open up new horizons, they release new powers within us. If the whole spirit is thus strengthened it does not matter how the play goes in the catalogue : it may be entitled historical-pastoral or tragical-historical or tragical-comical-historical-pastoral or what you will, but its true name is real gold. If through its agency a new plane is reached, a finer sensibility achieved, a deeper harmony experienced in the depths of our being, then something higher than either imagination or reason, born of the perfect marriage of these twain, has assumed governance over us. We then bow our heads in thankfulness, silent, as is right in the moment of miracle.

One has a touchstone by which to know such happy works, symphonies, plays, novels, or poems. It is this : Do we find ourselves drawn towards them when we are passing through or have just passed through a spiritual crisis : when we are putting off or have just put off the Old Man—when our every cell—physical and spiritual—is sensitive as the new-shorn lamb, or as the leafage of a May morning ? If only a very small portion of Synge's work stands such a testing, it is because his works were, nearly all, conceived in and wrought out in the thought that the drama was serious only inasmuch as it nourished the imagination.

IV.

It may be that Synge in so expressing himself had no other thought than that the dramatist should never attempt to jostle the preacher from his place. A right view, for the preacher may quite legitimately set out to strengthen one by one the powers of the human soul. He is fulfilling the whole duty of either day if to-day he aim at strengthening the will of his people and to-morrow seek to refine their imagination : while always the artist must deal with man as one and indivisible in his faculties. But if this, that the dramatist should not preach, was the length and breadth of Synge's thought, it is a pity that he chose to express it in the preface to, of all his plays, *The Tinker's Wedding*. That is a gaudy raree-show ; and one fears that his feeling about it was : This is an outrageous piece of work, but it must be taken as a work of art ; in fact, it *is* a work of art because of this very outrageousness. That high-coloured cheaply-imaginative gaudiness, outrageousness, which is like a stain upon so many of his pages, was not without its cause ; a cause, shall we say ? immanent in the depths of his being. That cause was his own reaction from the greyness of the world. The instant's escape from that sense of greyness was his moment of exaltation. And that his plays should bestow such happy moments on those who witnessed them was his kindly dream. How, therefore, could they be too gay with colour, or too bright with music, or too exciting with the antics of human beings liberated, like their creator, from the grey bondage of the world ? He really had no more philosophy than this, and this is scarcely to be spoken of as philosophy. In practice he did, here and there, outstep the tenets of his philosophy, which was a structure of mood rather than of thought ; and then he wrote far above what we, carelessly perhaps, reckon as his level. But generally he indulged his

mood. In the essays on the Aran Islands we find in a description of a voyage from one of the islands to another this
passage : " We had only a three-oared curagh, and if the
sea had gone much higher we should have run a good deal of
danger. Our progress was so slow that clouds came up with
a rise in the wind before we reached the shore, and rain began
to fall in large single drops. The black curagh working
slowly through this world of grey, and the soft hissing of the
rain, gave me one of the moods in which we realize with
immense distress the short moment we have left us to
experience all the wonder and beauty of the world." [1] And
perhaps there is no other passage in his works that so
immediately gives us to understand his build of character.
Not the wonder and beauty of the world as a thing in itself,
but as imagined and longed for in the midst of a world of
greyness that is fraught with inevitable and, it may be,
imminent death ! His apprehension of beauty is sudden,
fierce, ravenous : it trembles always with the excitement of
his thought that the beautiful thing that so enraptures him
is backed by an eternity of greyness into which, after a
moment, it will certainly withdraw again. " Thou wast not
born for death, immortal Bird " is a thought that never came
to him, or, if it did, was not fondled and taken into daily
companionship. His mind was like that of the soldier who
in the aftermath of battle, as also on the very eve of it, craves
for ' life '—life gaudy and violent with noise and spirit. It
was illogical of him to rail against old age, grey hairs, the
loss of beauty, or loneliness, for these were necessary to the
awakening of the mood in which alone the wonder of the
world shone ravishingly upon him. For Mr. Yeats to declare
that Synge was no mystic was supererogatory, since every
line of his work shows him to have been quite the opposite.
Inhibition of this world's phenomena is what the mystic
practises, while Synge contrariwise would fiercely hug them
to his bosom—not all of them, but such of them as in
appearance or nature strove valiantly against the dull and

[1] *The Aran Islands.* Part iii.

the featureless. The fierceness of his passion for them is due to his unforgetfulness of the vast orbit of greyness which is above them and below them and all around them, in time as in space. His characters, taking them all in all, express this heart's burden of his very adequately : his own favourites among them, even while they plunge fiercely onward in pursuit of their visionary joys, which are seldom or ever much different from what Wordsworth spoke of as ' animal movements,' cannot for all that ever empty their speech of references to old age, the fading of beauty, the advent of grey hairs, of loneliness, and death. Fundamentally they are untameable souls, dark and melancholy by nature or boisterous and wild. However, at the moment they break upon our sight, they are as perfervidly and as excitedly in reaction from the greyness of the world as Synge himself was on that stormy day in the curagh. He was of the race of brooders. It is visible in all his creations : in them he would express the opposite of the sullen depths whereinto his thoughts would fall when no excitement was at hand. However much he would have his men and women resemble not the grey sea but the bright bubbles that arise from its distress, iridescent in the flame of heaven, beneath their sporting all the time the sea is growling, intent on wreckage and death. Only once did he create a character which was not negative in its nature, which was integral—the old woman in *Riders to the Sea*. What concurrence of events, of thoughts, of reliefs, freeing him from his too great thraldom to his own moods, gave him to ally himself for once with the eternal modesty of nature in moulding out this Demeter-like figure, this fruitful mother, who can say ? He himself doubtless could not have said. But there she stands confronting the sea, the *real* sea, for ever, one thinks, while all the others act their little hours upon the stage, their parts contrived for them.

As in this case, the modesty of nature, had he only sufficiently reverenced it, would always have freed him from his self-imposed limitations. She, Maurya, of *Riders to the*

*Sea*, differs in many ways from all his other characters. The
'innocency,' which Professor Mair discovers in Synge's
characters, she knows nothing of, for unlike the others she
is not emptied of native content : she is not, like the others,
morally irresponsible—'escaped from the anchorage and
driving free.' When her thoughts hark away to other
worlds, we believe her, she speaks by her soul. But when
the others touch upon such worlds, they speak by the book ;
and we do not believe one word of what they say, not even
though they speak as, and are addressed as, saint or priest.
Their creator's powers were somehow self-strangled : they
could not range : the immodesty of the imagination, by which
Synge worked when creating them restricted, it appears,
where the modesty of nature as a guide would have liberated.
The immodesty of the imagination, curious paradox, reveals
nothing to him beyond what *caro et sanguis* reveals. The
modesty of nature, that is, his subject in its native wholeness,
integral, chastening the natural waywardness of his creative
genius, rewards him by opening the gates of life everlasting.
If it were not always so, we must startle at the strangeness
of it. The airy nothings that glow so magically in the poet's
mind can be brought to glow with the same brilliancy in
ours only when he maintains unslackeningly his grasp on
the two-by-four solidity that inspires them. It was the
knowledge of this that Dante shared with the humblest
stone-carver of the Middle Ages. But it was half-knowledge
to Synge : only once did he work humbly in the full light
of it.

## V.

To ask why Synge let this theory of the overwhelming
importance of the imagination waylay him into cheap things
when he had it in him to create *Riders to the Sea*, is very much
like asking why John M. Synge was John M. Synge. Even
had his advisers bidden him to write more plays like this
masterpiece, and fewer plays like *The Tinker's Wedding*, one
cannot feel that any good would have come of it.

It is not right for James Stephens to say he was a folk writer ; if he were a folk writer he would have attained to innocency rather than ' innocency,' which is what he did attain to. But one understands why Stephens said so. Synge was a modern writer, fairly learned in many languages ; a modern writer who, however, had come to detest all that modernity connotes. He had flung himself for comforting into the huts of the people, exposing every cell of his being to absorb that outlandish mentality of theirs, which, when the simple work of the day was over, was accustomed to make such strange holiday in folk-lore and song and fantastic guesses at truth. Folk-lore, and in general the literature of the folk-mind, is imagination at its most unrestrained. Writers on Synge have written of this and that characteristic of his mind, but one thinks that they should always have remembered that these characteristics were, if one be allowed the phrase, drunken with a new delight. If one thing is truer than another it is that Synge was more deeply moved by what he experienced in the Aran Islands than he had ever been before. One thinks that he always as he wrote his plays tried to see them through the eyes of the island people he loved. If they relished such folk songs as he had come to know in Hyde's *Love Songs of Connacht*, or if they delighted in the wild fantastic tale he had just been gathering from one of them, or if they gave their heart to that bout of coarse buffoonery he had witnessed, they surely in turn should relish this play he was making. One wonders if Synge ever so expressed it, but it comes to me, as I weld together the Essays on the islanders, the Plays, and the Prefaces, that so it may have been.

I prefer to account in this way for the general nature of his work than to attribute the air of moral irresponsibility in nearly all of it to the influence of the Ascendancy mind upon him. It is true that in Ascendancy literature the common Irish people are the comic relief ; that is their part ; moral responsibility would not go with such a part : they therefore are painted as if they were incapable of ever going beyond the teaching of mother wit. If one reads *The Real Charlotte*, Somerville and Ross's best book, or George Birmingham's funny stories, or Sean O'Casey's plays, or Charles Lever or Lover or . . . . or . . . . one knows this to be true. But Synge's work stands worlds apart from the works of these. In their works the irresponsibility of the common Irish people is a counterfoil not to Ascendancy virtue but to Ascendancy normality. Synge had no such thought. If he failed to give us a true reading of the people he would deal with, except in *Riders to the Sea*, it was not from any want of sympathy with them. His sympathy with them was true and deep ; but his range of mind was limited, and was not quite free from inherited prejudices. He saw in them what he had brought with him : he noted their delight in the miraculous, the unrestrained outbursts of emotion they indulged in ; he noted what their living so close to mother earth had made of them. He drenched himself in all the features of the physical world they moved in, but he made choice among the features of their mental environment. Of their spiritual environment he did not even do that same. Once of a Sunday morning he found himself alone in the cottage, the people having all gone to Mass : " I sat for nearly an hour beside the fire with a curious feeling that I should be quite alone in this little cottage. I am so used to sitting here with the people that I have never felt the room before as a place where any man might live and work by himself. After a while as I waited, with just light enough from the chimney to let me see the rafters and the greyness of the walls, I became indescribably mournful, for I felt that this little corner on the face of the world, and the people who live in it, have a peace and dignity from which we are shut out forever." [1] Now, if he had asked the people how they had come by that peace which so impressed him they would all have answered in the same way. We however cannot say he would have believed them ; he had his own thoughts about such matters ; but we are free to complain

[1] *The Aran Islands.* Part iv.

that having beheld this peace and dignity of theirs as an objective thing, he did not allow his mind to range freely or with sympathy over what *may*, at least, have accounted for it : a living faith in another world. In Aran there are, as everyone knows, prehistoric remains of surpassing interest. They had not even ordinary interest for Synge. To the vanished faith of the lost people who built some of them, as to the living faith of the people who on that Sunday morning left the little hut to himself, he gave no sympathy. But he gave every sympathy to the living folk-lore in which the grave islanders found relief. Therefore we say he made choice as to what in their mental background he gave attention to ; and remained cold to the spiritual. That folk-lore side was of a nature to strengthen in him what he had brought with him out of the modern world : a distaste for the mechanical, the commonplace, the didactic, a relish for the imaginative. If we hold that he did witness mentally his own plays performed before the islanders—such as he conceived them to be, emptied of most of their spiritual content—then we come to some increased understanding of the nature of his work.

## VI.

But there were other influences as well. There was not alone a narrow range of sympathies, there was his own constitutional delicacy which may well have bred in him swift admiration of the coarser virtues : daring, physical energy, high-heartedness, physical courage. Of spiritual sensitiveness he had little. In that—one regrets it—he was at one with all the Ascendancy writers, from Swift onwards to George Bernard Shaw. We can easily conceive how instinctively the islanders would shrink from exposing to the gaze of such a one the dearest thoughts of their souls. He almost quite succeeded in sounding the depths of their spirit in his *Riders to the Sea ;* and the wonder of that achievement is to us a far greater surprise than his rather reckless and wild-eyed view of the people in his other plays.

His view of imagination and the drama, then, may be understood if we recollect, first, his constitutional ill-health inclining him towards the grosser virtues and the physical strength, agility, and energy necessary to them ; secondly, his absorption in the folk mind with its bent towards the imaginative ; and thirdly, his own brooding and non-intellectual nature, with its necessarily limited range of sympathies.

## VII.

That the imaginativeness of a play was the measure of its seriousness was not however the whole of his creed. He also believed that the creative genius of the dramatist should choose for itself as material the profound and common interests of life. This idea it may be thought would act contrariwise to that already dealt with, would constrain his imagination to a jog-trot pace. But not necessarily so. The profound and common interests of life may be treated unimaginatively, as Edward Martyn had proved, or imaginatively, as Synge's own plays prove. His idea of what was fitting material for an artist had of course nothing to say to his idea of how it should be treated. His mind dictated the treatment, his heart the choice. That heart was big and simple ; and whatever is good in his work is due to it. It was his heart persuaded him that reality did not exist in literature unless it dealt with the profound and common interests of life. Drama was for him a matter of reality and joy. His imagination would see that it was bright ; his heart that it was human. It is this, the second article of his creed, that separates him from the Ascendancy writers. Only for it he had accomplished less than they, for there was not one of them who was not his superior in native mental equipment. It is true that for his special craft he had haphazardly come by a training that was not theirs, but one would be hard put to pick out any of his Ascendancy contemporaries who was not possessed of a keener brain and a wider range of ideas. It was his heart that differed. Those

F

others, had they been as fundamentally simple-minded as he, might also have come to be so moved by the national movement of their time. Not one of them but flirted with that movement ; but he alone gave to it his heart. It was through that movement he came into closer contact with the people than they : in a measure it aided him to overcome the defects of his Ascendancy upbringing, made him ever so much less of an outsider than they. Those others, outsiders, could not, even had they wished, come in contact with the profound and common interests of Irish life. Even Synge had his difficulties. But he was free of the peasant's hut if not of the peasant's soul, whereas the others had to take to literature for their themes, to the fairies and the ' demons of the air.' Synge's heart naturally made him scornful of A.E's ' skinny sidhe '—it had rather have a day's sporting with Red Dan Philly's bitch. It saved him from would-be literary Dublin's cynical attitude towards life, above all towards the life of the common people ; as also it saved him from that finicky refinement of craftsmanship in which literary workmen always indulge when no people or nation is behind them. It kept him reading Dr. Douglas Hyde while the others were making themselves adepts in the literary movements that were fashionable in London.

It was this impulsive heart of his that accounts for his slow development. Of precociousness there is not a sign in his works ; and because of the nature of this selfsame heart we may be quite certain that his early death was an untold calamity. Precocity is not capable of development but simplicity is never done growing.

More narrowly considered, it was this heart of his that urged warmth into every line he wrote. His imagery is often gaudy, but it is never cold ; even when it is mere fancifulness, it is never like Wilde's ; and it is more natural and more attractive than Musset's, although Musset's thought goes deeper. There is a surge of genuine emotion beneath Synge's writing even when his subject is harum-scarum.

He speaks of old poets like Villon, Herrick and Burns as
drawing upon all they had experienced of life; and so
assuredly he did himself. Mr. Yeats speaks of his
objectivity; Mr. Colum of his subjectivity; and those two
words we associate with mind; but what both these poets
would assert of their dead friend, each in his own way, is
perhaps more closely expressed in the word emotion. It is true
he was always subjective; because he was always emotional,
because he could not away from his own heart: the avocation
of his lonely hours was listening to its beating. It is true he
was objective, because he loved all spots of earth, all
implements of toil, all hearthsides, ditches, bushes and glens,
and birds and dogs—loved all such phenomena as were part
of the profound and common interests of the life of the
people he had come to know. But that examination of the
workings of one's own mind, which declares itself far more
certainly in relative clauses than in lyric phrases, he had no
heart for. And that keen examination of the object,
including men and women, as a thing in itself, existing apart
from our emotional life, that patient and vigorous casting
aside of first impressions, almost of last impressions, that
condensing of many phrases into the one piercing word, he
made but little practice of. It was his heart always gave
him the hint to speak. And the heart is a careless workman,
often putting the cart before the horse; wherefore, only for
his grounding in music—what discipline is severer—and his
toiling in languages and literatures, one cannot but think
that his work would have been but a shapeless mass—perhaps
not unlike Sean O'Casey's.

## VIII.

Knowing, as we now know, his attitude to literature—his
relish both of imagination and reality, his disinterestedness
in ideas, his liking for the non-moral atmosphere of folk-lore,
for the terrible sincerity of folk poetry,—one could almost
make a fair guess at the style of language that would appeal
to him. It is the lyric phrase that gives us the colour and

feel of things, liberally rather than precisely, strikingly rather than significantly, at the same time that it opens up for our imagination the most distant horizons. Although his plays are in prose form, lyric phrases, like gaudy bouquets, bestrew the pages : they are at once both his record of, and his incitement towards, a state of joyousness that cannot contain itself. His living characters are ever in a state of excited reaction against the greyness of the world, against old age, the fading of beauty, the quenching of passion ; their excitement is nervous, not spiritual : their language therefore is not secretive, such as spiritual passion religiously hides itself in, as in a reliquary ; it is contrariwise challengingly open, its music loud and shrill, with all its banners flauntingly outspread. Left to itself, the imagination will always on and on towards the farthest bourn of all qualities, seeking ever the *ultima thule* of all conceptions ; it grudges to express, for instance, mere whiteness, its acme is the whiteness of whiteness, as if mere whiteness was the norm. To say that imagination does nothing by half falls immeasurably short of the truth, since it projects all qualities into their own peculiar planes where they have in their own right unbounded sway, liberty really to be themselves ; and in that plane imagination apprehends them and would express them. Pantingly, imagination seeks to give us the very vastness of vastness, and, at the next moment, the very littleness of littleness. Synge was always impressed with this insatiable claim of the imagination to entire freedom, and was led by this conception into numerous errors of taste. He could not refrain from letting a ' good ' thing have utterance, no matter what pain might result from it. Reason can be callous for ulterior ends ; but imagination is callous for its own satisfaction. And no ulterior ends, such as the belittling of the Irish peasantry, for instance, lie behind Synge's callousness. Nothing but the satisfying of the lusts of his own imagination lies behind it. He was not a satirist ; neither was he ironic, for irony has always purpose behind it, and Synge had no intention of improving anything. His own lack of spiritual delicacy made him unaware of the wound his flippant use of holy words caused to sincere believers. The use of such words and phrases was in no wise necessary to the completion of the pattern ; and perhaps one cannot therefore help thinking that he took some illicit pleasure—illicit, that is, not æsthetic—from the surprise that he knew such phrases would produce in his audience. But we must also take account of the fact that he was himself in a state of protest against the narrow world of the theatre of his days, the four-walled drawingroom, the pallid words of Ibsen and Zola, the timid flirtations of A.E. and his Dublin school with Celtic mythology. Against all this he pitted his own vision of life in the west, a world where there are large spaces, both of time and place, in which the imagination is tempted to have its fling. He held that the language, if not the life itself, of rural Ireland had much in common with that of Elizabethan England. He had steeped himself in Ben Jonson and others of that time, was sure that some of their best phrases were snapped up by them as they fell from the lips of their own people, and he saw no reason why he should not make similar use of similar opportunities. Only that he kept no measure. That he should borrow from the folk in this manner was his all too simple idea of collaboration. Collaboration with a given people in a given time and a given place has produced all the classics in literature ; but the collaboration was far more deeply interfused than Synge dreamt of ; though one thinks of course that his practice of collaboration was more comprehensive than his statement of it. Collaboration really means the fertilizing of the whole region of conscious ideas by contact with the self-ineffable, self-incommunicable qualities of the unconscious. Already we have quoted Synge's description of his own feelings as he sat of a Sunday morning in a hut in the islands while the people of the house were at Mass. That was collaboration of the deeper kind. Is it possible to think that after such a moment of revelation he could write exactly as he would had it never come to him ? And could it ever have come had he contented himself with travelling through the land in a glassed coach, and not taken the trouble to come into some fair intimacy with the people's lives ? Travelling through our quiet midland solitudes in a railway carriage I have often thought how different an experience it was from walking intimately in these same places, knowing whose the cattle were, what fair was to come or had come, whose cottage the spire of smoke was rising from in the distance ; while all the time the nostrils were filled with the breathing of the earth and the ears with its stirrings. It is such essences of the landscape, of the people, of life itself, as will not pierce a sixteenth-inch pane of glass that makes the difference between national and what is now called international literature. In the fields—physical, mental, spiritual—of our own nation we walk abroad : through other countries we go glassed up, as it were. And another passage from Synge will perhaps clinch the argument : " This procession along the olive bogs, between the mountains and the sea, on this grey day of autumn, seemed to wring me with the pang of emotion one meets everywhere in Ireland—an emotion that is partly local and patriotic, and partly a share of the desolation that is mixed everywhere with the supreme beauty of the world." [1] Patriotic is the word he dares to use—a word his fellow-Ascendancy writers mostly smile at themselves, and coax others to smile at. There again he experienced what real collaboration means, something far deeper than the gathering of striking phrases into a notebook. We have seen a quotation from a Russian writer, Rozanov, which sums up another aspect of collaboration : " You look at a Russian with a shrewd eye . . . . He looks at you with a shrewd eye . . . . And all is said. And no words wanted. That is just the thing that is impossible with a foreigner." [2] The excitement in Synge's highly-flavoured phrases, the nervous tingle in all his words, is due to the build of the man himself, but the warmth in them is due to the fact that he had experienced such shrewd glances, and had

---

[1] *In Wicklow and West Kerry*, by J. M. Synge.
[2] *Contemporary Russian Literature*, by Prince D. S. Mirsky.

not been accustomed to such experiences. He had ceased
almost to be an outsider ; he had gained a *patria*. Yes, his
idea of what collaboration means was less than his practice
of it. His statement as to his having found his phrases in
the mouths of the people is meant to rebut the charge of
artificiality. Being live phrases, they should be serviceable.
Yet, after all, if commonness be the test of life, they are not
half so live as the pallid phrases of Ibsen and Zola. It is
best to take these phrases as an index to the state of lyric
excitement into which his conversion to Irish nationalism had
thrown him, imagination-ridden as he was. One might be
inclined to say : his conversion to nationalism as such, and
not to Irish nationality, if he himself in an enlightened mood
had not dared to use the word patriotic. Had he attempted
the same style without any such conversion, his phrases would
have been as cold as Wilde's in *Salomé*.

But whatever the fount of this copiousness of language,
this almost riotous lyricism, what we have chiefly to examine
is : Does he write as a dramatist ought ?

A dramatist has many implements at hand to help him to
communicate his message, and one of them is words. To ask
whether he uses the implement legitimately as such, or
whether he cannot help drawing our attention to the make
of trowel he is building with, is to inquire into his standing
both as playwright and man. Was not Synge's trowel too
shiny ?—a word he fancied. And moreover like that spade
James Fitzgerald, the smith, was to make for Eoghan Ruadh
O'Sullivan, the poet, had it not in it too bell-like a sweetness ?
Between its flash and its song it bedazzles and distracts us.
While looking at or reading certain portions of *The Well of
the Saints*, and *The Playboy*, one remembers Gautier's phrase :
' On chante ce qui ne vaut pas la peine d'être dit.' Sometimes indeed when the dramatist is especially annoying, one
is inclined to cry back at him in his own tongue : " If it's
the divil's job, let you mind it, and leave your speeches that
would choke a fool." [1]

[1] *The Tinker's Wedding.*

One can understand how Synge, in his lyric exaltation of having discovered a *patria* for himself, in his warmth of protest against contemporary dramatic methods, could, day after day, look on at the rehearsal of certain of his plays without cutting out many of the lyric passages in them, for it is not possible to get outside oneself. But surely it is not necessary for anyone else to sit out more than one performance of Synge's *Playboy* or Wilde's *Salomé* to make up his mind once for all that lyric phrases cannot ever be the warp and woof of dramatic speech. We find ourselves pitying the actors—and is not that enough? The poet writing these phrases, rolling them under his tongue, was revelling in his sweet toil; the choked up actor speaking them is certainly not revelling in his. Lyricism in drama has, of course, its uses; and the Greeks knew of them. Tragedy cries out for relief; and the choric passages in their plays, even while they deepen the significance of the catastrophe that is being unveiled, bring us that sense of relief. Music is music and dance is dance; and elements so shapely and so ordered, so gratifying in themselves to ear and eye as these are cannot take the place of outcry and wailing without a shifting of the planes—which thing is relief. To feel how necessary such shifting of the planes is one has but to witness a play like *Ghosts*, in which there is none. Perhaps there is a deeper reason. One thinks that a certain lyricism must accompany all tragedy in art—a ground bass so deep as to be felt rather than heard, or a flight of overtones so high that it is more like continuous shimmering than sound; for without something of this implied lyricism one can think of tragedy only as lawlessness or savagery. Nor can comedy dispense with it for long; for is there anything of which the mind so quickly tires as horseplay or knockabout fun, even when its quality is excellent? It needs a sequence of a different kind: speech low-toned and sweet: ' The moon shines bright—In such a night as this,' or that the ballet should glide across the stage. But one doubts if lyricism apart from this function of relief has any place in drama;

of which fact the theatre itself and not the book convinces
one. Reading some lyrical play, one may sometimes forget
that it is not Slender's *Book of Songs and Sonnets* one has
between the fingers ; we enjoy the trailing words, we can
linger on them even as the writer did ; and this feeling of
quiet satisfaction we carry with us to the theatre, only to
have it incontinently vanish. The theatre transforms either
us or the play. How little those phrases count for ! Are
these the words we memorized ? How unnoticed they have
passed by, as if they had lost their virtue. We sit guiltily
before the stage, we whisper ourselves the words are sweet
and, i' good faith, well-spoken ; yet somehow they are not
working upon us : the fault must be in ourselves we fancy ;
but we look at our neighbour ; and he, we unfortunately
discover, is no more enraptured than ourselves. Synge it
seems never noticed this. Such phrases he loved for their
own sake ; they gratified his spoiled imagination ; he thought
they could not be too good. But of course they can ; the
trowel can sing too sweetly and shine too dazzlingly. He
wanted each speech to be as full of flavour as a nut. Yes,
quite so, but the scene and not the speech is the unit : it is
the scene, using the word in the French sense, that must be
as full of flavour as a nut. It is the nature of the scene that
dictates the flavour of each and every speech in it ; and the
number of flavours is infinite. The true dramatist knows
this instinctively : each character with *him* speaks in the
spirit of the current situation ; yet never once ceases to be
himself ; the brain and the heart of each character remain
the same in all sorts of situations, but are never uninfluenced
by them. They may be quickened, lightened, depressed,
exalted or demeaned, grow weak or old, but they never
lose integrity. They never cease to be themselves. They
may under the stress of the situation, burst into lyricism, or
fling out snappy monosyllables, or even not speak at all ; to
assess their speeches, therefore, apart from the situation in
which they are uttered, is to work blindly. We may pick
out certain lyric passages from Synge and admire them

greatly as such, only to find that in the play they have not only little value but are even harmful. The flavour of the spices destroys the flavour of the cake.

Characteristically Synge's practice occasionally escaped from his theories at the bidding of his own sterling creative faculty. In the first act of *The Playboy* there is an example. The Playboy finds himself for the first time in his life the object of a handsome girl's praises.

> PEGEEN (*standing beside him, watching him with delight*)— You should have had great people in your family, I'm thinking, with the little small feet you have, and you with a kind of a quality name, the like of what you'd find on the great powers and potentates of France and Spain.
>
> CHRISTY (*with pride*)—We were great, surely, with wide and windy acres of rich Munster land.
>
> PEGEEN—Wasn't I telling you, and you a fine, handsome young fellow with a noble brow ?
>
> CHRISTY (*with a flash of delighted surprise*)—Is it me ?

' Is it me ? '—there is a full-flavoured speech ! Yet of lyric quality there is nothing in it. But we all share the speaker's surprise, we share in the half-incredulous, half-delighted lift of the brows ; we, too, sit up ! The speech requires an actor : when none is at hand, we create one in our brain.

And just at the end of the play we come on this. His father (Mahon) has freed the Playboy from the ropes with which the Mayo men had bound him :

> MAHON— . . . . but my son and myself will be going our own way, we'll have great times from this out telling stories of the villany of Mayo, and the fools is here. (*To Christy—the Playboy—who is freed*)—Come on, now.
>
> CHRISTY—Go with you, is it ? I will then, like a gallant captain with his heathen slave. Go on, now, and I'll see you from this day stewing my oatmeal and washing my spuds, for I'm master of all fights from now. (*Pushing Mahon*)— Go on, I'm saying.
>
> MAHON—Is it me ?

' Is it me ? '—the self-same phrase ! And again it is as full of flavour as a nut, but how different a flavour ! The phrase is right in both cases : no other collocation of words could serve so well ; nor is there need to go further to prove our statement, that phrases are not to be assessed apart from the situation in which they occur.

That creative urge which is in all his work, not always of course working at its maximum, maintains something of dramatic reality in all his scenes, lyric as well as non-lyric ; but who can reckon how often that urge is wilfully slowed down, chilled, choked up ? Yet it is also to be remembered that the scene is seldom struck cold in the sense that so many of the scenes in Wilde's *Salomé* are killed ; for unlike Wilde's, Synge's imagination was wont to make holiday in the fields of life, in the fields of one especial time and place, and not in the twilight meadows of literary asphodel. In emotional content those phrases of Synge's are richer than Musset's, if the insight in them be not so deep. For what he praised in Herrick, Burns and Villon, is true of himself ; his imagery is personal, at once objective and subjective, for the reason that it is emotional, as if he remembered only those things he gave his affection to. The images he uses have been not only observed by him but lived by him. Tennyson noted the colour of things, the shapes, the similarities, and worked his notebooks into his poetry. Synge may or may not have done the same, but one feels that he wrote them in his heart as well as in his book, and that with the warmth of the heart still about them they served him in his plays. His imagery is as concrete as that of the Bible : and only familiarity with the life dealt with enables a writer, nay forces a writer, to allow the subject so to declare itself. His gift was that which Pater praised in Wordsworth : the habit of impassioned contemplation. It is that gift which separates him from the recognised realists. Synge observed only what sent warmth along his heart ; but your true realist observes chiefly, and notes best, only that which sends there a warmth whose nature is perverse. Because of this impassioned contemplation it is that Synge's imagery is never devoid of emotional value even when that emotional value is not always of the temper required from the particular speaker in the particular situation. " I'll be getting my death now, I'm thinking, sitting alone in the cold air, hearing the night coming, and the blackbirds flying around in the briars crying to themselves, the time you'll hear one cart getting off a long way in the east, and another cart getting off a long way in the west, and a dog barking maybe, and a little wind turning the sticks." This perfect distillation of an Irish evening by the roadside is true to the situation in which it occurs ; but it also lives in its own right as a snatch of lyric music. Synge, like Hardy, was one to notice such things as the carts getting farther and farther away, and to record them in his heart. It is many years now since I first came on these words : and how often since, going about the roads in my own corner of this land, they have recurred to my memory—not oftener Sappho's lines about the evening star. That is what comes of impassioned contemplation—the only kind of contemplation which really serves the ends of art, inducing quintessential life in it. If this be true, we have come on further confirmation of the thought that an element of lyricism is necessary to all drama, for such contemplation issues naturally in music and in song.

Synge therefore is not a realist as the word is usually understood. He wrote of the virtues he loved—the grosser virtues—courage, high-heartedness, daring, rather than of the vices he despised—which is a rough and ready test. He did not, like the older Ibsen, set himself to examine the social structure for the purpose of exhibiting its defects. Because he wrote ever of what he loved, his work may live far longer than that of men reckoned cleverer. He was not a conventional realist, but he was a truer realist than such, inasmuch as he looked a little deeper into the life of things. As dramatist he might have much better imparted to us his recollection of his moments of vision, if only his methods were neither so wilful nor so lyric. But we must not let this flash and this song of his put us off the track: what here we need to recognise is: that all his work is instinct with genuine emotion. It is hard therefore to understand Mr. Forrest Reid's complaint: " The dramatic movement has produced Synge, who was an artist but certainly not a great writer. His sympathies lay too exclusively with what is exceptional for that. ' In a spirit of any fineness human things inspire but two feelings: admiration or pity '—*Les choses humaines n'inspirent que deux sentiments aux esprits bien faits: l'admiration ou la pitié*—(Anatole France, *La Vie Littéraire*)—and it is partly, but only partly, because these sentiments seem to me to be almost completely absent from that intense, hard, narrow, bizarre talent—and I say this quite remembering *Riders to the Sea*—that I think we do it an injustice in claiming for it more than it can carry." [1] We hold that beneath Synge's work there is genuine emotion, and we do not understand how this emotion can be anything else than the result of admiration and even of pity. It is not because he chose to present us with hard-grained people, like the old man in *The Shadow of the Glen* or even the old woman in *Riders to the Sea*, that he had not much feeling for them. As for his more freakish characters: had Cervantes no admiration, no pity, for Sancho as well as for the Don? Like Cervantes, Synge had such a genuine feeling for reality that it would not allow him to soften the edges, but this presentation of his subject does not carry with it any contempt of his subject. That his sympathies lay with the exceptional is a charge often brought against him, yet his own reply would have been that his sympathies were as broad as the profound and common interests of life, and had no other bourn. His sympathies were not with the exceptional; they were too overborne by the pressure of his heart for such a charge to be true. Where are the exceptional among his characters? They are no more exceptional than Molière's. The Playboy himself is, when all is said, rather a likeable piece of stuff: we are glad to learn

[1] *W. B. Yeats*, by Forrest Reid.

that he did not really kill his da. Synge's eye in the short period with which we have to deal was certainly somewhat earth-bound, was taken with the gaudy, leaving vast spiritual tracts of human life unvisited, but there was nothing inhuman in his genius. And it is this aptitude that seems to us to sum up Mr. Forrest Reid's complaint. It is curious that it is the same complaint of inhumanity that Synge brings against Shelley and Coleridge—writers with whom Mr. Reid would have more sympathy.

It was Synge's nationalism gave his heart the hint to speak in this way. It kept him close to Irish earth. Open his plays anywhere and there is the Irish countryside spread before us—wide and windy acres of rich Munster land or the plains of Meath or the mountains eastwards from Aran or the Wicklow hills,—the Irish landscape, and it thick with weather—mists or frosty stars or rain or sunshine, or the Irish seas with the strength of the Atlantic beneath them. How much of his imagery is referable to those roads he loved, the furry glens, the hills ! And how the native salt keeps it fresh ! Without this wholesome love of Irish earth his imagery might have become dainty, refined, literary. It remains an imagery, not as significant as Yeats's later imagery, nor as personal, yet it is far more spontaneous, and one does not hear the scraping of the file in it.

### IX.

His sense of reality—which is really the quality in him that the Belfast sentimentalists cannot abide—makes humanly valuable then his imaginative outpourings. But one does not maintain that his sense of reality and his imagination worked always in harmony. His love of colour, of sound, often enticed him beyond the modesty of things. So too his sense of rhythm far too often calls attention to itself. Blank verse rhythms become so frequent in certain portions of *The Playboy* that unconsciously, by dint of reading them, we find ourselves forcing certain likely-looking sentences into blank verse moulds  There is not a character in the play we can quite trust to speak prose from beginning to end. Widow Quinn startles us with a Miltonic strain : ' From Binghamstown unto the plains of Meath ! ' and old Mahon, who had so little of the *gentilesse* of poetry in him, has ' picking cockles till the hour of death.'

Note the end of this line—' the hour of death.' It would be no small task to reckon the number of times Synge used this favourite cadence of his. In three pages of *The Playboy* we come on it more than twenty times : to bring in this close he kept at hand a set of counters which in the end he used almost mechanically, as if he hardly knew he was doing so : ' the dawn of day,' ' the dews of dawn,' ' the noon of day,' ' the dead of night,' ' the noon of May,' ' the fall of night,' ' the moon of dawn,' ' the fall of dark,' ' the fogs of dawn,' etc., etc.—and among this set of counters he had of course certain favourites, ' dawn of day,' and ' stars of night,' being perhaps the two he affectioned most. Every musician, however, has his own chords and his own dying falls, and there are places in drama where a little pinch of opium does but little harm.

A graver fault, of course, is the choking of the actor for the sake of a full ending, though indeed his love of gaudy adjectives is often as much to blame as his love of pattern. It needs no small knowledge of breath control to speak this sentence : " It's little you'll think if my love's a poacher's, or an earl's itself, when you'll feel my two hands stretched around you, and I squeezing kisses on your puckered lips, till I'd feel a kind of pity for the Lord God is all ages sitting lonesome in His golden chair ; " [1] or this : " If the mitred bishops seen you that time, they'd be the like of the holy prophets, I'm thinking, do be straining the bars of Paradise to lay eyes on the Lady Helen of Troy, and she abroad, pacing back and forward, with a nosegay in her golden shawl." [2] In the heyday of passion the Playboy may well grab at more than his hand can hold : incoherence is not,

[1] *Playboy of the Western World.* Act iii.
[2] *Playboy of the Western World.* Act iii.

however, the fault one finds in such passages, but simply that they are not truly passionate at all. At such times Synge is attempting the impossible : he will have the intensity of delight, the ecstasy, but he will also have copiousness and lusciousness of language, forgetting that ecstasy is spare of speech. In such places his love of colour dims the vision. Against those two loves of his, colour and sentence-patterns, his dramatic sense had often to struggle violently. The trailing sentence-pattern is seen at its best in his books on the Aran Islands and on Kerry and Wicklow. In these one finds variety and subtlety, and one can rest on them for better enjoyment ; a thing the headlong rush in a play forbids. Perhaps the prevailing note with him is a reflection of Loti's ' wailing grace,' as Thomas Beer described it.[1] Indeed there are pages in Synge's prose works where one might fancy oneself to be reading *Pêcheur d'Islande* or *Figures et Choses Qui Passaient*. That ' wailing grace ' is found of course in excess in *The Shadow of the Glen ;* while in *The Well of the Saints* it slows down the current of the whole work almost to lifelessness. Against the time he wrote *The Playboy* he had, one thinks, begun to weary of it, for in that play the dramatist is constantly asserting himself ; and in *Deirdre of the Sorrows*, his unfinished play, the note is only rarely heard. The Elizabethans and Hyde's *Love Songs of Connacht* had come to his aid.

The somewhat nerveless rhythms of Loti Synge applied to a living speech ; but that living speech had also of course certain characteristics of its own which equally appealed to him. He found in it what Dr. Douglas Hyde with his books of folk poetry had taught him to look for—a directness, and an absence of the merely literary. It is admitted that it was Dr. Hyde who created this Anglo-Irish speech, the writers who followed in his path, Lady Gregory and Synge, loosening it out, so to speak. Loti's ' wailing grace ' and the strangeness of the English of the Irish peasant with its Irish constructions and, in certain districts, numerous survivals

1 Quoted in *Portraits : Real and Imaginary*, by E. A. Boyd.

from Tudor English—these two are the foundation stones of Synge's way of writing. Afterwards he came to add 'the verbal debauch' of Elizabethan literature. Naturally in the plays we find only echoes from his preoccupation with Loti while the prose books remind us of him on every page. Or perhaps we should say that it is chiefly the more descriptive pages in these books which remind us of *Figures et Choses Qui Passaient* and *Jérusalem* and *Pêcheur d'Islande*. In those pages which are not descriptive, which have something dramatic in them—and the dramatic note is hardly ever to be found in Loti—we come, perhaps, on the influence of Borrow. Here is an example :

"One evening, on the high ground near the Avonbeg, I met a young tramp just as an extraordinary sunset had begun to fade, and a low white mist was rising from the bogs. He had a sort of table in his hands that he seemed to have made himself out of twisted rushes and a few branches of osier. His clothes were more than usually ragged, and I could see by his face that he was suffering from some terrible disease. When he was quite close he held out the table.

'Would you give me a few pence for that thing ? ' he said. 'I'm after working at it all day by the river, and for the love of God give me something now, the way I can get a drink and lodging for the night.'

I felt my pockets, and could find nothing but a shilling piece.

'I wouldn't wish to give you so much,' I said, holding it out to him, ' but it is all I have, and I don't like to give you nothing at all, and the darkness coming on. Keep the table ; it's no use to me, and you'll maybe sell it for something in the morning.'

The shilling was more than he expected, and his eyes flamed with joy.

'May the Almighty God preserve you and watch over you and reward you this night,' he said, ' but you'll take the table ; I wouldn't keep it at all, and you after stretching out your hand with a shilling to me, and the darkness coming on.' "

97

G

This is pure Borrow. It has the romantic excitement, the hurry, the touch of exaggeration that are his characteristics. In Synge himself there was something akin to both Loti and Borrow. Or it may be that it was they who had trained his eyes. Borrow himself quested with the eager eye of a healthy boy in a strange countryside : in the telling of his adventures the salient he made more salient. But the salient had lost all attraction for Loti, he had travelled over such wide spaces : it was the quiet tones he rested his eyes on, and in the recording of his pleasure he dimmed them even a little more. Synge, too, deeply felt the charm of a countryside, especially if the scene breathed melancholy : that melancholy he could well depict for us with wailing words. Let however a couple of tramps heave themselves above the horizon and his pulses quicken towards a new life ; the dramatist surges to the surface.

Taught of these masters, Dr. Douglas Hyde, Loti, Borrow, and afterward Ben Jonson and other Elizabethans, he created from the living speech about him an idiom which has won universal praise. It is only when one compares it with the peasant speech used by his predecessors in Anglo-Irish letters, or with contemporary efforts in England and elsewhere to give the peasant utterance in his own idiom, that one becomes fully aware of its distinction. Synge's speech is more unified than theirs, has been more thoroughly kneaded by a more strongly creative spirit. It does not please everybody, such philologists for instance as taken too much by their own trade, resent the creative process in language ; and of course there are blunders in Synge's 'Anglo-Irish' which displease everybody, for instance, the frequent use of the Perfect— 'I've been'—a phrase never heard from the peasants ; as also a way of using 'should' unknown to them, 'Naisi should be stale and weary.' But these are only small points, Synge's memory betraying him. There have been writers who never made such errors, Kickham for instance, but those writers hardly ever achieved distinction in their dialect passages, for the simple reason that they had no keen sense of style.

Only pedants will examine such writers as Synge phrase by phrase, eager to convict them of inconsistency. One can pick out passages where dialect is laid on somewhat too thick and slab, but in the choicer places it is certainly a beautiful speech and deserves the praise Mr. E. A. Boyd has given it : " It is evident that Anglo-Irish is to Synge a medium in which he has obtained absolute freedom, he uses it with the same effect as the Elizabethans used English. The savour and freshness of a language that is still unexploited, the wealth of imagery and the verbal magnificence of the Elizabethan tongue are felt and heard again in *The Playboy of the Western World.*" [1] Professor Mair praised it even still more warmly : " He had at his command an instrument of incomparable fineness and range in the language which he fashioned out of the speech of the common people amongst whom he lived. In his dramatic writings this language took on a kind of rhythm which had the effect of producing a certain remoteness of the highest possible artistic value. The people of his imagination appear a little disembodied. They talk with that straightforward and simple kind of innocency which makes strange and impressive the dialogue of Maeterlinck's earlier plays." [2] A French writer even more warmly still : " Mais Synge est le premier qui éleva vraiment le dialecte anglo-irlandais—dont Lady Gregory s'était déjà remarquablement servie—à la dignité de langue littéraire. Il fit pour l'Irlande au vingtième siècle ce que Dante avait fait pour la langue en Italie au quatorzième." [3]

While agreeing with those writers as to the value of Synge's achievement, one is at the same time conscious that Synge would have outgrown this style. It is his folk period style, one feels, and it is not really Synge's own style. It is a transition style. The ease with which it can be parodied shows that it is a style in the making, not made. Had he lived longer, won gradually from the nationalistic fervour

[1] *Ireland's Literary Renaissance*, by E. A. Boyd.
[2] *English Literature : Modern* (Home University Series), G. H. Mair.
[3] *L'île des bardes*, by Simone Téry.

that possessed him, won anyway from the folk-mind obsession which held him, he would probably have evolved a speech not unlike Mr. Yeats's own, or even like Mr. George Moore's : one thing at least is certain, a spirit so strongly creative would not have lacked for a medium.

How much under the sway of the living mind of the people he had come is evident not only in the more overt features of his work, but is also to be felt in unimportant details. It was his custom not to make any effort to give the pronunciation of his dialect by phonetic spelling : most writers of dialect in English have followed him in this : there was one word however which Synge often wrote phonetically— ' divil.' Who that knows our people will hold that he did wrong in thus breaking his own rule ? He also uses ' paralatic,' but in this case the word properly spelled would not convey the right meaning.

Admiration for Synge's dialect, as we have seen, has been expressed openly by foreign and native writers. Foreign musicians have been freely expressing admiration for the arrangements of Irish airs that are now going out from Ireland : they have said that they know no folk music so sympathetically arranged. In earnest endeavour to explore our own place names we have also done pioneer work of some value. In all these endeavours—the raising of the spoken speech into a literary language, the arranging of our folk melodies, the explaining of our place-names — a nationalistic impulse has directed the effort. The national virtue of the country had been laid astray, *perdu*, in some wayside cavern : only the temerity of lovers could reach to it and rescue it. In all cases the Irish language was the key to the cavern.

## X.

Synge's feeling for character was simple : the subtleties, the inconsistencies, the apparent contradictions that may lodge within the one cranium he made no search after. The finer types were beyond his ken. For the *Brands*—those who for the sake of an ideal will lacerate not only their own flesh but that of those they love—he had no feeling, if indeed he had ever become aware that such types existed at all. Had he lived long enough to write a *St. Joan,* he would have made the saint even a more ' gamey ' sort of person than Mr. Shaw has, for his sense of the spiritual was just as odd. He could conceive of character clouded over by a mood, but apparently not stiffened by a faith. It is curious to note how his eye, which seems so sterling when it seeks after the inwardness of a landscape, is almost inept, or at least easily satisfied, when its traffic is with human character. One cannot imagine him writing even a second-rate novel. Perhaps a gradual winning away from his folk obsession, perhaps that schooling which suffering brings, would have in riper years brought him dissatisfaction with such simple readings of the human soul as he had made. One cannot tell. We must accept what he did. The rather boyish or even tomboyish types he chose accord with his own outlook on art and life : they suffer from no physical aches or pains, and are untroubled with conscience ; only the natural virtues they are aware of. In none of them is any delicacy of mind, any willingness to deny themselves, any sensitiveness to the claims of the spirit as against those of the flesh. The riddle of the universe they read, as did that returned island girl Synge had met : Everything is queer ! Queer, however, only when their romping time of youth is interfered with. They are all very much the same. " I wouldn't give a thraneen for a lad hadn't a mighty spirit in him and a gamey heart," says Pegeen in *The Playboy of the Western World,* and in these words she utters the whole law and the prophets as far as her creator is concerned. " But you've a fine bit of talk, stranger, and it's with yourself I'll go," says Nora Burke in *The Shadow of the Glen,* and if we add the fine bit of talk to the gamey heart, we have the type to which Synge gave all his affections—folk imaginative and adventurous. Nora Burke herself, the Tramp in the same play, and indeed also the old man, her husband, there's something of the adventurous spirit in them all. They will not abide where they are. They must after the gamey heart and the poetry talk. In *The Well of the Saints* we find Martin Doul, his wife, although perhaps to a less degree, and Molly Byrne, to be all of the same kindred. Mary Byrne in *The Tinker's Wedding* in spite of her years is as game as ever she was : she breaks into ribald song, and would not surprise us if she broke into ribald dances as well. She might have mothered at least three-fourths of Synge's characters. The *Playboy* at his entrance is immature ; but perfected, what is he ?—master of all fights from this ! And his tongue has also learned a trick or two. Pegeen without her own gifts could of course never have brought such transformation about. She is the child of Michael James, who might have fathered all that old Mary Byrne might have mothered. Deirdre is Pegeen's true sister, and Owen, in the same play, true brother of the *Playboy* with a little more of old Mahon in him than has Christy, his true-begotten son.

Little else do they possess, except their tomboyish spirits. By the fitful light of their unruly hearts they live. The only evil they fear is the quenching of that light. Old age may quench it, bringing not lack of love so much as lack of lovers. Nothing matters only the retaining of their good looks, by virtue of which their lovers may be retained. They are a natural crew, almost a naturalistic crew. Yet, surprising us, Mr. Howe can write : " If he had lived, he could not but have added to the number of his plays ; and yet in the six plays he has left us, what that is essential in life has he failed to include ? "

We find inelasticity of mind, then, in the creator of those oft-repeated character patterns. And we find a want of depth in his treatment of the patterns. He is himself become free of the physical hinterland from which those characters emerge : they bring with them its winds and rains, its fogs, its fall of night, its moons and dawnings, because Synge has been with them in the open. To a certain extent he shares their mental background, he has taken the trouble to write

down their local histories, their memories, their folk-lore.
But their spiritual background—this he not alone ignores
but almost denies. One would not object so much if they
had not been peasants, and Irish peasants at that. Because
of this lack of sympathy in their creator, they come to us
not only more or less emptied of spiritual content, but peculiar
in their gropings after what they have lost. To those who
know them better than Synge they act strangely and speak
strangely too. They are not at one with themselves ; they
are not homogeneous. One thinks Synge did not very
earnestly seek to know their beliefs ; and in Irish peasant
life there are so many features to set the outsider astray. In
almost any Irish countryside one can hear a good deal of
banter that verges on blasphemy, or at least so one might
imagine ; the plenitude of that banter however, and the
terms in which it expresses itself, are in themselves but so
much implicit testimony to the strong religious consciousness
of the people. Of recent years that religious consciousness
runs rather to pietism than to moralism ; and this perpetual
banter in which holy names and religious terms may be tossed
about, almost recklessly one thinks, is the obverse of the warm-
hearted piety of the folk. . . . I am in Macroom. I see
an old man, half-cracked, making a speech, more or less
political, to a laughing crowd. I inquire who he is : I am
answered in tones of surprise, as if I might have known :
' Why, that's St. Joseph ! ' If there is one saint more
beloved than another in Ireland it is St. Joseph. ' Poor
St. Joseph ' he is called for very love. Synge would have
drawn his own inference from the people's willingness to
nickname a cracked old man St. Joseph just because he had
a long beard. And that inference would have been wrong.
An Irish teacher tells me he went recently to an old woman
he had been told of as a treasure house of Irish folk-lore and
poetry. 'Are you always alone ? ' he said to her. 'Always,
except for the God of Glory and His Blessed Mother, and
what company could be better ? ' But that old woman
would not have answered every one in that strain. Synge

of course did not fail to see that side of his people ; he did little or nothing however to make his own of it ; and indeed he may well have distrusted his own powers of dealing with it. Anyway to leave it out is the Ascendancy convention. It is because he did scant it that one is inclined to agree to some extent with Mr. Lynd's description of Synge's characters as decorations. To his scanting of it is also due much of that ' innocency ' which Professor Mair finds in them. Of his neglect of the spiritual background which his type of character demanded, Synge would probably have taken Martin Doul's apology as his own : " I'm thinking it's a good right ourselves have to be sitting blind, hearing a soft wind turning round the little leaves of the spring and feeling the sun, and we not tormenting our souls with the sight of grey days and holy men, and the dirty feet is trampling the world."

His elimination of Catholicity from his men and women has naturally been noticed by Continental rather than by English critics. M. Maurice Bourgeois writes : " One would never suspect on reading these essays, that the Irish country folk are Christian worshippers whose religious feeling is often carried to an absurd excess of superstition and almost to fetishism. To Synge the Irish peasant is a latter-day Pagan, on whose old-time heathendom the Christian faith has been artificially and superficially grafted." [1]

' These essays,'—but he might as surely have added : ' and these plays.' And Mme. Simone Téry writes : " C'est l'esprit du plus pur paganisme qui souffle dans l'œuvre de Synge. Il semble qu'à travers le Christianisme il ait retrouvé l'âme primitive des anciens Celtes. . . . . Lui-même ne voit dans le paysan irlandais, sous la couche superficielle des rites catholiques, qu'un païen qui s'ignore." [2]

It may be objected that to stress this shortcoming of his in dealing with all the facts—and the Catholicism of the Irish peasant is a mighty fact—is to examine his men and women

[1] *John Millington Synge*, by Maurice Bourgeois.
[2] *L'île des bardes*, Simone Téry.

not as such but as Irish men and women. Well, he did not choose to write plays about international stock and share brokers or political chiefs or commercial magnates, in whose lives, it is taken for granted, not altogether rightly, the spiritual must wither away under the pressure of the business of the day. He chose on the other hand to deal with simple men and women living in the Irish countryside where the clock gives ample time for long prayers and long meditations. His plays are mostly comedies, it is true, and one does not look for mention of prayer or meditation in such : in them one is satisfied if such an atmosphere is not created as outrages not only what we know of Irish peasants but of peasants in general, for whom the skies have not been emptied of their heavenly powers. If in a writer one finds the peasants emptied of their spiritual content how can one maintain that the profound and common interests of their lives have been the subject matter dealt with ? Obviously it is not the profound interests of their lives that have been dealt with.

It is not quite true to say that Synge's characters have no spiritual background. They are however allowed to have only a child's gaudy idea of the spiritual ; which is little better than none. They make use of holy names for effect, as a Dublin minor or even major poet might, and so bring in an artificial atmosphere, the trifling air of literary padding. Now, there is obviously one of Synge's plays which in this matter of the spiritual, as in many other matters, stands apart from the rest. That is of course *Riders to the Sea*. This play we shall discuss in its turn, but here it is necessary to deal with it if only to complete our survey of Synge as a writer. In all the others there is a certain gaudiness about the chief characters, but in this there is none. The characters in the other plays are non-moral ; when they refer to other worlds they speak for effect, but when old Maurya in *Riders to the Sea* says : ' May the Almighty God have mercy on Bartley's soul,' there is a feeling quite different. Only in one line in *Deirdre of the Sorrows* is the same amplitude invoked : ' Keep back, Conchubor ; for the High King who is your master has put his hands between us.' This is paganism, but anyway the ' heavenly powers ' for a moment are about us. This line excepted, *Deirdre of the Sorrows* takes its stand with the others : it is drenched with mortality. In this respect all his work is Elizabethan, or more generally, Renaissance. But *Riders to the Sea* is a play as truly Greek as it is truly Irish in genuine religious feeling. The old woman in it, to say so once more, moves us more deeply than any of his other characters, sets free a more profound fund of reflection ; yet she is almost characterless. This brings us to the difficulties of Mr. Yeats and others about the characterless nature of great tragedy. [1] Mr. Yeats sees a vast difference between the Greeks and Shakespeare, the Greeks seeming to set little store on character, while with Shakespeare it is· everything. Between Shakespeare and Racine he finds the same difference, only less in degree. Racine is almost free of character and Shakespeare's own great characters, Mr. Yeats points out, doff their characters in the great moments. He concludes that in great tragedy there is an essential feeling against the presence of character. Mr. Forrest Reid does not agree with him. He writes : " Turning again to Shakespeare, Mr. Yeats urges that in the ' great moments ' of his drama, in the moments of supreme passion, character is forgotten. But can there, we might reply, really *be* such moments at all, if the persons who experience it are not there for us ? Is it not principally by character that. our feelings are moved, our sympathies awakened ? It is so in life ; how, then, can it be otherwise in art ? Granting that the two genres exist—for we have always Racine—does the difference between them really spring from any deliberate choice that has been made by the writers of ' tragedy ' ? Is it not rather the result of a lack of power in one particular direction ? *Could* Racine have written as Shakespeare wrote—that is, *could* he have created Hamlet, or Coriolanus, or Brutus, or Richard II, or Lady Macbeth ? Did not the Greeks, who worked under far

[1] *The Cutting of an Agate.*

stricter limitations than those imposed on any modern writer, try for as much character as they could get ? " [1] Mr. Reid asks two questions (1) Can there be such moments . . . . if the persons are not there for us ? Is it not by character that our feelings are moved ? (2) Could Racine have written as Shakespeare wrote ?—Did not the Greeks . . . . try for as much character as they could get ? Are those questions to the point ? Is personality the same as character ? Character in drama is complex : it is personality *plus* variation. Hamlet—the Prince himself—is rich in character because he is not a simple personality. Variation is stressed in his case more than usual. With the Greeks variation was not stressed at all : they contented themselves with personality. In their sculptures they contented themselves with planes, avoiding such kinks, wrinkles, minor surfaces as would give *character* to their creations. They sculptured the same type of face always. They satisfied themselves in drama with the just man, the religious man, the impious man—planes of humanity rather than kinks. Therefore instead of asking : Is it not principally by character that our feelings are moved, our sympathies awakened ? Mr. Reid should have asked : Is it not by variation (kinks, wrinkles, pockets) that our feelings are moved ? And we should have answered—Yes—our *feelings ;* but our *spirit,* no ! Our spirit is moved only when we have reached a plane in which only personality counts, not variation. Who at the end cares any longer for the blemishes in Cordelia or Lear or Othello or Lady Macbeth ? It is *we* who have reached a different plane : no longer our feelings, but our whole spirit must the dramatist satisfy. In these moments to stress variation is to do our spirits outrage. 'Could Racine . . . could the Greeks ?'—We can never tell. The difference between a Greek tragedian and an Elizabethan is this : The Greek tried to keep our *spirit* in play *all the time.* The Elizabethans, often after much floundering, reached the Greek plane, usually only towards the end of the play. Sometimes they never

1 *W. B. Yeats,* by Forrest Reid.

reached it at all. Racine matched himself against the Greeks.[1]

To get back to Synge. The greatness of *Riders to the Sea* lies in this : that it is one of the few modern plays written, and successfully written, in the Greek genre. It is a religious play, for the heavenly powers brood upon the action, as they do both in the Greek tragedies and in those of Racine, and as they do *not*, except at moments, in the Elizabethan. It is therefore written in that high plane which disdains ' character.'

It may seem more fitting to postpone such discussion until it is come to us to discuss this play among the others, but since we are dealing with Synge as writer, we cannot fix his stature without taking account of the powers he gives evidence of in this play. If he had not written *Riders to the Sea* he would not only have been a less great writer, but he would have been an infinitely less great writer, as those who work only on our feelings are immeasurably inferior to those who work upon our spirit.

Note also that to write this play he had to shed his little personal prejudices against the religion of the people. He allows it to play its natural part in the unfolding of the action ; and immediately how the spheres open !

Fixing his stature then as writer, it is necessary always to keep this great even if small piece of work in mind. Arnold remarks how, sometimes, it seems as if nature itself took the pen from Wordsworth's fingers : it happened only at those blessed moments, we may be sure, when some fortunate theme had energised to the maximum all the faculties of the poet's soul. This too is what occurred when Synge wrote *Riders to the Sea*. The theme aroused in him to a new strength all the love he had felt time and again sweep over him for the islanders ; it solemnised him too—and his spirit was such as sadly needed chastening—so that the inherited

[1] Mr. Yeats sees the fact, but does not see the reason ; yet almost stumbles on it when he writes : " The persons upon the stage, let us say, greaten till they are humanity itself."

petulancies, insolencies, prejudices, fell utterly away from him. He wrote then above his native strength, one may say, yet not above the level to which he had been raised by his great desire to express his love for those people he had lived among.

## XI.

We have now looked at Synge as writer from many different angles. His theory of what was serious drama had in it the narrowness of protest. It was a theory that prevented him from looking as comprehensively at life as one so gifted might have done. It made him overvalue the high-coloured gewgaws both of life and language. Yet, fortunately, that other article in his creed which held him fast to the profound and common interests of life saved him from becoming such a *fantaisiste* as his bent towards the imaginative would have urged him : he might have become a Lord Dunsany. His conversion to nationalism taught him the value of collaboration ; also by giving him a *patria* it gave him material on which the profound depths of emotion natively in him could work. Whatever is of value in his writings arises from the genuine affection he bestowed upon the land and the people he had made his own. That emotion would have functioned more purely as an element in his creative processes were it not that certain inherited prejudices as well as an inherent lack of spiritual delicacy held him back from reading as deeply in life as he might have done. Greatly moved on one occasion, he achieved the shedding of these prejudices, and wrote his masterpiece : *Riders to the Sea*. It is the unique example where an Ascendancy writer entered with any effective intimacy into the life of the Catholic Gaelic people.

# CHAPTER IV.

## THE ESSAYS

### " The Aran Islands."   " In Wicklow and West Kerry."

ESSAYS is not a good word to describe Synge's book *The Aran Islands*, nor that other book of his *In Wicklow and West Kerry;* yet to call them note books, as Mr. Howe does,[1] is worse. They are too carefully wrought out for note books, too elaborated into simplicity, directness, and unity. One can see that the prose in them, with its freedom from all trace of journalese and looseness of expression, is the result of long and anxious toil. They have usually been searched through for the evidences they contain of his way of collaborating with the folk in the making of his plays ; in them we come upon either his plots or hints for his plots ; we also find fragments of racy speech, isolated incidents, fragments of folk-lore, which, usually with only slight change, he was afterwards to use as dramatist. But one thinks that if he had never written any plays, or never had written them in the way he did, those essays would still be valuable. During the last two hundred years very many books have been written by travellers in the strange regions of this island, many of them good books, when one is aware of the travellers' limitations. Yet from all these, Synge's essays easily draw apart. He was a poet and he therefore saw more deeply into the life of things. Of knowledge of the usual kind he had less than the others ; he had, one thinks, like most of his class, read little or nothing about Ireland. Fortunately however, as has been noted, he had lived abroad, had shed many of his prejudices, and even still more fortunately, perhaps, whatever reading he had done was in

1 *J. M. Synge*, by P. P. Howe.

creative literature. Because of the type of mind such reading had formed in him, what he was to observe in Aran was already, without his knowing it, set apart for him, simplified, freed from the criss-cross of the insignificant. How much more intimate, more truly informative than masses of facts and figures, is such a passage as this in which he tells of the effects of a spell of bad weather in the islands :

> "At first the people do not give much attention to the wildness that is round them, but after a few days their voices sink in the kitchen, and their endless talk of pigs and cattle falls to the whisper of men who are telling stories in a haunted house." [1]

In such a passage we come on the real spirit of the place ; and other passages equally invaluable surround it.

We have been offered various explanations why he consented to go to those impoverished and lonely places, why he returned to them time after time, why, unlike almost all other writers on such places, he never makes any mention of the physical discomforts he must have suffered from in the pilgrimages. It is surely clear that he went to them as a writer, that as a writer he was glad to come upon them in the same way a landscape painter is glad to discover a terrain that is not only full of character, but has never been explored by other artists, appealing therefore not only to the æsthetic sense but also to the pioneer spirit which is in every child of Adam. As an artist Synge went about his work, searching always for the character of things, animate, inanimate ; and not only with his mind but with his heart, for character is to be felt as well as seen, trickles into the refining chambers of our mind through the very pores of the body. Partisans in later years questioned the islanders about him, and were glad to learn that he spent most of his days lying alone in the sun or, equally alone, moping around under the stars ! What kind of study was this ? What could that sort of person have learned about the islanders ? They discovered also that he did not frequent the really authoritative people on

[1] *The Aran Islands.* Part i.

the islands who could have told him everything about everything. He preferred the happy-go-lucky folks who were not
authorities on anything : the simple ones were friends of
his ; blind men and callow youths he would spend long hours
with ; he preferred rambling stories that had not a word of
truth in them to the pronouncements of the wise. Those
partisans in the statements they have made make us aware
of nothing except their own simplicity ; there are so many
strange pathways unknown to them into the world of wisdom.
" Perhaps the facts most astounding and most real are never
communicated by man to man. The true harvest of my
daily life is somewhat as intangible and indescribable as the
tints of morning or evening. It is a little star-dust caught,
a segment of the rainbow which I have clutched." That
little star-dust, that clutching of the rainbow's end, which
Thoreau knew was true wisdom, we experience with a sudden
awareness, only when we have thought ourselves, or more
correctly perhaps, felt ourselves into our surroundings,
established ourselves among them in peace. Because Synge
had let the mists and the tides, the rocks, the seas, the stars
of Aran make him their own in some such way as they had
all the long years been making the islanders their own, he
had thought himself more deeply into the island consciousness
than one could have hoped for : the lounging in the sun, the
dreaming beneath the stars had indeed helped him towards
considerable riches. But those who noted down how he had
rather spend the afternoon with a ne'er-do-well than with a
man of substance, of whom indeed the islands might well
have been proud, what conception could they ever have had
of the wealth he was seeking ?

In the recollection of all this is the right approach to these
essays. So come upon, they yield us all they have ; we
perceive at once what separates them from other such studies,
with their slickness and their woodenness, written by people
who had never dreamt of thinking themselves into the life
of the region they dealt with. And portion of what they
yield us when so approached is an apprehension more intimate

than any study of the plays alone could induce in us. Such passages in these books as give us direct, actual information about the islands themselves or their inhabitants, are so rare that they seem to have found entry into them only by chance. But surely far more valuable than mere information is the feeling we attain to of acquaintanceship with the consciousness of the island people as also with the various factors that have brought that consciousness to be what it is. We must not think that Synge plumbed that consciousness to its depths, leaving nothing for other inquirers. Being what he was, coming whence he did, he had his limitations ; and these narrowed his outlook ; but even so, he brought also with him the recompense of much travel, of literary study, of long brooding, an inner eye full of sympathy for man as man, man child-begetting, craving affection, toiling and moiling, yet never quite despoiled of the stir of spirit or of the inner wildness of dreams. And this inner eye, when it was pleased, as it was whenever it lighted upon colour, extravagance of gesture or deed, upon the simple natural virtues, or upon natural religion, had the power of communicating to us the warmth of its own satisfactions. It is not therefore the thought or the knowledge in these books that makes them valuable : it is their outwelling human sympathy that for a little while wins us away from the world wherein we so uselessly waste our powers.

Those aptitudes of his, his sense of colour, his relish of whatever had spirit in it, word or gesture, his sympathy with whatever was traditional, enrich almost every page he writes. As for his eye for colour, we come frequently on such passages as these :

> " The kitchen itself, where I will spend most of my time, is full of beauty and distinction. The red dresses of the women who cluster round the fire on their stools give a glow of almost Eastern richness, and the walls have been toned by the turf-smoke to a soft brown that blends with the grey earth-colour of the floor." [1]

[1] *The Aran Islands.* Part i.

H

"A few days ago, when I was visiting a cottage where there are the most beautiful children in the island, the eldest daughter, a girl of about fourteen, went and sat down on a heap of straw by the doorway. A ray of sunlight fell on her and on a portion of the rye, giving her figure and red dress with the straw under it a curious relief against the nets and oil-skins, and forming a natural picture of exquisite harmony and colour." [1]

"No one who has not lived for weeks among those grey clouds and seas can realize the joy with which the eye rests on the red dresses of the women, especially when a number of them are to be found together, as happened early this morning." [2]

And often we come on a picture that Jack Yeats or Paul Henry might have painted : it is easy to know that he had lived much among painters and pictures :

"In the evening, as I was coming home, I got a glimpse that seemed to have the whole character of Corkaguiney—a little line of low cottages with yellow roofs, and an elder tree without leaves behind them, standing out against a high mountain that seemed far away, yet was near enough to be dense and rich and wonderful in its colour." [3]

Those quotations show him at his most objective : we find him perhaps more truly himself when he is setting down something that not only charmed him but also excited him, as where he tells of the passing of a storm. The whole description must be read to feel how closely the nervousness of the writing reflects the disturbance in his own mind ; but we must satisfy ourselves with a short passage :

"After sunset the clouds broke and the storm turned to a hurricane. Bars of purple cloud stretched across the sound where immense waves were rolling from the west, wreathed with snowy phantasies of spray. Then there was the bay full of green delirium, and the Twelve Pins touched with mauve and scarlet in the east. The suggestion from this world of inarticulate power was immense, and now at midnight, when the wind is abating, I am still trembling and

[1] *The Aran Islands.* Part iii.
[2] *The Aran Islands.* Part i.
[3] *In West Kerry and Wicklow.*

flushed with exultation. I have been walking through the
wet lanes in my pampooties in spite of the rain, and I have
brought on a feverish cold. The wind is terrific. If anything serious should happen to me I might die here and be
nailed in my box, and shoved down into a wet crevice in the
graveyard before anyone could know it on the mainland." [1]

He was a colourist ; he was even a sensationist. He noted
how ravenously the people, while engaged in their daily work,
would snatch at the excitement incidental to it, enlarging it,
intensifying it by gesture, outcry and the flashing of the
eyes. He tells of the whirlwind of excitement in which the
shipping of cattle, of ponies, is carried on, work exciting in
itself owing to the use of primitive gear, made doubly exciting
by the outcries and violent gestures of the workers. Even
when no excitement is incidental to the work, he notes how
they induce it, and all who know those people will remember
similar instances. A hooker has arrived from Connemara :

"All the men sat along the edge of the pier and made
remarks upon the rottenness of her timbers till the owners
grew wild with rage." [2]

So too he writes of a crowd, many intoxicated, on a railway
platform in Galway :

" It gave me a better instance than I had yet seen of the
half-savage temperament of Connaught. The tension of
human excitement seemed greater in this insignificant crowd
than anything I have felt among enormous mobs in Rome
or Paris." [3]

He is attracted by that capability of excitement in the
people ; he does not argue about it. So also when he notes
how the simple, almost annual re-thatching of the roofs
becomes a festival, he makes no generalisation : he does not
wonder whether it is the too-great organisation of sport has
banished all trace of excitement from our daily labour in
cities, making it so joyless, or whether it is the necessary
elimination of excitement from their daily toil has enforced

[1] *The Aran Islands.* Part ii.
[2] *The Aran Islands.* Part i.
[3] *The Aran Islands.* Part ii.

the workers to organise their pleasures, to organise them so effectively that at last they too become pallid.

As he brought an eye for colour, for violence, so too he brought a feeling, but not more than that, for the ' wild mythology,' the vestiges of ancient beliefs that remained in the mind of the people. For their living faith, however, we have found him with scarcely any sympathy at all ; and whatever he had no sympathy for he hardly noticed. Of the old blind man who was his first teacher of Irish on the islands, he writes :

> "As we talked he sat huddled together over the fire, shaking and blind, yet his face was indescribably pliant, lighting up with an ecstasy of humour when he told me anything that had a point of wit or malice, and growing sombre and desolate again when he spoke of religion or the fairies."

From this one infers that for the old man there was no difference in his feeling for both fairies and religion. In reality, we may be sure, his feeling was quite different. When speaking of the fairies a peasant's face grows desolate and sombre, for to him they are evil spirits ; it is only to the poets of Dublin town that the fairies are dainty creatures bright in companionship. The peasant's face, on the other hand, does not grow sombre when speaking of his religion, for it is his religion he opposes to those malign spirits that waylay his feet in the night time. This is a matter of simple observation. So also Synge writes :

> "As we set out I noticed among the groups of girls who smiled at our friendship . . . a beautiful oval face with the singularly spiritual expression that is so marked in one type of the West Ireland women. Later in the day, as the old man talked continually of the fairies and women they have taken, it seemed that there was a possible link between the wild mythology that is accepted on the islands and the strange beauty of the women."

—' It *seemed*,' and so one is debarred from comment ; but one may surely be allowed to think that the religion openly professed and practised for well over a thousand years on the islands may also have had something to do with the look in the women's faces. Where Synge gave his heart, he observed with warmth, but for religion, even for the fairy religion, he had only little feeling ; and such fragments of folk-lore as he came upon he valued less for their own sake than for the light they threw on the island consciousness. For one whose sympathies were so circumscribed he is as fair as one could expect. He notes the peace that is in the people's lives, the peace and the dignity ; and it is while they are at Mass on a Sunday morning he makes his comment on it.

For the simplicity of the people's character, for their skill in many crafts, as also in two languages, for their readiness to face risk and danger without any show of bravado, he is full of admiration. Little by little he became aware of how much in their character was due to their dependence for livelihood on the weather conditions about them ; nature, through her constant dealing with them, had given them the temperament of the artist :

> "The continual passing in this island beween the misery of last night and the splendour of to-day, seems to create an affinity between the moods of these people and the moods of varying rapture and dismay that are frequent in artists, and in certain forms of alienation. Yet it is in the intonation of a few sentences or some old fragment of melody that I catch the real spirit of the island." [1]

> "I am only beginning to understand the nights of Inishmaan and the influence they have had in giving distinction to these men, who do most of their work after nightfall." [2]

Elsewhere he speaks of the education the waves had given them.

> "This continual danger, which can only be escaped by extraordinary personal dexterity, has had considerable influence on the local character, as the waves have made it impossible for clumsy, foolhardy, or timid men to live on these islands." [3]

[1] *The Aran Islands.* Part i.
[2] *The Aran Islands.* Part iii.
[3] *The Aran Islands.* Part i.

These quotations are not the most striking passages in the books ; but it is from them and similar passages we come to know that the consciousness of the people was what he really was studying all the time—that consciousness as it had been fashioned by the buffetings of winds and waves upon their bodies as well as on their huts and their curraghs, fashioned also by their inherited faith, their immemorial traditions. It was the artist in Synge that undertook such a quest ; and this fact is clear in every line of the books themselves.

But this is equally clear, and in every page almost, if not in every line, that although it was as an artist he went to those people, the spirit of the islands, meeting with some stirrings that had been taking place within his own spirit, some hunger there, won upon him and at last induced in him a feeling for the barren rocks and the dwellers on them that no one could have foreseen. And that is why those books draw so easily away from those others of a similar nature.

If we turn back to that passage in which he describes the effect of a storm we see it for a piece of still-life painting until we come to the words : " and now at midnight, when the wind is abating, I am still trembling and flushed with exultation." Immediately we read these words, the purple clouds, the mauve and scarlet colours on the hills, the green delirium of the waters, become in the backward glance alive, powerful over our own spirits. It is so with the whole book ; we are after every page or two coming on short passages, a line or two, a phrase, that informs with an inner stir of life whatever simple-seeming observations he has previously been making. In the earlier pages on the Aran Islands, we come on such words as :

> " It gave me a moment of exquisite satisfaction to find myself moving away from civilisation in this rude canvas canoe of a model that has served primitive races since men first went on the sea."

Yes, we say, here speaks one who has been having too much of the life of Paris and other huge cities ; but even already

are we not aware of something more sincere in the manner
of the expression than we find with those whose trade it is to
hasten from sensation to sensation ? ' Exquisite satisfaction '
seem the right words. And on his return to Galway from this
visit to the islands he writes :

> "The sort of yearning I feel towards those lonely rocks is
> indescribably acute. This town that is usually so full of
> wild human interest, seems in my present mood a tawdry
> medley of all that is crudest in modern life. The nullity of
> the rich and the squalor of the poor give me the same pang
> of wondering disgust ; yet the islands are fading already, and
> I can hardly realize that the smell of the seaweed and the
> drone of the Atlantic are still moving round them." [1]

The words, ' indescribably acute,' we again accept without
question ; and it is such phrases recurring often, yet not so
often as to become a mannerism, that make the whole of
these books pregnant with inner life. His exquisite delight
becomes still more exquisite ; it is of his visit the next year
he writes here :

> "The lamp had burned low, and another terrible gale was
> howling and shrieking over the island. It seemed like a
> dream that I should be sitting here among these men and
> women, listening to this rude and beautiful poetry that is
> filled with the oldest passions of the world."

And it was during this second year that he began to
experience not only an exquisite delight but an exquisite
distress. That distress arose in him from a new-found
consciousness that there was a gap between himself and the
islanders that could not be crossed.

> "On some days I feel this island as a perfect home and
> resting place ; on other days I feel that I am a waif among
> the people."

To be at home it seems he must be at one with the folk.
That thought henceforth is to recur again and again, filling
the pages with a curious poignancy. Yet he only half
fathoms the meaning of the recurring mood ; he does not

[1] *The Aran Islands.* Part i.

ask himself why he should not be content to be a waif in their midst, as presumably he was content in the midst of the people of France and Germany. On his parting from the islands after his second visit he writes :

> " I have left Aran . . . . Again I saw the three low rocks sink down into the sea with a moment of inconceivable distress."

Two years go by and he is back again :

> "As I sat down on my stool and lit my pipe with the corner of a sod, I could have cried out with the feeling of festivity that this return procured me."

His nature being what it was, reticent and tongue-tied, it is clear he must have been stirred very deeply before he permitted such words to remain in the printed page. In the book on West Kerry and Wicklow he does not so plainly set down his feelings, yet it is in a page of the West Kerry book he lets fall the word that gives us to understand he had been asking himself why his emotional being should so react to such places. This passage has already been noted by us, yet it may be fitting to deal more fully with it. It is a Sunday morning, he has been wandering about on the roads around Dunquin, talking Irish with the people while they waited, as their custom is, on the roadside for the Mass to begin in the church :

> " I got on a long road running through a bog, with a smooth mountain on one side and the sea on the other, and Brandon in front of me, partly covered with clouds. As far as I could see there were little groups of people on their way to the chapel in Ballyferriter, the men in homespun and the women wearing blue cloaks, or, more often, black shawls twisted over their heads. This procession along the olive bogs, between the mountains and the sea, on this grey day of autumn, seemed to wring me with the pang of emotion one meets everywhere in Ireland—an emotion that is partly local and patriotic, and partly a share of the desolation that is mixed everywhere with the supreme beauty of the world."

—The pang of emotion that is partly local and patriotic—

there of course is the "little more" confessed, the added keenness that makes sensation, whether of distress or rapture, exquisite. And it is because Synge felt this so deeply, and only, as one thinks, in the places and among the people that were most truly Irish, that Synge is a portent in Anglo-Irish literature. To the note that is in these pages, surely it is a far cry from writers like Lever and Maginn, or even Somerville and Ross of our own day, to all of whom the Irish peasant, but more especially the Irish-speaking peasant, was a figure of fun. On returning to the peasants, on finding himself once more seated by the turf fire in one of their huts, Synge could have cried out with joy; at the same time he was conscious that he was not really one with them. The disturbance set up in his mind as a consequence is written plainly in the pages on West Kerry, and more plainly still in those on the Aran Islands; and those papers therefore seem to me to be of more value than those others on Wicklow, wherein we discover none of that pious uneasiness, although they are, as critics have noted, the better written pages and the more interesting; unless one is eager to come rather on the writer's own self than on anything else.

Those papers then are valuable for their own sake as descriptive of the consciousness of the people. They are perhaps more valuable still for the insight they give us into Synge's own consciousness, his fundamentally emotional nature, his awareness only of whatever would stimulate that nature—colour, violence, dramatic incident. We find in them also, hinted rather than said, his quest for a fatherland, a spiritual home, whether he himself ever fully realised it or not. But those essays are, of course, also the note books where we may find the raw material on which the dramatist was afterwards to try his creative powers. Because of what we discover in these papers, we come to feel how sterling were those creative powers of his, sterling even when they fail sufficiently to chasten the materials with which they would deal, as in the case of *The Tinker's Wedding* and perhaps *The Playboy of the Western World*. We are taught in them what he meant by collaboration. From the bald statement in one of the prefaces one would take it that he meant no more by the word than the weaving into his plays of such expressions as he had gathered from the lips of the people ; we cannot however read those papers without learning that he knew the necessity of drenching himself with all the influences of the place—the folk-lore ; the weather ; the home life ; life on the sea, in the fields ; the nights ; the winds ; the stars—all those influences, especially such of them as were purely natural,—which have been time out of mind working their will on the consciousness of the people. The spiritual influences which escaped him—at moments he felt that they were escaping him : and for one with such antecedents this was not little.

These papers, then, are valuable in many ways. Sometimes I have the idea that the book on the Aran Islands will outlive all else that came from Synge's pen.

# CHAPTER V.

## "THE SHADOW OF THE GLEN"

### I.

WHETHER first-written or not this was the first of his plays to be performed. It is as truly a piece of himself as anything he was afterwards to write. The theme is as old as the hills : an old husband, a young wife ; and Synge came by the story in the Aran Islands ; but there is no peasant community in the world where it is not to be found. From old Pat Dirane, one of the islanders with whom he used to practise his Irish, Synge heard it. In the tale the elderly husband lets on to be dead that he may discover the unfaithfulness of his youthful wife. From his bed of sham death he arises and slays both his wife and the young lover she has brought into the house.[1]

The thing to note is that in all such traditional stories, wherever told, in whatever tongue, the *raison d'être* is the wonder in the matter itself. The peasant mind cannot conceive why any other justification for tale telling should be sought for. Beyond the incident itself folk-lore looks neither before nor after. And in that is the difficulty when a modern writer makes such a tale his theme. The mere wonder in the incident is not enough for him. Shifting the centre of interest from action to character, the wonder in the tale becomes of secondary value. The degree to which the surprise that is in the original shows through the texture of the play will then naturally depend on the place folk-lore holds in the dramatist's mind.

This particular tale which Synge chose is comedy with a dash of the illicit in it. As looked at by the folk, it deals not with love, but with what Croce calls the game of love,

[1] In *Once A Week* (July-December 1860, page 374) appeared a short story, *A Night Adventure in Ireland*, by a Soldier, with the same theme.

that selfsame love which Bacon tells us is ever the matter of comedies. What is likely to happen then if the playwright, one truly under the spell of the folk mind, cannot rightly settle for himself whether his play, based on such a story, is to be comedy or tragedy ? As one might have expected, the happy-go-lucky comedy in the folk-tale breaks to the surface again and again in Synge's drama ; when all is said, those parts of it which make the audience laugh the loudest—the ' dead ' man sitting up in the bed, the lovers, certain he is dead, discussing their affairs in his presence—these are really the best things in it whatever ' poetry ' has been written about the young wife and her desire for a fuller life. In his elaboration of the character of the woman, Nora Burke, Synge introduced so many elements that were contrary to the spirit of the comedy that one scarcely knows whether to call his play tragic or comic. Neither did Synge himself ; neither does the audience. There is no passage without its titter or laugh, but so clearly does Synge wish to win our sympathies for the young wife, that when we laugh, especially in the theatre, (for it is a play that the acting improves), we are not comfortable in our laughter. This Nora Burke has surely been taken by the critics too much *au sérieux.* One can but smile at what Mr. Yeats has written of her : " When he brought *The Shadow of the Glen,* his first play, to the Irish National Theatre Society, the players were puzzled by the rhythm, but gradually they became certain that his woman of the glens, as melancholy as a curlew, driven to distraction by her own sensitiveness, her own fineness, could not speak with any other tongue." [1] 'As melancholy as a curlew ' is so pretty one wishes to let it pass, but what can one say to ' her own sensitiveness,' ' her own fineness ? ' If Synge had succeeded in harmonising a fine and sensitive creature with a story so integrally rough and comic, he would indeed have achieved a miracle. His woman is dark and melancholy, but as for her fineness and sensitiveness, are we to forget that she speaks in this strain : " What

[1] Preface to the First Edition of *The Well of the Saints.*

way would I live, and I an old woman, if I didn't marry a
man with a bit of a farm, and cows on it, and sheep on the
back hills ? " It is curious language for a fine and sensitive
soul, as also this : " He's after dying on me, God forgive
him, and there I am now with a hundred sheep beyond on
the hills and no turf drawn for the winter." As also this :
" . . . . and if it's a power of men I'm after knowing
they were fine men, for I was a hard child to please, and a
hard girl to please, and it's a hard woman I am to please
this day, Michael Dara, and it's no lie I'm telling you." Nor
would such a woman as Mr. Yeats pictures for himself spread
out the old man's money on the table under the eye of her
young lover knowing him to be the commonest sort of clay.
Synge of course made no effort to create a fine and sensitive
woman : in his folk-lore mood such people had no appeal
for him. What he created was a piece of naturalistic flesh
and blood, wearing her lusts upon her sleeve, a being all
appetite and no faculty, a woman after his own literary
fancy, full of physical courage, daring and bold. And being
such, she retains in her much of the feeling in the old tale,
the spirit of which is frankly naturalistic, as is the way with
folk-lore. On the other hand the melancholy that is in her,
conflicts with the mood of the tale ; and it is this incongruity
that keeps the play swinging between comedy and tragedy.
Since it altogether occupies only twenty or twenty-five
minutes in the acting, scarcely is one mood established in
our minds, scarcely is it beginning to colour them, which
means that æsthetic pleasure is being attained to, when
another mood pounces upon us, and again we are in the
doldrums. The melancholy is not really fundamental in the
woman ; it is too much played upon for its own sake ; it
has in no way spiritualised her, as we have seen from her
own words : she makes poetry-talk like most of Synge's
other creations, but she conducts herself like the common
creatures of the earth, who, living within themselves, self-
centred, think but little of the winds crying in the bushes or
the mists that roll through the glens.

The play is too small for such changes of mood as occur in it ; and, to use a musical term, there are no bridges between mood and mood. Nora Burke's disparate character is the reason of this uncertainty. The others, exactly to the degree they bring with them the feeling of the tale, are congruous, Dan Burke, the hard old man, who has been enriched with a grim sense of humour quite in tone, being the best of them. His scornful repetition of the poetry-talk he has been listening to while ' dead ' is not only the very stuff of comedy everywhere and in every time but has that added quality—the intensity of the local instance—which Synge himself valued so much. The Tramp, with whom Nora Burke goes away in the end, is a very parfit gentil knight, not a bit like any tramp that ever was even in the county Wicklow. It is he who speaks the best of the poetry-talk which gives the play its peculiar atmosphere : " Come along with me now, lady of the house, and it's not my blather you'll be hearing only, but you'll be hearing the herons crying out over the black lakes, and you'll be hearing the grouse and the owls with them, and the larks and the big thrushes when the days are warm." To all of which what can Nora Burke answer only : " You've a fine bit of talk, stranger, and it's with yourself I'll go." Her husband has ordered her out, her lover, now that she is penniless, shrinks aside ; yet for all that one finds it hard to reconcile this Nora Burke with the woman who a few moments before could not brook the idea of growing old without a bit of a farm, and cows on it, and sheep on the back hills. It is not that a new, the real Nora Burke, has come to the surface, for if that were so, she would not have waited for the dismissal. She had established herself in our minds as true peasant ; and everywhere your peasant is the very antithesis of the stroller. To have lived in the farm houses of our people is to have no doubt about this. Yet she takes to the road as if she had never indulged the Irish peasant's dream of stability and comfort. But in a drama we must seek not the type, but the exception to it. Synge himself writes, as if foreseeing the charge : " In all the circumstances of this tramp life there is a certain wildness that gives it romance and a peculiar value for those who look at life in Ireland with an eye that is aware of the arts also. In all the healthy movements of art, variations from the ordinary types of manhood are made interesting for the ordinary man, and in this way only the higher arts are universal. Beside this art, however, founded on the variations which are a condition and effect of all vigorous life, there is another art—sometimes confounded with it—founded on the freak of nature, in itself a mere sign of atavism or disease. This latter art, which is occupied with the antics of the freak, is of interest only to the variation from ordinary minds, and for this reason is never universal. To be quite plain, the tramp in real life, Hamlet and Faust in the arts, are variations ; but the maniac in real life, and Des Esseintes and all his ugly crew in the arts, are freaks only." [1] If Nora Burke is to be considered by us as a variation, earnest to get free, we must forget her horror at the idea of an unpropertied old age. Her variation one would think would most signally show itself in a long indulged recklessness about and contempt for those typical peasant ideas which had induced her to join her life with an aged man. In her we find no trace of this scorn for the peasant's dream of everlasting stability. What we do find is the dream itself, four square and well set. The mind, it is true, does leap from positive to negative, but only in moments of collapse ; and one is not certain which is the collapsed condition in Nora's case ; the vision of an old age with a farm, or freedom with some poetry-talk thrown in ; and it is because Synge himself did not know, that we do not know.

He had not yet acquired certainty of touch. The play is a sketch, with some passages as good as any he was afterwards to write ; but all of it has the mark of not having been sufficiently thought through. When the old husband rises from his bed of ' death ' the craven lover takes great

1 *In Wicklow and West Kerry.*

fright, and implores Nora, who, fine and sensitive as she is, takes but little fright, to rescue him: " Get me out of it, Nora, for the love of God. He always did what you bid him, and I'm thinking he would do it now." Here is a backward glance into the married life of the old man and the young wife for which nothing in either character prepares us. It is perhaps the only touch in the play with genuine human feeling in it. So indeed would it have been with two so mated; and now when the time for parting had come to them, certainly it is that past endeavouring of theirs towards felicity that would rise into consciousness. If Synge had settled that the play was to be a tragedy, appealing intimately to our own reading of life, this recollection of the past years would not have been dismissed by him so summarily: if he had definitely decided for comedy, the touch would never have been introduced, he would have felt its disturbing effect.

All the way through there is uncertain psychology. When Nora leaves the house to fetch her lover, the 'dead' man sits up and explains to the Tramp how he is about to trap his wife. The wife returns with her lover in tow. She asks the Tramp to retire into the next room, leaving herself and the lover alone with the dead man. Obviously the Tramp would have done so, rather pleased that the plot should be given such a chance of working itself out. In the play, however, he refuses to withdraw, and one does not know why. If he wished to save Nora he could have prevented her from entering at all. The straightforward current of the play is interfered with, it tumbles and tosses for some time before making again forward.

The outstanding weakness of the play, however, is the aforesaid too rapid transitions from mood to mood that occur in it, no single mood being given the chance thoroughly to infect the mind with its own colour. The play rocks all the time upon its base; and we do nothing but wait for the rocking to cease.

## II.

One finds the whole of Synge in this play, sketch as it is. In it we become familiar with his methods as also with the strains he loved to weave into his compositions. The characters in it are true brothers and sisters of all those he was afterwards to create.

The story is folk-lore. That story he deprived to some degree of its elemental folk flavour when he elaborated the humanity of the young wife, changing it from personality to character, from the Old Man's Wife to Nora Burke. He moreover omitted both the murder and the adultery; and the Tramp, who is but an onlooker in the old story, when he is there at all, he made the hero of it. This last change was perhaps the most characteristic: almost any other modern playwright would have made the other two. The scene he placed in Wicklow, and one is doubtful whether it was this choice decided the tramp's part in it, or whether the choosing of a tramp as hero led him to Wicklow for his scene. That county he associated with vagrants. And they were not ordinary vagrants, he would have us know. They really were the natural aristocracy of the place. Their abundance in Wicklow has been regretted, he says, and he continues: " Yet in one sense it is an interesting sign, for wherever the labourer of a country has preserved his vitality, and begets an occasional temperament of distinction, a certain number of vagrants are to be looked for. In the middle classes the gifted son of a family is always the poorest—usually a writer or artist with no sense for speculation—and in a family of peasants, where the average comfort is just over penury, the gifted son sinks also, and is soon a tramp on the roadside." [1] One may think the sympathy that so beheld the tramps of Wicklow somewhat overweening, one may think that there are gifts and gifts ; anyhow the passage helps us more truly to understand the Tramp as well as why Nora went with

[1] *In Wicklow and West Kerry.*

I

him than we should from the play itself alone. He has, as
Nora says, a fine bit of talk. So conceived of, one is glad
that the natural if submerged distinction in the man is not
overdrawn, for, except for the bit of talk about the herons,
the grouse, and the owls, the larks and the thrushes—except
for this simple feeling for the poetry of earth, the reflex of
Synge's own feeling, he exhibits no other distinction whatever. His is a case of variation, not of freakishness. While
he wrote of him, Synge may have had some remembered
figure in his inner eye. Whether or no, he was anyhow quick
with the feel of the Wicklow glens. In his papers on that
county he speaks of the influence of particular localities on
the people :

> " These people live for the most part beside old roads and
> pathways where hardly one man passes in the day, and look
> out all the year on unbroken barriers of heath. At every
> season heavy rains fall for often a week at a time, till the
> thatch drips with water stained to a dull chestnut, and the
> floor in the cottages seems to be going back to the condition
> of the bogs near it. Then the clouds break, and there is a
> night of terrific storm from the south-west—all the larches
> that survive in these places are bowed and twisted towards
> the point where the sun rises in June—when the winds come
> down through the narrow glens with the congested whirl and
> roar of a torrent, breaking at times for sudden moments of
> silence that keep up the tension of the mind. At such times
> the people crouch all night over a few sods of turf, and the
> dogs howl in the lanes." [1]

Elsewhere in the book—in the paper on Glencree—one
comes on a description of the effect of the mists on
the mind :

> " The fog has come down in places ; I am meeting
> multitudes of hares that run round me at a little distance—
> looking enormous in the mists—or sit up on their ends against
> the sky line to watch me going by. When I sit down for a
> moment the sense of loneliness has no equal. I can hear
> nothing but the slow running of water and the grouse crowing
> and chuckling underneath the band of cloud. Then the fog

[1] *In Wicklow and West Kerry.*

lifts and shows the white empty roads winding everywhere, with the added sense of desolation one gets passing an empty house on the side of a road. When I turn back again the air has got stuffy and heavy and calm, with a cloud still down upon the glen; there is a dead heat in the air that is not natural so high up, and the silence is so great three or four wrens that are singing near the lake seem to fill the valley with sound. In most places I can see the straight ending of the cloud, but above the lake grey fingers are coming up and down, like a hand that is clasping and opening again. One longs for rain or wind or thunder. The very ewes and lambs have stopped bleating, and are slinking round among the stacks of turf . . . . All one's senses are disturbed. As I walk backwards and forwards, a few yards above and below the door, the little stream I do not see seems to roar out of the cloud." [1]

What helped Synge always towards distinction in his dramatic work was his own intimate feeling for the matter dealt with, his gift of impassioned contemplation; of which this passage is so evident. Before he began his play, his mind had been already charged with the humanity of the people in it, their appearance, their speech, their labouring, as also with their environment—this environment and the folk harmonising in a rich colour scheme, which harmony was indeed the chiefest pleasure perhaps that Synge himself experienced. He had enriched the characters by dreaming upon them, and as for the places, he loved the very names of them—" places with curiously melodious names, such as Aughavanna, Glenmalure, Annamoe, or Lough Nahanagan." [2] He had willy-nilly to work the names into the pattern, as also the scraps of folk-lore, the racy turns of speech, he had gathered in these or other countrysides. From the passages just quoted we learn how truly this play was an abstract of the Wicklow glens, their people, their mists, his reading of them very much his own. The Tramp born into higher circles would have been a writer or artist; and Nora Burke suffers terribly from that tension of mind the mists of these mountain regions induce in one. And these two, Nora and

[1] *In Wicklow and West Kerry.*
[2] *In Wicklow and West Kerry.*

the Tramp, who most closely cleave to the scene are the leading figures in the piece.

We discover quite sufficiently, then, what play-making meant for him from this one example ; and we come also in it on the naturalistic nature of his moody philosophy. The ordinary Catholic people of Dublin have been frequently lectured for not taking to this play with any enthusiasm. They have been informed, with topical instances culled from newspapers, that women do leave their husbands in Ireland and go off with other men. They have been reminded that Synge lessened the venom of the old tale by omitting both the adultery and the murder. But of course such apologists are not answering in any way the people's case against the dramatist. The people do not deny that crimes are committed in their midst. They feel, however, in looking at a great many Abbey plays, that something is wrong. And of course there is. They really, whether they know it or not, go to the work of a native dramatist to experience a focussing and a clarifying of all their own entangled thoughts, impressions, desires, ideals ; and they find that they really might as well have gone to the work of an outlander. This play is enough to show that this is so. As the people watch this play develop, the word conscience, the question of right and wrong, looms before their minds. Here is an Irish peasant woman going off with another man, doing so without the least trouble of conscience. How she, or any other peasant woman in Wicklow could do such a thing without sore trouble of mind is what the people of Ireland cannot understand. The play turning out as it does, this question of right and wrong is for them the thrilling thing in it, the big thing, and, wonderful to tell, it is not even as much as hinted at by any person on the stage ! It is the old inability of Anglo-Irish literature to deal with the facts. How can the people take serious interest in that literature until the questions that arise in their own consciousness, as they read it, exist also in a natural way in the minds of those who write it ?

But here one may be asked : How comes it then that the common people, the peasants, have kept the old tale, which also scants those questions, alive from generation to generation ? And the answer is that the old tale begins with some such phrase as : Once upon a time ; that is, the action is shifted on to a plane wherein the mind takes holiday. The incidents in such a tale then are conceived of as having only just as little bearing on life as those in the *Arabian Nights*. It is a different thing when the nameless woman in the folk tale is indeed none other than Nora Burke having her being in county Wicklow in our own days. When the dramatist gives so much information to his audience, they are agog to have their own ideas of right and wrong dealt with, rather than their ideas and feelings about old husbands and young wives and the influence of long periods of fogs and mists on the minds of the dwellers in the glens.

The play has been spoken of as ironic comedy. As we have seen, Nora Burke is a curious figure in a comedy ; when folk in comedies are melancholy it is the selfish melancholy of Malvolio they inherit, not that unity with the moods of nature, from which Nora suffers. It is certainly not an ironic comedy. It has no purpose, it does not warn against the mating of youth and age. Certainly, however, it has in it the bite of reality ; old Dan Burke is four square to the winds. And this reality is the result of Synge's liking for the directness that is so often the be-all of folk literature. The play was practically the first of those peasant plays in the Abbey repertoire which were afterwards to put a special seal on the work of that theatre. Other such plays followed, plays written by Padraic Colum, Lennox Robinson, Thomas C. Murray, and others, nearly all of which had something of this bite of peasant realism in them. It is by these plays that the Abbey has influenced in some degree the drama in English-speaking countries—Eugene O'Neill in America, for instance, and John Masefield in England. Its importance as a piece of drama, coming where and when it did, is that it so strongly brought back the feel of folk literature, its directness, and brought also back to the drama of those days, afflicted as it was either with the artificiality of the drawing room or the sophistication of 'poetic' playwrights, the free airs of the hills, as well as human souls who felt really only the penalty of Adam.

# CHAPTER VI.

## "RIDERS TO THE SEA"

### I.

AS we have seen *The Shadow of the Glen* is not single-minded. Such warm understanding as Synge had for nature's infection of the mind with its own gloomy and mysterious moods chilled the true genius of the tale, which was reckless, if not comic. It was strange that one whose thoughts were full to overflowing of the nonchalant interplay of nature on the soul of man should set his mind to comedy ; for in comedy the ways of men and women among themselves, the stirrings within the human ant-hill, are nearly always the whole of 'nature.' If its writers be, as Synge was in this case, absorbed at the same time in the vision of the larger world, the whole universe, it is likely that too frequent an *arrière pensée* will chill the fun ; almost as if the memory of night time should live on during the day :

> Die Welt is tief,
> und tiefer, als der Tag gedacht.

*The Shadow of the Glen* shows us therefore a playwright unhappy in his theme, inasmuch as the body of his thoughts at that period had a movement in it that was both too slow and too vast for the rhythm this theme demanded. *Riders to the Sea*, his next play, on the other hand shows us that same playwright not only happy (inasmuch as the provenance of thought and theme was identical) but inspired, wrought upon so deeply, so intensely, that such wilful human frailties as were in the way of nature his, solemnly quieted, ceased for the time to show themselves. He had happened on a theme that came in four square with all that he himself was at his best. He had become free enough of the consciousness of the islanders to feel within his bones, almost as they felt it, the immemorial malignity of the sea towards them. Not only that, but, in this play too, and in this play alone, he also shows himself as aware that sheer distraction must follow on such sense as was theirs of this malignity if they had not as well a world over and beyond the warfare of wind and wave to rest their thoughts upon. He shows himself conscious of this, but not, we should say, fully conscious. The Penal Laws had one effect—one almost writes one beautiful effect on the consciousness of the Irish people : spiritual reticence. The people are now being gradually trained into open and public expression of their religious beliefs, they are being encouraged to give them to the light of day. This movement has not yet reached the backward places, least of all places like Aran, and in Synge's time had hardly begun anywhere, so that for him it was no easy thing to come upon the islanders' unspoken thoughts. They loudly lamented the loss of a friend—they could do so without any parade of their religion ; but silently they hoped and prayed that his soul might be saved. The lament Synge was aware of, but not the unceasing and intensely earnest praying that did not declare itself. Even in this play where he most of all shows himself alert to the totality of the people's consciousness, one may notice that the thoughts the peasants would not loudly cry out, have escaped him. He was still to some degree an outsider ; yet of such as he then was this play is the complete epitome, emotional, sincere, and solemn. Its theme is the unavailing struggle of the fisherfolk against the sea. Little by little Synge had come to realise how terrible was this warfare, how constantly the terror of it was in the thoughts of the islanders. We have from him a description of the burial of a young man whose body after being for weeks in the sea had been washed ashore : when the grave had been covered Synge had walked away and had come on a group of men fishing with a drag net :

"As they talked to me and gave me a little poteen and a little bread when they thought I was hungry, I could not help feeling that I was talking with men who were under a judgment of death. I knew that every one of them would be drowned in the sea in a few years and battered naked on the rocks, or would die in his own cottage and be buried with another fearful scene in the graveyard I had come from." [1]

In an earlier page of the same book he tells us of the keening he had heard raised over the body of an old woman who was being buried :

"This grief of the keen is no personal complaint for the death of one woman over eighty years, but seems to contain the whole passionate rage that lurks somewhere in every native of the island. In this cry of pain the inner consciousness of the people seems to lay itself bare for an instant, and to reveal the mood of beings who feel their isolation in the face of a universe that wars on them with winds and seas. They are usually silent, but in the presence of death all outward show of indifference or patience is forgotten, and they shriek with pitiable despair before the horror of the fate to which they all are doomed." [2]

In these two passages we breathe the fateful atmosphere that is in the play. But he had also noted another trait in the island consciousness which helped him to understand more fully the old-established horror of those people towards the sea : "On these islands," he writes, "the women live only for their children," [3] and elsewhere : "The maternal feeling is so powerful on these islands that it gives a life of torment to the women. Their sons grow up to be banished as soon as they are of age, or to live here in continual danger of the sea." [4] These notes tell us why the principal figure in the play is rather a mother crying out over her drowned children than a wife crying out over her drowned husband. But indeed fittingly to realise how compact an epitome of his understanding of Aran the play is, not only stray notes from it, but the whole book must be kept in one's mind. For instance we may learn how he happened on the rather

[1] *The Aran Islands* (iv).
[2] *The Aran Islands* (i).
[3] *The Aran Islands* (i).
[4] *The Aran Islands* (i).

curious name : " When the horses were coming down to the ship an old woman saw her son, that was drowned a while ago, riding on one of them." [1] Not only did he thus find himself a name for the play, but the incident itself he also introduced. In the same way, we may take it, there is scarce an incident, an action, in the drama that he had not, with warm sympathy, observed as daily taking place in the life of the cabins. He had noted how often the hearth has to be replenished with turf ; he had seen someone contrive a halter, talking at the same time ; Bartley's words, " The blessing of God on you," are just right ; as also is his changing of his old coat for his new one ; he had seen the island girls counting the stitches, noted the tying up of the bread in a piece of cloth ; many other little daily occurrences in which only the poet's eye could behold not only charm but significance. Of itself the play is sufficient evidence of his gift of impassioned contemplation : it was that gift that enabled him to make use of such daily happenings as we ordinarily do not notice, to interpret the humanity of his characters. That gift, we may learn, is the be-all of the thaumaturgy the creative artist practises. The process of impassioned contemplation in an artist's mind is a ruthless, although seemingly undirected, sifting of his gathered observations, knowledge, what you will :—in the process the insignificant sinks below the threshold of consciousness ; to the onlooker—were such onlooking possible—it would seem as if the *summum bonum* of the artist's gatherings was vanishing out of sight, that only a tiny residue was being left. Yes, but every particle of that residue is kinetic in its nature, powerful to move us to the depths of our being when the artist bares it to our vision. Those little incidents in the play not only keep it alive ; they are in truth so many such kinetic particles, charged with significance, and therefore symbolic ; for the true artist cannot help but make use of symbols : almost unconsciously he does so. Truly significant, truly symbolic, and truly universal are all synonymous

[1] *The Aran Islands* (iv).

terms ; and any one of them may be applied to the con-
stituents of that residue that remains when the process of
impassioned contemplation has taken place. We do not
know how an artist can exercise this gift unless he has
immersed himself in the matter, in the life, he deals with ;
and therefore we conceive that what is known as International Art—it is surely right to grant the name the sloganic
efficiency of capitals—and impassioned contemplation are
disparate in their nature : we can not see the one resulting
from the other. It was Synge's thorough immersion in the
matter he dealt with, his feeling for it, the surrender of
himself to its genius, that in this case enabled him to create
a piece of art that is at once local and universal in
its appeal.

## II.

The play is in one act, the story as simple as possible.
From time to time the father and five sons of the one household have all been drowned. Nine days before the play opens
the fifth son, Michael, was drowned ; his body has not yet
been recovered from the sea. But a bundle of clothes has
arrived at the hut—' got off a drowned man in Donegal.'
This bundle is Michael's clothes. Only one son, Bartley,
now remains. It is turning to a wild night : " that wind is
raising the sea, and there was a star up against the moon,
and it rising in the night," says the old mother, yet the
last son will not be dissuaded from crossing to the mainland.
That some disaster will overtake him we feel as certain as
the old woman, his mother, who foresees it and foretells it.
As Bartley leaves the house he instructs his sister : " If the
west wind holds with the last bit of the moon let you and
Nora get up weed enough for another cock for the kelp. It's
hard set we'll be from this day and no one in it but one man
to work." To these words the old woman replies : " It's
hard set we'll be surely the day you're drowned with the
rest." And when he has left the house her words are : " He's
gone now, God spare us, and we'll not see him again. He's

gone now, and when the black night is falling I'll have no son left me in the world." At nightfall Bartley's corpse is brought in to her from the sea. This is the whole of the story.

Where is the drama ? Nowhere, if we do not conceive of the sea as the inhuman protagonist with which this old woman, whose husband and five sons have been its prey, is striving. Brunetière tells us that the germ of every drama lies in some person's coveting of some other person or thing. In *Riders to the Sea* the sea itself is the coveting agent, the mother the sufferer. When we become aware of this we are as certain as when we read a Greek play that the end is at hand : and, again as in a Greek play, we find that though that ending has terrible and final disaster in it, the human spirit that is privileged to view it goes away into the living world not with a more resolved hardness but with a new tenderness upon its lips.

In this play the sea is fearful ; almost unconsciously however, we become impressed that the mother who confronts it is so firm set and integral in her nature that in spite of all its victories over her she is still herself and will remain herself, not distracted, not frenzied. It is through her husband and her six sons that the sea assails her, as if she herself in her own nature were indefeasible. How Synge brings us to realise the malignity of the sea is worth noting : he brings us to view it, to apprehend it, through the island consciousness. King Lear bellows against the storm, the thunder and lightning, naturally, for to him, dispossessed, these elemental powers are all a new revelation : undisciplined and untaught he vaingloriously pits himself against them. It is all otherwise with the fisherfolk. For them the sea is no new revelation : its worst is of old and familiar : in Aran the voices are not raised against the whirlwind : as the whirlwind rises, their voices sink to a lower whispering. Synge makes the old woman, mother of many fishermen, never refer to the sea except as—the sea. Her phrases are : the sea ; on the sea ; in the sea ; by the sea. There is never an adjective ; no personification ; no synonym. The word ocean does not occur. Yet how terribly aware of the malice of the sea we become ! When one daughter says to the other : " Didn't the young priest say the Almighty God won't leave her destitute with no son living," the old mother replies in a low voice : " It's little the like of him knows of the sea." That is all, but how effective it is ! And in another place the old woman speaks, not with any wildness, but merely as explaining a previous statement, a few words that open for us the very maw of the sea : " There does be a power of young men floating around in the sea." With unforced yet effective touches he brings its malice so much home to us, that we ourselves, like the islanders, feel like dropping our voices as we speak of it.

Equally unforced is the means by which he induces in us a feeling that this old Aran peasant fisherwife is the universal mother : if our minds rest on her, try to image her forth plastically, the form that shapes itself in our vision is large-limbed, rugged, stern, rock-set, not unlike the figure of Demeter herself. Her words are always simple yet big with imaginative power : " If it was a hundred horses, or a thousand horses you had itself, what is the price of a thousand horses against a son where there is one son only ? " It is only at the close of the play, however, where her relations with the sea are openly declared, that we realise her bigness : " They're all gone now and there isn't any more the sea can do to me." So strongly established in us is the mood of the play by this time that we feel no disproportion in these words ; in our sense of the great struggle that has been taking place our minds are enlarged and renewed : with the old woman herself we almost share the calmness of despair, that blank feeling of restfulness that ensues when all that we feared has happened and there is an end : " I'll have no call now to be up crying and praying when the wind breaks from the south, and you can hear the surf is in the east, and the surf is in the west, making a great stir with the two noises, and they hitting one on the other . . . . It's a great rest

I'll have now, and great sleeping in the long nights after Samhain, if it's only a bit of wet flour we do have to eat, and maybe a fish that would be stinking." The words find response in the depths of our heart, yet the passage that follows removes us still further from our customary state of being, leaving us so stirred, so thrilled, if we may use a word that has been spoiled by too much use, that we never more can doubt the power of great drama to effect purification through pity and fear, for we have experienced it in a way we could not ever have foreseen : " They're all together this time, and the end is come. May the Almighty God have mercy on Bartley's soul, and on Michael's soul, and on the souls of Sheumas and Patch, and Stephen and Shawn ; and may He have mercy on my soul, Nora, and on the soul of every one is left living in the world. Michael has a clean burial in the far north, by the grace of the Almighty God. Bartley will have a fine coffin out of the white boards, and a deep grave surely. What more can we want than that ? No man at all can be living for ever, and we must be satisfied." 'And on the soul of every one is left living in the world.' We do not think that it is a new Synge that perhaps only half consciously let these words slip from his pen ; we think rather that it is the real Synge, himself purified in the fire of his own vision. Of itself the passage, but more especially these words, so full of insight into the life he was dealing with, mark him off not only from the type in Anglo-Irish letters, but almost from them all, both in the mass and individually. The others are never able to say Amen ! when the simple people of Ireland utter the cry that is in their heart.

### III.

The play, as a play, is almost perfect, unless one maintains a very rigid idea of what a piece of dramatic work should be. All the way through there is a succession of those little happenings that make for life, every one of them charged with significance. We may note how the bundle of clothes is used. At the beginning, our attention is concentrated on

it : unopened, its contents guessed at however, it is hidden
away from us. When at last it does come to be untied our
eyes strain to see what is in it ; for we have since become
one with those whose fingers tremble to open it. We may
note by what simple means we are made aware how great
have been the old woman's sufferings : before she enters at
all, one daughter says : " Where is she ? " and the other
answers : " She's lying down, God help her, and maybe
sleeping, if she's able." Simpler the words could not be, yet
how effective ! Then we may note how Bartley's corpse is
not brought in until after the old woman has described an
exactly similar home-coming, and the description is an
example of perfect visualization : " I was sitting here with
Bartley, and he a baby lying on my two knees, and I seen
two women, and three women, and four women coming in,
and they crossing themselves and not saying a word. I looked
out then, and there were men coming after them, and they
holding a thing in the half of a red sail, and water dripping
out of it . . . . and leaving a track to the door." The
words have scarcely fallen when we behold a number of
hooded women, who are making the sign of the cross on
themselves, stealing in without raising their heads, without
speaking a word. With awful immediacy the vision the
words have raised in us is dramatised for us : the effect is
terrible, but not intolerable, for the sense of poetry established
in the air by the old woman's words, by the very rhythm of
them, has not died away. In all the books on play-making
we are given the French saying, that dramas are made of
actions, not of words ; but great drama, we may be quite
sure, has never been achieved except when both means are
employed in perfect harmony, as in this instance.

IV.

As may be perceived from these quotations the touch is
perfect. Here and there a passage strikes one as being a
little too rounded, a sentence as being too carefully balanced :
" He went down to see would there be another boat sailing

in the week, and I'm thinking it won't be long till he's here now, for the tide's turning at the green head, and the hooker's tacking from the east." In such cases, if one has a feeling for the fall of a sentence, one almost forgets to gather the meaning ; and in such a play this is a defect.

But such defects are too slight and too rare to take from the greatness of the play, which, deeply emotional in its nature, demanded that delicacy of touch of which the intellectual playwright who discards emotion, as if it were beneath him, has no need, it seems. Had Synge lived long enough he might perhaps have excelled it in *Deirdre of the Sorrows*, for in that play there certainly are very wonderful passages ; this however one may doubt because it is not certain that his approach to the Deirdre theme was anything more happy than his approach to the theme in *The Shadow of the Glen*. For touch, neither *The Well of the Saints* nor *The Playboy of the Western World* can be compared with *Riders to the Sea* : indeed beside it *The Playboy* seems flashy, overwrought yet unfinished, unachieved. Indeed one would be hard put to it to find half a dozen one-act plays in English fittingly to companion it. Where in modern work shall one find the simple words of the language used with such cleanly directness, producing vast effects with the most economic means ? It is curious to note how few dramatists have ever learnt so to choose, and so to use the English language as to leave us with the sense of the thing, and not with the sense of words : yet immediacy, one imagines, is or ought to be the very note of dramatic writing. The old woman's words in *Riders to the Sea* are infected all through with this immediacy : " It's a great rest I'll have now, and great sleeping in the long nights after Samhain, if it's only a bit of wet flour we do have to eat, and maybe a fish that would be stinking." Synge could have learnt, perhaps unconsciously did learn, this way of using speech from Racine, but from him only when at his best ; we may however be quite certain that consciously he came by it in his study of the poetry in the Irish language, almost every line of which, in good examples, pierces the imagination once for all and deeply. One might perhaps think it the Irish way of using words, as also, perhaps, the Greek.

Beyond this virtue, yet perhaps not unconnected with it, if we think clearly enough, is that other power in the play to move us not only in our feelings but in our spirit. This characteristic even still more decisively sets it apart from modern drama in English; from Shaw, from Galsworthy, from Barrie, Bennett, Masefield, the others. To achieve it one knows that all these should come by a different manner of using words. Synge made always for the fundamental; and in this play, at least, went near achieving it. He had happened, as has been said, on a theme which moved himself so profoundly that it left him freed of that tendency towards the overstatement, the flashy, towards bad taste, indeed, which the imaginative artist is always prone to. In none of the other plays do we come on quite the same writer: in them all he is always less; yet he had laid by him, all the time while he was writing these others, another theme that might equally have raised him to his best. That theme is to be found in those pages in *The Aran Islands* where he describes an eviction scene on Inishmaan:

> "She belonged to one of the most primitive families on the island, and she shook with uncontrollable fury as she saw the strange armed men, who spoke a language she could not understand, driving her from the hearth she had brooded on for thirty years. For these people the outrage to the hearth is the supreme catastrophe. They live here in a world of grey, where there are wild rains and mists every week in the year, and their warm chimney corners, filled with children and young girls, grow into the consciousness of each family in a way it is not easy to understand in more civilised places.
>
> "The outrage to a tomb in China probably gives no greater shock to the Chinese than the outrage to a hearth in Inishmaan gives to the people.
>
> "When the few trifles had been carried out, and the door blocked with stones, the old woman sat down by the threshold and covered her head with her shawl." [1]

[1] *The Aran Islands.* (i).

J

This theme he did not handle. From the context, however, we become certain that he was as deeply moved by it as he was when he realised one day that he had been talking with men who were living in the shadow of death.

### V.

Synge is, I repeat, a portent in Anglo-Irish literature inasmuch as he made a serious attempt to fathom the native consciousness. It is in *Riders to the Sea* we have the most convincing proof that he made that attempt. We find in it, moreover, the reflex of the soul of the writer when he had a theme that raised him, as one cannot help saying, a little beyond his best ; for in it he exhibits an integrity of thought and feeling that is very rare in these days of ours, undisciplined by tradition as they are.

# CHAPTER VII.

## " THE TINKER'S WEDDING "

IN this two-act comedy we have only four characters:
Michael Byrne, tinker; Sarah Casey, his doxy; Mary
Byrne, his mother; and a Priest. We learn that Sarah
Casey and Michael Byrne have been living together for many
years, but that Sarah is now minded to be married to him
properly in a church by a priest. Although reluctant,
Michael Byrne gives his consent. The priest they bargain
with over the fees, settling at last on paying him ten shillings
together with the new tin can Michael Byrne has been
working at. The marriage is to take place in the morning.
While the two younger folk, Sarah Casey and Michael Byrne,
are abroad rifling the farm yards of the countryside, old
Mary Byrne, ' die immer durstige Mary,' as Krieger [1] describes
her, steals the new tin can, replacing it by a few empty porter
bottles, and sells it for drink to Jemmy Neill, the publican.
In the morning—and we are now in Act ii—the marrying
pair unsuspectingly hand the priest the parcel containing the
empty porter bottles, as also the half-sovereign. He opens
the parcel, flies into a rage at the deception, and threatens
to have in the police. Fearing the coming of the " peelers,"
the three tinkers tackle him and tie him up in a bag. There
he growls and struggles. Michael is for throwing him into
a bog hole, but Mary reminds him that that might mean
hanging for them all. They offer to release him if only he
swear not to inform on them. This he promises, whereupon
they untie him. Then he lifts his hand: " I've sworn not
to call the hand of man upon your crimes to-day; but I
haven't sworn I wouldn't call the fire of heaven from the

---

[1] *John Millington Synge, ein dichter der keltischen renaissance,* von Hans
Krieger.

hand of the Almighty God,"—and with this he begins a Latin malediction—the words are not given—in a loud ecclesiastical voice, before which the tinkers fly for their very lives.

In Synge's sketches we come with certainty on the provenance of this play. A man " on this side of a mountain to the east of Aughavanna in Wicklow " gave him this account of the tinkers to be met with in that county :

> " They're gallous lads for walking round through the world. One time I seen fifty of them above on the road to Rathdangan, and they all matchmaking and marrying themselves for the year that was to come. One man would take such a woman, and say he was going such roads and places, stopping at this fair and another fair, till he'd meet them again at such a place, when the spring was coming on. Another, maybe, would swap the woman he had with one from another man, with as much talk as you'd be selling a cow. It's two hours I was there watching them from the bog underneath, where I was cutting turf, and the like of the crying and kissing, and the singing and shouting began when they went off this way and that way, you never heard in your life. Sometimes when a party would be gone a bit down over the hill, a girl would begin crying out and wanting to go back to her ma." [1]

From the play itself one scarcely understands why Sarah having lived many years with Michael Byrne and borne him many children wishes at last to be properly married to him. She babbles, it is true, about the spring time, and the queer thoughts it excites in one ; from the above passage, however, one learns that the season has its own special anxieties for tinker communities.

In another passage in the same book we come closer to the fable. It is a herd encountered near Aughrim in Wicklow who is speaking :

> " One time he (a tinker) and his woman went up to a priest in the hills and asked him would he wed them for half a sovereign, I think it was. The priest said it was a poor price, but he'd wed them surely if they'd make him a tin

[1] *In Wicklow and West Kerry.*

can along with it. 'I will, faith,' said the tinker, 'and I'll come back when it's done.' "They went off then, and in three weeks they came back, and they asked the priest a second time would he wed them?" 'Have you the can?' said the priest. 'We have not,' said the tinker; 'we had it made at the fall of night, but the ass gave it a kick this morning the way it isn't fit for you at all.' 'Go on now,' says the priest, 'it's a pair of rogues and schemers you are, and I won't wed you at all.' They went off then, and they were never married to this day."

In the material so come upon, Synge made but little change. This play was written at the same time as *Riders to the Sea* and *In the Shadow of the Glen*, preceding them, it is thought, in conception, but not finished off until long after they had been produced. For obvious reasons it has never been performed in Ireland. Mr. Yeats tells us that the riotous reception given to *The Playboy* urged Synge to strengthen rather than to soften such features in it as were likely to give offence. Only in a few passages do we come on the deeper Synge, and those few passages apart, the play is scarcely worth considering either as a piece of stagecraft or as a piece of literature.

That tin can to which, very foolishly, such a leading part is assigned, played havoc with Synge's creative powers. It tied them down. In no other play of his do we come on that air of contrivance which always hangs above the action when mechanical aids are called in: how one wishes to forget all that handkerchief business in *Othello*! In the preface to the play Synge, with a lack of proportion not common with him, wrote that on the stage one must have both reality and joy. Either word, no matter how meagre a signification we give it, is too big, for there is no reality in the play, and such knockabout fun as is in it, is so obviously contrived that it has even a depressing effect. Reality does not need defence, neither does joy if reality be its foundation, even such joy as may be found in a play that laughs at those priests who stray so ludicrously from the normal as to become comic variations. The old woman in the play—the ' ever thirsty Mary '—is the one character that has a trace of roundness in her, of such abundancy as we find in Martin Doul in *The Well of the Saints*. The others are the merest puppets. Lacking reality, the play is barren of such joy as is deepened by our recollections of life : and as an element in drama joy must be assessed by the self-same tests we apply to terror in a play : we are to be moved by it in the totality of our being, toughened as we have been by living among men and women. Only a coarse-grained hobbledehoy could relish either the character-drawing of the priest or the general shindy in which *The Tinker's Wedding* ends. There is hardly a note of poetry in the play, which is tantamount to saying there is scarcely a trace of John Synge in it, for John Synge, it is clear, was overflowing with poetry in those years when, perhaps to his own surprise, he had happened on a channel into which he could pour his genius with every chance of preserving the integrity of that genius— the boon of all others the true artist most desires. Failing to put his real self into it, the play lacks central fire, the fire that fuses all elements into a comely and harmonious whole. In a sense its weakness is a tribute to the natural depths within himself, which would not give up their treasures until his own spirit had been moved by some vision of life as transfigured by poetry. His plays are sterling, exactly to the degree in which they record the happy incidence of such visions upon him.

In one place in *The Tinker's Wedding* we come on the true John Synge : it is Mary Byrne's monologue :

> " It's gone they are, and I with my feet that weak under me you'd knock me down with a rush ; and my head with a noise in it the like of what you'd hear in a stream and it running between two rocks and rain falling. What good am I this night, God help me ? What good are the grand stories I have when it's few would listen to an old woman, few but a girl maybe would be in great fear the time her hour was come, or a little child wouldn't be sleeping with the hunger on a cold night ? Maybe the two of them have a good right to be walking out the little short while they'd

be young ; but if they have itself, they'll not keep Mary
Byrne from her full pint when the night's fine, and there's a
dry moon in the sky. Jemmy Neill's a decent lad, and he'll
give me a good drop for the can, and maybe if I keep near
the peelers to-morrow for the first bit of the fair, herself
won't strike me at all ; and if she does itself, what's a little
stroke on your head beside sitting lonesome on a fine night,
hearing the dogs barking, and the bats squeaking, and you
saying over, it's a short while only till you die."

There is little else in the play on the level of this, little
else that gives us an idea of background, of a life lived within
that lonely contrivance which is everyman. The passage
dies away into continuing soliloquy within Mary's own self ;
this anyway we naturally think, until, unfortunately for us,
we discover from a stage direction that Mary is to go off
singing : *The night before Larry was stretched* ! So that even
here we seem to find Synge's creative powers working inter-
mittently, and not with that integrity they worked with,
say, in *The Well of the Saints*. The passage may have been
heightened when Synge was preparing the play for
publication, for it has in it the same feeling,—the horror of
old age, the sense of humanity's loneliness,—as is everywhere
in *Deirdre*, the only play he was afterwards to write. Except
old Mary Byrne, there is hardly a character in *The Tinker's
Wedding* worth a comment. Sarah Casey, at the beginning,
says : " The spring time is a queer time, and it's queer
thoughts maybe I do think at whiles," but we fail to find
in her any further confirmation of the idea we immediately
form of her as one whom the moods of nature play on as
on an instrument. As we have seen, the words testify
more to Synge's knowledge of the ways of tinkers than to
Sarah Casey's character. Michael Byrne says but little one
recalls ; and in the words of the German commentator the
priest is merely a figure of fun : " Der priester ist als reine
possenfigur, aber ohne jede tendenz gezeichnet." In this
character Synge does not laugh at the Irish priesthood. To
judge by his passing remarks on them, the priests he met
with in his travels he seemed to like ; it is nevertheless true

that no one reared in an Irish Catholic household would dream of creating a similar figure, unless of course he were, like Liam O'Flaherty, a mere sensationalist, for he would know that such a character would not be accepted. Even variations must keep measure ; and literature, and more especially dramatic literature, is a game played by two parties, the writer and the public. One cannot imagine an English writer of comedy putting on the stage, let us say, an English prime minister whose shirt tail was protruding through a hole in his pants ; yet such a character would make a really interesting variation from the run of English premiers, whose sense of public propriety has always been so overwhelming. English writers, happily born into a naturally developed national tradition, are not tempted to such blunders ; such liberties are unthinkable ; yet we find foreign critics, English critics among them, rather patronizingly wondering why this rather poor play has never been performed in Ireland ! A variation in England, or anywhere else except Ireland, must keep within bounds, and the national mind in those places is allowed to determine these bounds ; no such privilege is, however, to be allowed the Irish people. Though it is their way to observe their priests with far shrewder, far keener eyes, than clergymen are observed with in England, they are for all that to say nothing when a priest on the stage is made so absurdly ludicrous that they cannot accept him without jettisoning the experience of all their lives. One is sorry Synge ever wrote so poor a thing, and one fails to understand why it ever should have been staged anywhere.

# CHAPTER VIII.

## "THE WELL OF THE SAINTS"

IF *The Well of the Saints* be not a play of rare quality there are few such in English. None of Synge's other works has a flavour so likely to puzzle us, if not to elude us. If one cares for him at all, one relishes his *Playboy of the Western World ;* it wins as naturally upon one as a bright day in early summer, wilful with wind and sunshine. In the quiet months of autumn, however, in October, there may come certain unchanging days, as free of wind as of sun, that the multitude take no heed of because their spirits are not attentive. So is it with *The Well of the Saints :* it is dreamy, slow-pulsed, with here and there unexpectedly violent passages, not unlike the sudden outcries and scurrying that startle us if, on such days as these, we walk by the edge of still waters. The goodness of the play seems then to be one rather of flavour than of more sterling qualities. And, therefore, if we truly know the play, we give it our affection, for we have discovered a personal appeal in it, while to sheer excellence, as in the case of *Riders to the Sea,* we give admiration, sharing it, we flatter ourselves, with the whole world of the elect.

### I.

*The Well of the Saints* is in three acts, and the story may thus be summarized : Two blind beggars, Martin and Mary Doul,[1] husband and wife, are informed of the approach of a holy man who bears with him a vessel of miracle-working Water from the Well of the Saints. This holy man by the use of this water restores their sight to them. Misery and not happiness is for them the result. After long years of married

---

[1] *Doul,* that is *Dall,* Irish for *Blind.*

life they even drift apart. Blindness, however, overtakes them again. Once again also the holy man approaches and the neighbours, as before, urge them to avail of his powers ; wiser this time they refuse, preferring, united, to wander off into the wilderness, to destruction itself, it may be, lapped in the security of their own dreams.

It is well to state the subject to ourselves thus starkly, the better to estimate how strikingly the play, as we have it, illustrates the richness of Synge's genius.

Where, if anywhere, he came upon the fable is not certain. Mr. Padraic Colum tells us that Synge spoke to him of a mediæval French farce as having suggested the play to him ; [1] but that indefatigable researcher, M. Bourgeois, when he sought out this early farce, failed to track it down. Many other origins have, by one writer and another, been hinted at. Chaucer's *The Merchant's Tale*, Maeterlinck's *Les Aveugles*, Zola's *Lourdes*, as also Huysman's book on the same subject, Clemenceau's *Le Voile du Bonheur*, and a chapter in Lord Lytton's *The Pilgrims of the Rhine*,[2] have all been thought of as likely sources. *The Cricket on the Hearth* has also, of course, been mentioned. It would certainly be interesting to know definitely what fragment or story set Synge's mind working on the theme, but we cannot think that such knowledge, however certain, could make us much wiser than we are about Synge's self. His mind was actively creative, which is to say that whatever it seized upon, it made truly its own, the matter seized upon becoming not more but less refined, less abstract, less a thought or idea and more a gesturing, quaint-spoken boon companion of the whole tatterdemalion gipsy-gaudy crew his memory had already gathered from byeway and tavern, keeping them in fee as an old-time king his dwarfs and fools. The thoroughness with which a writer makes his own of what he seizes upon, is a measure of the thaumaturgic quality of his creative powers. Synge's genius was so truly creative

1 *The Road Round Ireland.*
2 Chapter IV. : *The Maid of Malines.*

that *Le Voile du Bonheur*, coldly artificial as it is, worked upon by it, might conceivably have become transformed into *The Well of the Saints ;* and with less difficulty, any of the other suggested origins might also, one thinks, through the same genius, have been raised and kindled to such warmth and colour as bedizen its simple and rural pomp. Yes, one would like to know where and when such a mind happened upon its prey in each particular adventuring, but those who petulantly undertake such inquiry for the malicious pleasure of proving the adventurer a mere thief and plagiarist, are surely piteously misunderstanding people. In Synge's own lifetime, sad to record, it was often with such squint-eyed zeal that the sources of *The Well of the Saints* were sought out. It is difficult to refrain from rejoicing when such mis-directed energy brings home such doubtful results. Synge may have lighted upon the fable more or less complete, as we have it in the play, but what we think did happen is that from his meeting with certain characters on our Irish roads, some of them blind, his imagination had become charged with images that clamoured for form, for ordered life ; and that some lucky chance, perhaps his happening on some mere phrase or verse, suddenly enlightened him as to how all these images might be fused and brought forth, no longer disparate, but unified and filled from a common fount of life. That verse in *The Love Songs of Connacht*, a book that he liked to frequent, might well have served to such an end :

> Happy 'tis, thou blind, for thee
> That thou seest not our star ;
> Could'st thou see as we now see
> Thou would'st be as we now are.

only that Synge, and very naturally for him, read the lines backwards. A mediæval pre-Renaissance farce might, of course, equally have fused the disparate elements, or, for that matter, some flying gleam that Synge might afterwards find himself unable to recall. Whatever it was, old French play or new French play, or story, or poem, the framework he decided to work upon was meagre enough and rickety enough. The form of the play is too slight for the life it contains, from which one may guess that this framework he did not discover in a genuine piece of folklore, as his custom was, for a genuine folk-tale is strongly jointed, as with fore-knowledge of the many adventurings it must endure, like the scenery of a travelling theatre. In *The Well of the Saints* it is the content rather than the form that resembles folk-lore. We believe then that Synge fashioned, in this case, his own fable, although of course he may have taken hints for it from many sources.

Of those images that were alive in his imagination and that are the real provenance of the play, we have many indications from his own pen. Early in the book on the Aran Islands we come on names and phrases that later were to be used in the play. "A couple of miles from this village we turned aside to look at an old ruined church of the Ceathair Aluinn (The Four Beautiful Persons), and a holy well near it that is famous for cures of blindness and epilepsy." [1] Just a little later :

'A woman of Sligo had a son who was born blind, and one night she dreamed that she saw an island with a blessed well in it that could cure her son. She told her son in the morning, and an old man said it was of Aran she was after dreaming.

' She brought her son down by the coast of Galway, and came out in a curagh, and landed below where you see a bit of a cove.

' She walked up then to the house of my father—God rest his soul !—and she told them what she was looking for.

' My father said that there was a well like what she was dreaming of, and that he would send a boy along with her to show her the way.

' " There's no need at all," she said, " haven't I seen it all in my dream ? "

' Then she went out with the child and walked up to this well, and she kneeled down and began saying her prayers. Then she put her hand out for the water, and put it on his eyes, and the moment it touched him he called out : " O Mother, look at the pretty flowers ! " '

[1] *The Aran Islands.* (i.) In the play : " Timmy, did you ever hear tell of a place across a bit of the sea, where there is an island, and the grave of the four beautiful saints," etc.

Here we have account of Synge's having actually seen a well whose waters were held to cure blindness. And fancy is bred now, as ever, in the eye. In this tale a writer of finer sensibilities than Synge would have been attracted, not so much to the cure itself, as to the mother who had seen the well in her dream and knew, because of her love, that she could discover it for herself. But anyone under the thraldom of the folk mind would have done as Synge did.

Perhaps we might also quote the following as among the sources from which the play derives :

> "About six o'clock I was going into the schoolmaster's house, and I heard a fierce wrangle going on between a man and a woman near the cottages to the west, that lie below the road. While I was listening to them several women came down to listen also from behind the wall, and told me that the people who were fighting were near relations who lived side by side and often quarrelled about trifles, though they were as good friends as ever the next day." [1]

Synge has frequently been blamed for setting himself to study such scenes, for eavesdropping, for spying on the people, as if he ever had any other interest in listening than to catch the turn of phrase used and the methods of working natural to unsophisticated minds. The two principal characters in *The Well of the Saints* quarrel also, for hours, one understands, over simple things, providing drama for themselves, breaking the tedium of life-long familiarity, in the same way as, in Lady Gregory's excellent little comedy *Workhouse Ward*, the bed-ridden pair quarrel, and with as little real malignity.

More important than these indications of the provenance of the play, is the account he gives in his book *In Wicklow and West Kerry* of a very remarkable vagrant he had come upon in Wicklow who had lived to be 102 or thereabouts, who had married often and had had so many children that in his old age he could not remember the age or sex of some of them.

---

[1] *The Aran Islands.* (iv.)

"When he was over ninety he married an old woman of eighty-five. Before many days, however, they quarrelled so fiercely that he beat her with his stick, and came out again on the roads. In a few hours he was arrested at her complaint, and sentenced to a month in Kilmainham. He cared nothing for the plank-bed and uncomfortable diet; but he always gathered himself together, and cursed with extraordinary rage, as he told how they had cut off the white hair which had grown down upon his shoulders. All his pride and his half-conscious feeling for the dignity of his age seemed to have set themselves on this long hair, which marked him out from the other people of his district; and I have often heard him saying to himself, as he sat beside me under a ditch: 'What use is an old man without his hair? A man has only his bloom like the trees; and what use is an old man without his white hair?'" [1]

This discovery by Synge that an old man may find compensation in what the years bring—the dignity of white hair—for what they have taken away, is one of the leading *motifs* in the play. The eighth line in it may indeed be thought of as the first significant line in it: "You were that length plaiting your yellow hair," says Martin Doul to his wife, "you have the morning lost on us," and afterwards, when he comes to describe her, of all her illusory gifts it is her hair he mentions first: "I've heard tell her yellow hair, and her white skin, and her big eyes are a wonder." When his sight is restored, the first woman he lays his eyes on he takes for his wife, because of her yellow hair: "The blessing of God on this day, and them that brought me the Saint, for it's grand hair you have." Discovering his mistake, he fastens on another, and again it s her hair he speaks of first: "Is it you is Mary Doul? I'm thinking you're more the like of what they said. For you've yellow hair, and white skin, and it's the smell of my own turf is rising from your shawl." And again, later, he informs us why he, as he says, drove her from him: "But there's one thing I'm telling you, if she walked off away from me, it wasn't because of seeing me, and I no more than I am, but because I was looking

---

[1] *In Wicklow and West Kerry.* (*The Vagrants of Wicklow*).

on her with my two eyes, and she getting up, and eating her food, and combing her hair, and lying down for her sleep." It is no different with Mary Doul herself; it is always her hair she mentions as her crowning charm: " If I'm not so fine as some of them said I have my hair, and big eyes, etc. . . . ."

It is Mary indeed who first makes the discovery that an old person needs no other charm ; she pictures herself with white locks, " the way when I'm an old woman there won't be the like of me surely in the seven counties of the east." Whereupon her spouse looks also into the future : " I'll be letting my beard grow in a short while, a beautiful, long, white, silken, streamy beard, you wouldn't see the like of in the eastern world . . . . Ah, a white beard's a grand thing on an old man, a grand thing for making the quality stop and be stretching out their hands with good silver or gold." The reason why the playwright stresses so much the hair right through, is, of course, because it is the discovery by the pair of them of the value and dignity of the beautiful white hair of old age that later on becomes the very *deus ex machina* of the piece.

We may assure ourselves, it would seem, that whether or not Synge came upon the fable in old French drama or in Irish folklore, it was his discovery of the old vainglorious vagrant in County Wicklow that impregnated it with life, causing it to stir and blossom.

The old blind man, Pat Dirane, who used to help Synge in his study of the Irish language, and who, in character, does not seem to have been quite unlike the blind man in the play, must also be reckoned as among the origins. It was perhaps his familiarity with Pat Dirane that gave Synge such certainty of himself in dealing with the dream-world which the sightless build up for themselves either from their own recollections of the past, or from the hints that reach them from the world of light, or from both. To recall Synge's intercourse with this old blind teacher of his ; his meeting with the Wicklow ancient whose hair was his glory ;

to recall his browsing ·on the folk songs Dr. Hyde had newly published ; to note also his own gathering of wayside legends ; to find him studiously and indeed joyously lending his ears to the quarrelling of the neighbours in Aran—to know Synge in such connections is of more importance to us than to come on some meagre tale where disillusionment follows the restoration of sight—a theme both hackneyed and old—for our task is not so much to determine the cold pattern that helped him in laying out his materials, as to feel our way into his mind, sharing a little in the creative warmth natural to it.

II.

*The Well of the Saints* comes third in the collected edition of Synge's plays ; it is not agreed, however, that it was the third of his plays in point of time. Mr. Howe speaks of it as his earliest play ; M. Bourgeois says it was composed in 1902-3 ; while Krieger says it was begun in 1903, but that the ill-health from which Synge so often suffered delayed its completion. It was performed for the first time, Feb. 4th, 1905, at the newly-opened Abbey Theatre to a house of barely two dozen. It was given seven performances.

We easily accept the statement that its writing was spread over a long time, and that it grew contemporaneously with his other early plays. In it he is obviously feeling his way towards a style of his own ; while its orchestration, its under-song, its texture, have the richness we find only in those works whose gestation period was not curtailed—works that almost unknown to their creators became one with their own very flesh and blood. The treatment of the Hair *motif*, already set out, assures us of this, it is done so naturally. Analysing it, one does not feel that those references to the hair, both of the old man and old woman, were distributed at due intervals in a mechanically efficient way as pointers, to use the word in the text books ; one feels rather that this *motif* had become instinctive in the characters themselves from their long ripening in the dramatist's mind, and had not been added to them for ulterior purposes, although of course those frequent references to the hair, those pointers, do strengthen the *dénouement* when it is reached. If the undersong in this play is richer and more deeply interfused than that of the *Playboy*, it is due, one thinks, to the lengthier period Synge indulged the characters within the warmth of his own brain.

III.

Whether Synge himself invented the fable or came upon it in his wanderings among men or books, it is clear that in it he found a theme after his own heart. If not actually a fragment of folklore (and anyone who knows the theme only in Clemenceau's pages, or in those of Lytton, would not associate it with folklore) it had anyhow the element of wonder largely in it, of miracle, which is the root of all folklore. Synge certainly treated it as if it were truly such. Time and place are practically unfixed. His direction is: "Some lonely mountainous district in the east of Ireland one or more centuries ago." He might as well have begun with : Once upon a time. The scheme of life in the play is so simple that the exact number of centuries does not matter ; anachronisms get no chance of showing themselves ; while his east of Ireland might as well be the west of Ireland, for one cannot discover any significance in the choice. But, for all this vagueness, the drama is simply drenched in the perennial atmosphere of the Irish countryside, as of course all Irish folklore is, the narrators knowing no other. It is as homely, as real, a piece of work as Clemenceau's, with its insipid effort at local colour, is alien and artificial. Moreover, it has the callousness of the folk-tale in it—the mockery of the blind pair by the neighbours, for instance. So treated it could not of course be any serious contribution to the question of the confrontation of the ideal with the real.

Not only did the theme fall naturally within the province of folklore, so commending itself to Synge, but it also allowed him to indulge his fancy for vagrants and their happy-go-

161

lucky ways. His whole conception of drama was Dionysiac, and folklore is no halfway house. We have seen in our consideration of *The Shadow of the Glen* that, in his view, the vagrants to be met with on the Irish roads were very often nothing else than gods in exile. In using vagrants on his stage he could indulge at the one time his feeling both for the Dionysiac and the natural, the homely, even the quaint. Indeed all his work may be described in such terms. It is at once both Dionysiac and homely. Naïveté is integral in *The Well of the Saints*. Saint and all, the characters are genuinely quaint ; the same homogeneous current of life flows through them all, whatever be their station in life. This homogeneity is characteristic of everything that Synge wrote ; more than anything else it shows him to have been always the intuitive artist, just as the frequent lack of it shows Shaw and, to take a lesser figure, Sean O'Casey, not to have been born in the purple, whatever gaudy shreds of it they may in their passage through life have gathered about their usurping limbs. The complacency of the blind couple in *The Well of the Saints*, displayed to us who see them for what they really are, is so thick and slab that it moves us to that sort of affection we bestow on a dog that is at once not only hideously ugly in his expression but vain-glorious as well : in doing so we perhaps experience the pleasure of living for the nonce by an outlandish, topsy-turvy, set of values. It is the pleasure we take in seeing Socrates off his perch. Yet quaint and homely as Synge's pair are, Martin and Mary Doul, there is in both, and more especially in Martin, who is on the stage practically from the opening to the close, a daemon which we do not laugh at. In all Synge's favourite characters there is this central unaccountable element that affects all those others round about them. Dionysiac, as well as quaint, it was possible for Synge to use deeper stops than are often to be found on the comedian's organ. The end of *The Well of the Saints* is not comedy at all. In spite of this, the subject matter is the true stuff of comedy. There are in it two views of one or more characters : the characters' own view, absurd, yet from their own standpoint, not quite foundationless ; and the spectator's privileged view from the outside, which, we flatter ourselves, we share with the gods, the eternal verities. This was Molière's idea of comedy ; and it is because his practice of it was so assiduous that we find no *Taming of the Shrew* in his pages, a play that is very thin gruel indeed.

In many ways then Synge in *The Well of the Saints* had a subject after his own heart. And we know of that heart that it had become very full indeed of affection for what was native to Ireland, for what was really Irish as distinguished from what was merely Anglo-Irish. We may, therefore, consider next whether this play is not the most Irish of all he wrote.

### IV.

That it is so is conceded by most of those who have asked themselves the question at all. Yet one does not always agree with the reasons they give for their choice. In the play they find one other illustration of the Celt's refusal to be dominated by the fact. The blind beggars, irritated by the real world to which the Saint has restored them, voluntarily choose afterwards to have no more to do with that real world preferring the dreaminess of the world of blindness. Says Krieger : " Zwei welten stossen hier aufeinander, und der konflikt zwischen diesen beiden grundverschiedenen anschauungen ist so irisch, wie ihn sich herr O'Donoghue nur wünschen könnte." [1] And practically all the other commentators agree that it is the clashing of the two worlds— the real and the ideal—in the play that stamps it as Irish, or as some of them write, Celtic. Mr. Boyd says : " *The Well of the Saints* is the only occasion in Synge's career where he appears to express the traditional revolt of the Celtic mind against the despotism of fact." [2] And M. Bourgeois writes : "At the same time the play . . . . beautifully expresses . . . . the oft-noted tendency in the Celtic temperament

---

[1] *John Millington Synge, ein dichter der keltischen renaissance*, von Hans Krieger.

[2] *The Contemporary Drama of Ireland*, by Ernest A. Boyd.

to take refuge in a world of dreams away from the foulness of an actuality transfigured, fortunately, by imaginative illusion." [1]

If a piece of literary work is Irish because it deals with the clashing of real and ideal, then Cervantes was as Irish a writer as ever lived ; but perhaps we are, after all, to understand that he was a Celt. What however are we to say of *Le Voile du Bonheur*, in which there is nothing except this selfsame clashing ? What one feels like saying is that anything less Irish, or indeed less Celtic, than that piece of insipidity could not well be imagined. If that same clashing is the subject matter of Synge's play, what a curious idealist we have in Martin Doul ! It is true that Krieger writes of him : " Ein idealist mit reichem gefühlsleben, will er sich nicht in die enge welt des philisters einzwängen lassen." [2] It is true one can force oneself to think of Martin Doul in these terms, even as one might think of Polonius as a moral philosopher, but only a German can do these things without smiling. In *Le Voile du Bonheur* the principal character is truly an idealist, and nothing else, by his ideas he lives ; but Martin Doul does not know what either ideas or ideals are ; he knows, however, what appetites are, by them he would live, if he could. He may be taken as the fullest expression of Synge's very simple and very homogeneous philosophy of life. But it is not because Martin Doul fundamentally is this or that or t'other, with or against the Philistines, that the play is Irish. Padraic Colum gives us the true reason when he writes : " *The Playboy of the Western World* dramatises what is most characteristic in Gaelic life, the Gaelic delight in vivid personality " [3]—a true saying, sanctioned by two thousand years of Irish literature, from the sagas, with their every figure vivid and bitingly alive, to the poems of the eighteenth century, *Cúirt an Mheadhon Oidhche* for instance, or *Eachtra Ghiolla an Amaráin*. And

1 *John Millington Synge and the Irish Theatre*, by M. Bourgeois.
2 *John Millington Synge, ein dichter der keltischen renaissance*, von Hans Krieger.
3 *The Road Round Ireland*, by Padraic Colum.

it is because Martin Doul is a more real and vivid personality than the Playboy, who is only a lyric boy, that this play has a more Gaelic feeling in it than *The Playboy of the Western World*. And it is the utter absence of vivid personality in *Le Voile du Bonheur* that sets that play apart from anything that an Irishman could take interest in. Clemenceau's play may be taken as an extreme example of the insipidity that usually attaches to the treatment of blindness in literature, *The Cricket on the Hearth* serving as an example of the sentimentality that attaches to it. Irish literature of all ages may be searched without yielding scarce a line that can be described as either insipid or sentimental—if we except some poems written in certain districts in the eighteenth century where the literary tradition of the language had almost died. This liking for the vivid, the biting, in literature persisted in Irish when, through the influence of the Renaissance, with its alien, far-off, literary values, it had long died out in the main languages of Europe. Irish literature never drew away from its own folklore or from its own folk, even when the writers of it were Earls of Kildare or Earls of Desmond; never withdrew itself into classical colleges; and if it had a poetic diction among its resources, as it had, that poetic diction, unlike that of other languages, was as truly native, and as much a part of the mother tongue, as the ordinary household words in daily use. We may, therefore, understand how the folklore character that is so obvious in the play still further helps to bring Gaelic feeling into it. Nor must we fail further to notice the setting—the ruined church, as also the blessed well, the simple-minded saint, the hand-bell he carries about with him, as all furthermore assisting to separate the play from others which even more truly deal with the clashing of real and ideal. The Gaelic feeling then in the play has been induced in it not by the nature of the theme but by the treatment given to that theme. The writer at the time was deeply under the influence of the living folk-mind of the unschooled people of Aran, as also under the influence of Irish literature with its affiliations to pre-Renaissance standards both of thought and style.

If most critics, for whatever reasons, reckon the play as the most Irish of Synge's works, certain others protest that it is the least Irish because of certain phrases and incidents that occur in it. Thus M. Bourgeois writes : " Last but not least, we regard as utterly untrue to the Irish nature Martin Doul's gesture when he dashes the holy water can from the saint's hand ; an Irish Catholic would no more do ' the like of that ' than would a priest like Father Hart in Mr. Yeats's *Land of Heart's Desire* consent to hide a crucifix at the request of an evil fairy."

One wonders if the point of view so expressed be not too simple to argue against. In Ireland there is, and there must unfortunately continue to be, an overweening sensitiveness about the portrayal of the national character ; with this sensitiveness we shall deal in the chapter on *The Playboy of the Western World*, the play that, on account of its stormy reception, most aptly raises the question. This sensitiveness would have expressed itself in Anglo-Irish literature if that literature were native and not alien to the genius of the isle ; lacking such expression, lacking indeed any intelligent medium of expression at all, the people themselves have protested in open riots and at public meeting. Such words as we have quoted from M. Bourgeois, no unliterary person, are to be heard every other day from people in our midst who have never given a thought to literature. They feel, and no wonder, that they are not being truly exhibited either in novel or play, and so they break out recalcitrant, not knowing quite what is wrong. They have no acquaintance with mediæval or even with their own Irish literature ; they, therefore, are unlearned in what Catholic literature expresses naturally, as also with what their own particular branch of Catholic literature expressed naturally when it was intact and not put upon from without. They are equally uninstructed in what a serious writer finds himself driven to express through his characters if he would earnestly delineate his own people. Many points have to be considered that those unliterary people, as also those who speak for them, never think of. Does the writer, dramatist or novelist, introduce such words, such incidents as give offence, for the purpose of shocking his public ?—a charge Miss Rebecca West brings against James Joyce. If he does, it is not worth while protesting, for inasmuch as he indulges in such puerile wantonness, his work is weak and not sterling. Or is he squint-eyed ? He is squint-eyed if his backgrounds are perennially awry. We have read novels dealing with our people in which no single character was ordinarily sane or ordinarily moral: the writers seemed to have no sense of the value of relief or of the need for contrast, not to speak of such higher considerations as the influence of an all-embracing sympathy on creation, or the influence on style of the supreme gift of seeing life in the round. Squint-eyed work is as little worthy of protest as is wanton work : the odd, as Dr. Johnson pointed out, does not last long. Again, is the writer doctrinaire ? Is he writing dramas or novels *à thèse*, and has he become fanatic in his quest ? The discussion of such plays we had better leave to experts and moralists : the audience that relishes such work will as equally relish the protest, not seeing much difference between one and the other.

To come to Synge : he was bluntly insensitive to the finer spiritual values. Incidents in the plays, words and phrases, not to mention the vast tracts of human thinking and endeavour that escaped him, give us to understand this. He is in his plays occasionally wanton, not grossly wanton ; we catch him at the childish sport of shocking his audience ; nevertheless in spite of this insensitiveness he is on the whole a sane and healthy writer, saner and healthier than many a writer who cannot at all be charged with such offences. He is healthy because the mass of his people are so ordinarily sane and moral that to play even with the edge of misdemeanour is an adventure for them. A writer is to be tested in such matters rather by his backgrounds than by

those principal characters of his that occupy the foreground.
For in his understanding of the background we have his sense
of balance, his sense of the totality of life as lived, whereas
his leading men and women delineate for us his sense of life
as overtaken by disaster all too great, or by ecstasy all too
overwhelming. In dealing with life so overcome he is
in reality dealing with not only the ineffable but the
unknowable. No wonder then Hugo defined genius as a
promontory into the unknown. In this particular play of
Synge's, as indeed in all his plays, we have the sense of
ordinarily sane standards of living in the background. And
we may therefore whole-heartedly accept Synge's own statement : " In all the healthy movements of art, variations
from the ordinary types of manhood are made interesting for
the ordinary man, and in this way only the higher arts are
universal. Beside this art, however, founded on the variations
which are a condition and effect of all vigorous life, there is
another art—sometimes confounded with it—founded on the
freak of nature, in itself a mere sign of atavism or disease.
This latter art, which is occupied with the antics of the freak,
is of interest only to the variation from ordinary minds, and
for this reason is never universal. To be quite plain, the
tramp in real life, Hamlet and Faust in the arts, are
variations ; but the maniac in real life, and Des Esseintes
and all his crew in the arts, are freaks only." [1] This is a
sane man's view of writing, and Synge's practice agreed
with his theory. To have Synge's work such as *The Well
of the Saints* described as un-Irish because his ' variations '
do what is surprising, that is, act as variations, is not helpful
to any cause or theory. ' No Irishman would do the like
of that '—those who urge such a consideration are really
arguing against themselves, for have we not seen that Synge
held the same view ? Variations from the ' Irishman '—
would not they ' do the like of that ? ' Thank heaven, in
Irish literature, we have many Irishmen—that is variations,
whose place it is not to exhibit the depth and height and

[1] *In Wicklow and West Kerry.*

strangeness and beauty of Irish life so much as of life itself, Irishmen who ' do the like of that ; ' and we do not read that the Irish public of those days protested against their creators, though of course they may have, the protest of the shallow being one thinks as sempiternal as the instinct of the artist. We may then, as Irishmen, accept with an easy conscience Martin Doul's flinging aside of the holy water. The action springs directly out of the character of the man, as also out of the nature of the situation : Martin Doul is an unspiritual creature : the repercussions that might follow from an act of impiety have no existence for him. What is really expressed in the action is not his contempt for holy things, but the tyranny of his imaginings over himself. To the world of blindness he will, at any cost, cleave, his adventuring in the world of light having had such disastrous consequences. There are passages, however, in this play, as also in others, where Synge is simply wanton—we have for instance the first part of Martin Doul's set speech at the end of the play. Here the writer imposes his own mind on the mind of the character : we feel Synge himself behind the words rather than Martin Doul ; and this is the test-stone in such cases. But such a test the unliterary cannot understand.

V.

It is the folklore atmosphere in it, an untender atmosphere in which the sentimental cannot breathe, that gives flavour to the play ; but it is the richness and integrity of the character study in it that gives it its coherence and strength. Mr. Yeats very aptly points out that those dramatists who treat of politics or social passions fail to create what he calls ' abundant ' characters.[1] Ibsen did not do so, nor does Shaw. In Martin Doul, in this wayside beggar, illiterate, one may think, without a thought in his head, foolish even to look upon or to listen to, we have the most abundant character created by Synge. Deirdre, in his play *Deirdre of the Sorrows*, we might name as the nearest to him in roundness

[1] *Essays.*

and integrity. Martin Doul is purely naturalistic—appetite without intelligence. He can think of nothing the whole day long if in the morning he has listened to the voice of Molly Byrne, for the sound of her voice of itself creates within him an image he would enjoy; when his sight is restored, despite the self-knowledge so attained to, he makes love to her with such an intensity and passion as makes the love scenes in *The Playboy* seem the merest play-acting. In the love-making of Martin Doul there is a double opposition, his own self—'an old, wicked, coaxing fool,' 'a little dark stump of a fellow looks the fool of the world;' there is also the fact that Molly Byrne is set against him; whereas in the love-making of Christy Mahon and Pegeen in *The Playboy*, there is no opposition at all. We, therefore, understand why, in spite of ourselves, we are moved far more by the love scene in *The Well of the Saints* than by that in *The Playboy of the Western World*: the headlong energy in the love-making of Martin Doul blinds us for the moment to the wantonness he urges. There is in him an active principle that will not rest nor let others rest. The gift of sight he uses to set the world by the ears—Timmy the smith he shames into washing his face! He does the devil's work, maddening the people, filling them with a strange spirit, setting every person in the place, "and up beyond Rathvanna, talking of nothing but the way they do be looking in the face." He is everything that, in literature, a wayside beggar, whether blind or not, should not be. If he lays such strong hands upon us it is because he lives his own life. He is moreover genuinely part and parcel of the poetry of earth; the beauty of night-fall he feels as also the terror of the unseen. There is a significant passage, which one might easily read through or listen to without seizing on all that is in it; it occurs when he has reached the very depths of disillusionment:

Martin Doul (*gloomily*). The devil mend Mary Doul for putting lies on me, and letting on she was grand. The devil mend the old Saint for letting me see it was lies. (*He sits down near her*). The devil mend Timmy the smith for killing me with hard work, and keeping me with an empty, windy stomach in me, in the day and in the night. Ten thousand devils mend the soul of Molly Byrne—(*Mary Doul nods her head with approval*)—and the bad, wicked souls is hidden in all the women of the world. (*He rocks himself, with his hand over his face*). It's lonesome I'll be from this day, and if living people is a bad lot, yet Mary Doul, herself, and she a dirty, wrinkled-looking hag, was better maybe to be sitting along with than no one at all. I'll be getting my death now, I'm thinking, sitting alone in the cold air, hearing the night coming, and the blackbirds flying round in the briars crying to themselves, the time you'll hear one cart getting off a long way in the east, and another cart getting off a long way in the west, and a dog barking maybe, and a little wind turning the sticks. (*He listens and sighs heavily*). I'll be destroyed sitting alone and losing my senses this time the way I'm after losing my sight, for it'd make any person afeared to be sitting up hearing the sound of his breath— (*he moves his feet on the stones*)—and the noise of his feet, when it's a power of queer things do be stirring, little sticks breaking, and the grass moving—(*Mary Doul half sighs, and he turns on her in horror*)—till you'd take your dying oath on sun and moon a thing was breathing on the stones. (*He listens towards her for a moment, then starts up nervously, and gropes about for his stick*). I'll be going now, I'm thinking, and I'm destroyed with terror and dread. (*He touches her face as he is groping about and cries out*) : There's a thing with a cold, living face on it sitting up at my side. (*He turns to run away, but misses his path and stumbles in against the wall*). My road is lost on me now ! Oh, merciful God, set my foot on the path this day, and I'll be saying prayers morning and night, and not straining my ear after young girls, or doing any bad thing till I die.

Here surely is an abundant character. We have first the wanton passionate creature who knows no bounds. Then we have the lonely outcast sighing even for the company of Mary Doul, on whom with suddenly opened eyes he had looked with unutterable disgust. We have then the lyric poet : " I'll be getting my death now "—and, later, the imaginative human being for whom the darkness is filled with terrors. And then the craven, as abject in his desolation as he had been fierce a moment before when no curse he could frame was wild enough to relieve his spirit. Yes, an abundant character, ringing true, all the time, however, convincing us not of any theories but of his own existence among the wayward intermingling currents both of life as lived and life as dreamt upon. How thin-drawn in comparison appear those clever ones whom Mr. Shaw has given us, with their pertness in explaining, so intolerably clearly, the depth and height of life—Life, we should have said—itself, or those more humble creatures Mr. Galsworthy has so carefully turned out, social types, well-pressed and juiceless epitomes !

So much for the character of Martin Doul. Mary Doul, his wife, is of an opposed type, yet not so opposite as to suggest that both could never have lived together nor have suffered individually the same malign fate. Mary's character, as well as Martin's, has been moulded by long years of blindness. The inner principle in Martin's character is out-going : he will touch other people, his dreams are of others : others he would enjoy. Mary's principle is self-centred : she will sit with her hands crossed, like an eastern deity, and, showing no sign, overhear the praises of those who cannot help admiring her. She is complacency itself. Indeed her features I might picture to myself as resembling those of Epstein's ' Night ' if only I did not recall that she was nothing but a wayside beggar, accustomed to hold out her hand for alms. But one does not imagine her either as cringing for alms or petulantly or violently uttering her disappointment when nothing is dropped in her hand. She is too rooted in self-satisfaction for that. She therefore, in current speech, never gives herself away, whereas her headlong and scatter-brained spouse is always doing so, getting into hot water now with herself, Mary Doul, and then with Molly Byrne or with Timmy the smith, even with the benign and simple-hearted Saint himself. Her delineation is never out of drawing. Martin Doul awaiting the miracle that is to restore his sight breaks out : "And we'll be seeing ourselves this day. Oh, glory be to God, is it true surely ? " But Mary's anxiety is different : " Maybe I'd have time to walk down and get the big shawl I have below, for I do look my best, I've heard them say, when I'm dressed up with that thing on my head." When Molly Byrne, the young handsome girl, tells her why the Saint has entrusted her with the holy water : " for young girls," says he, " are the cleanest holy people you'd see walking the world," Mary Doul, as she sits down, laughs quietly to herself, and says : " Well, the Saint's a simple fellow, and it's no lie,"—a comment that would be hard to beat.

The remaining characters in the play are all slightly yet sufficiently drawn. The Saint is an innocent. He is indeed what our country people would call ' a bit of a gom.' Of intellect he has scarcely any, in speech he is no keener than the villagers about him. Yet Synge must have had some feeling for him since he granted him the great virtue of being able to see the beauty of God in the beauties of nature. Synge, it may be, was thinking of those old-time Gaelic saints who recorded their love of blackbird and blossoming wood in lyric strains that anticipated those of St. Francis by hundreds of years.

Timmy the smith, Molly Byrne, and the few others in the play, are brought in simply to carry on the action. Martin Doul and Mary Doul are the play. Synge had through long and affectionate brooding on them come to know them to the quick ; they had attained to a full and deep life before he wrote them down. In comparison with them Christy Mahon and Pegeen Mike in *The Playboy* are inventions, with but little substance in them. It is curious to note how impossible it is, however keen of brain we may be, to invent scene or character in play or tale that has not been invented a thousand times already ; whereas if our affections lead us to the discovery of something in life itself, our portrayals are never quite flat or insipid. Almost any writer might have created, if this be not too big a word, either the Playboy or Pegeen, but nobody except Synge himself could have spied out in the swirling currents of life around us, those two blind creatures, fastening on them with a keen eye, and rescuing them in all their integrity, not only for our entertainment but also for our enlightenment as to the depths and riches of those selfsame swirling tides.

VI.

Whether first or third of his plays, *The Well of the Saints* is quite certainly his first three-act play. To notice that each of the three acts is complete in itself is to guess as much. Act I. is finished so roundly that it is not possible to see from it how the action is to have further development. In it we have a quite sufficient theme : Two blind beggars, living their own life, making of the whole world what they will, are cured by a wandering saint ; instead of being what the neighbours have been saying they are, they discover that they are and always have been ugly and dirty ; the play ends, as comic plays so often end, in the husband and wife falling on each other with bitter words and blows. So too Act II., almost without the addition of even another expositional phrase, is self-contained, the theme again sufficient. We learn that these two, man and wife, have been cured of blindness ; that their custom had been to sit by the wayside exciting sympathy in the passers-by, but that these passers-by they had rather despised, so self-centred and rich with vain dreaming had been the inner life they indulged within their darkness. This aloof and self-wrought existence they have exchanged, we learn, for one of common drudgery ; they must now work with their hands, like everybody else, so strange are the blessings of sight ! This drudgery they could bear if only the wonted fires of their blind existence would die down ; but they will not die down ; they break out, not only to their own undoing but to the disturbance of the whole countryside. Blindness rather mercifully overtakes them again and the discord is resolved. In this Act therefore we have a complete little play. As for Act III., it is not only a finished one-act play, but may be taken as a model of such. Characteristic of the writer, it is a lyric outcry. Here are two blind people repossessing themselves of the happy kingdom they lost as soon as the Saint touched their lids with the holy water. Sight had brought them unhappiness, even desolation. Blindness, however, has restored them to unity and the exaltation of dreams. The Saint comes once more into their neighbourhood : they are tempted once more to try the blessed water ; but they resist, choosing voluntarily and exultantly to stand by their dreams. In this mood they leave the stage, although we foresee destruction for them.

Three one-act plays do not make a good three-act play. There is no rising line of interest to be followed with excitement. A fourth act might as aptly, we may think, follow the third as that followed the second. This accounts partly for the want of enthusiasm with which the play has always been received in the theatre. Perhaps also the language, all the way through, swings to a rhythm that is too slow for drama : the conception of Martin Doul and Mary Doul is the work of a dramatist, but the rhythms in the play mirror for us a lyric poet, and a young lyric poet at that. Yet one of the charms of the play is that it is in these slow rhythms and these lyric words we come to know of the restless energy, even the violence, that is in Martin Doul's central being. The language of the play, chiefly because of these rhythms, but also because of the texture and colour in it, the frequency of image—homely yet beautiful—for instance, comes benignly between us and the threadbare economy of the life dealt with, disguising it from us, arousing our affections, as the most featureless countryside, if only an amber-coloured sunshine rest upon it, may entice us to happy contemplation. What is this to say only that the play is a piece of literature ? We may, if we are foolish enough to allow the passion of analysis to overcome us, fix our attention on the illiteracy of the characters, their want of depth, their crudeness, their want of balance, even their foolishness, viewing the action as if we had bartered the tenderness, the many-sidedness of sensibility for the hardness and the close focus of mere brain. It is the well-made play, in the bad sense of the term, that

keeps the average audience alert and joyous—God help us !—
no matter how patchy the raiment of mood surrounding the
action may be, or how disparate the elements themselves
within the raiment. *The Well of the Saints* is possessed
almost too richly of the virtues that the ' well-made play '
knows so little of. The elements within the raiment may be
meagre enough, circumscribed, even undignified, but they
are not dissonant : they are harmonious ; while the raiment
is rich, deep-toned, and woven of one piece, integral from
opening to close.¹ It breathes music, a strange and rare
music, in the texture of which we are ever experiencing
reality as well as dream.

But if *The Well of the Saints* be anything but a ' well-made
play,' it is also anything but a play for the closet, which is
nearly always the very negation of drama. If it shows the
'prentice-hand in the want of carry-over between act and
act, it also shows the intuitive dramatist on almost every
page. In the first act we may note the preparation for the
Saint's entry. Out of the simplest materials there is created
a feeling of processional ritual that is just right : Molly Byrne
and Bride approach, carrying individually the Saint's water
can, bell and cloak. The Saint's entry is delayed. There is
a little play-acting with his bell and cloak, exactly the harm-
less sort of play-acting that is so common not only in Irish
folklore but even in Irish life, as probably in the life of every
other deeply Catholic people as well.² This play-acting, this
dressing-up, develops into one of those almost hourly quarrels
between Martin and Mary Doul that keep time itself from

1 But Synge should not have allowed Martin Doul to use that overworked
expression " dreaming dreams ! "—one of the very few places in which Synge
writes like a journalist, however respectable the ancestry of the phrase
may be.
  Nor should he have allowed Molly Byrne the expression " . . . . and
what does any man care for a wife, when it's two weeks, or three, he is looking
in her face " A young, fine-looking girl, about to be married, would not
allow herself to think such a thought, let alone express it.

2 I have just been listening to a tale in Irish telling of the high jinks
Saint Patrick, Conan Maol, and others of such Gaels as live in the folk
imagination, some of them Christian, some pagan, carry on in heaven on
Saint Patrick's Day !

rotting on their hands ; and this quarrel, this unexpected sequence on the appearance of the Saint's cloak and blessed water and bell, distracts our minds from simply waiting for his own arrival. When he does come, he comes with a certain suddenness ; his coming serves also to shift the planes ; we see the company present struck into sudden demureness, patent to us, unsuspected of the simple Saint ; we are also agog as to what is to happen next. It is homely, unforced yet effective comedy.

Act II. is like a movement in a sonata, Martin Doul the principal, almost the usurping theme, in it. At the opening the theme is unhappy, snatchy, tossing hither and thither, presently to develop into unforeseen strength and passion— Martin's love-making—which being broken in upon, struggles to resume its onward rush—the movement concluding with tumultuous chords struck all over the keyboard—disillusionments, recapturings, mad hopes, and last of all, wild and headlong cursing.

The first half of Act III. the mutual discovery of each other by man and wife, they each having, in their new blindness, crept back to their old wayside station ; Mary's silence while Martin gropes his way about, confessing to himself his desire for any company at all, even that of his own wife ;—all this is again unforced yet effective comedy, having in it besides the fine salt of significance. It is no new thing in stagecraft, yet here it has no appearance of having been contrived. Their mutual happiness becomes a spring-time lyric when suddenly, in the distance, they catch once more the sound of the Saint's bell—a fine touch. The end of the act is not so good. That wind that begins to rise is merely hinted at ; one thinks it should suddenly strike at the company with wild bellowings : we seem to require more than a doubtful catastrophe, for the end of the play is not comedy at all. It may be questioned whether comedies should so end, but it is the fact that the greatest comedians, Shakespeare and Molière, somehow fall into them—and what then can a theorist say ? The effort at pointing the moral at the end is amiss. It is the nearest approach in Synge to a direct lesson : his plays, truly literary, teach only through the sympathies and antipathies, when, as we say, his hand is in.

The abundance in Martin's character, the mellowness of the medium through which we are given that character : these are the two main features in the play which account for its flavour.

# CHAPTER IX.

## "THE PLAYBOY OF THE WESTERN WORLD"

### I.

WE have now come to *The Playboy of the Western World*. It is Synge's most famous piece of work, so famous indeed that one can hardly deal with it without becoming entangled in legend. To grow is of the nature of legend. "There were riots in Dublin when this play was first produced," and the foreigner, not knowing these for words out of a legend, sees, in his mind's eye, a tumult-ridden city, with chargings and counter-chargings in its streets and squares. Both inside and outside the Abbey Theatre during the first few performances of the play there certainly were squabbles and protestings, but to speak of them as riots is to use the very accents of the Playboy himself. Mr. Padraic Colum writes of the first performance: "I remember well how the play nearly got past the dubiousness of that first-night audience. The third act was near its close when the line that drew the first hiss was spoken,—'A drift of the finest women in the County Mayo standing in their shifts around me.' That hiss was a signal for a riot in the theatre. They had been disconcerted and impatient before this, but the audience, I think, would not have made any interruption if this line had not been spoken. Still, they had been growing hostile to the play from the point where Christy's father enters. That scene was too representational. There stood a man with horribly-bloodied bandage upon his head, making a figure that took the whole thing out of the atmosphere of high comedy." [1] Mr. Yeats takes up the

[1] *The Road Round Ireland*, by Padraic Colum.

tale : " On the second performance of *The Playboy of the Western World*, about forty men who sat in the middle of the pit succeeded in making the play entirely inaudible. Some of them brought tin trumpets, and the noise began immediately on the rise of the curtain. For days articles in the Press called for the withdrawal of the play, but we played for the seven nights we had announced ; and before the week's end opinion had turned in our favour. There were, however, nightly disturbances and a good deal of rioting in the surrounding streets. On the last night of the play there were, I believe, five hundred police keeping order in the theatre and in its neighbourhood." [1]

The protest made with such heat was two-fold. It was religious. It was nationalistic. And only such outsiders as have lived in countries where an alien Ascendancy, for two centuries or more, have been casting ridicule on everything native, can really understand it. Do not psychologists tell us that if an occurrence, which causes us mental pain, is repeated, every repetition brings not only its own particular amount of pain but brings, as well, recollection of our former sufferings from the same cause, that is, brings more than the amount of pain intrinsic in the event. The *Playboy* incident, then, was not unrelated : it awakened within the national consciousness ancestral disturbances. The new protest was portion of the old. Wherever there is an alien Ascendancy there is such an attendant protest, perennial, and on occasions quickening into noise and violence.

As to its cause and its nature, we may find instruction in these words :

" If an Irishman of any distinction be found a blackleg, a knave, a traitor or a coward, there arises a certain mirth in the discovery among strangers of all kinds, especially the English, as if they were glad to light upon an example in that nation of what is a pretty general rule in most countries at this time of day. But where they dare joke upon it, the single blot is imputed with great gaiety to that whole people. Thus all Ireland is made answerable for the faults of every

1 *Plays and Controversies*, by W. B. Yeats.

one of her children, and every one of these bears the whole weight of the country upon his shoulders. Therefore, the Irishman must, in his own defence, and that of his whole country, be braver and more nice in regard to his reputation than is necessary for any other man to be. If there is any mistake or crime in his conduct, not only he but his whole country is sure to pay for it. All this is owing to the calumny dispersed, time out of mind, by the tongues and pens of two neighbouring nations, in order to justify their own barbarous proceedings in regard to that unhappy people."

Will it be believed that these words were written two hundred years ago ? They are to be found in a letter from Chevalier Wogan, an Irish soldier of fortune abroad on the continent, to his friend Dean Swift.[1] They contain the simple truth. To sit among the audience in the Abbey Theatre when one of, say, Sean O'Casey's plays is on the stage, is to learn how true it is that the single blot is, *with great gaiety*, attributed to the whole people. To remain silent in the midst of that noisy gaiety, even to fling brickbats about, protesting against it, is, one thinks, to avoid the deeper vulgarity.

The protest attending on an alien Ascendancy's callous caperings is, of course, always most active in a period of national revival. In 1907, when *The Playboy* was first produced, the Irish revival was rapidly gathering momentum— we who were then fairly young murmur when we recall the period, ' Bliss was it in that dawn to be alive,'—and therefore Ireland's young men were become, perhaps, oversensitive where the representation of the native Ireland was concerned. Religion and nationality are not separable in Ireland. If in any piece of work there occur not only incidents which reflect, or seem to reflect, on the native Ireland, but also words and phrases which hurt the religious consciousness of that Ireland, then the offence of that piece of work is reckoned, in such periods, doubly gross, and not deserving of any fine consideration or afterthought. So was it with *The Playboy*.

[1] *The Life of Chevalier Charles Wogan*, by J. M. Flood.

It is too easily taken for granted by those who have since written on the whole matter that the protest was without foundation : that they who made it simply wrote themselves down barbarians. These superior people forget that the play is not now given the same representation as then ; nor are all the offensive phrases spoken : the fact is they are usually all omitted. When the play was broadcast from London[1] not only were such phrases as offended in Dublin omitted, but many others as well, for instance, " I wouldn't be fearing the looséd kharki cut-throats, or the walking dead," a sentence which the English censor also cut out when the Abbey company took the play for the first time to London. If, therefore, there are motes in the eyes of the Irish people, there are whole beams in the eyes of the English people. Then we fortunately have an outsider's account of the impression a performance of the play in Paris made on those present—a literary audience we may assume:

> Les acteurs qui ont joué à Paris il y a quelques années une traduction du *Baladin* n'ont pas semblé comprendre tout ce qu'il y a de délicatesse et de poésie profonde dans l'âme fruste de ces simples et leur langage savoureux. Ils ont poussé à la caricature et ont fait du *Baladin* une farce brutale et dégoûtante, sous prétexte que les personnages étaient des paysans. C'est que, lorsque nous représentons les paysans au théâtre, en France, nous en faisons de fades soupirants de bergeries, vêtus de velours et de soie, et la houlette enrubannée—ou bien des lourdauds ridicules. Notre théâtre est un théâtre de salon, la France ne connaît pas le paysan. En Irlande au contraire, le théâtre est presque tout entier paysan et, en vérité, c'est un art solide et profond que celui dont les racines sont fixées dans la terre et dont l'âme est celle du peuple.[2]

The actors seem to have given the play in somewhat the same way as it was first given in the Abbey Theatre itself. Now, it will be admitted that the Irish people had many urgings, ancestral voices among them, towards protests that neither the French nor the English could scarcely realize, yet

---

[1] January 19th, 1928.
[2] *L'île des bardes :* Simone Téry.

these peoples also, as we have seen, even if silently and through other channels, made their protest. They have not, however, been called barbarians for doing so. Of the protest in America it is better to take no account. Mr. Shaw felt called upon to write a pamphlet on it for the comforting of his own and England's soul : it was the pseudo-Irish who protested ! They would, one must think, have proved themselves real Irish if they had done quite otherwise from what their brothers in Dublin had done !

The protest, at any rate in Dublin, was inevitable. The natural, the inevitable, needs no apology. The fault lies not in the native Ireland but in Ascendancy Ireland, which has played the game of literature not for its own eyes, such as they have been and are, but for English eyes, not expressing Ireland to itself but exploiting it for others. Had Ascendancy Ireland treated Ireland fairly, serving up, without any ulterior motives, in literary form, the life of the country, had Ireland been long accustomed to see its own life so served up, so looked at and commented on, honestly from many standpoints, always, however, from indigenous, that is, natural standpoints, *The Playboy*, instead of being greeted with outcry and passion, would have been taken for what it was worth.

In it Synge probably did give way to a desire to shock his audience ; yet of this one cannot be quite certain. It may be that he expected a Dublin audience to look at the spectacle of the play as a purely folk audience in the West, self-contained and not conscious that their neighbour in the next seat in the theatre was English-eyed, might conceivably have done, for Synge was simple about many things, and was amorous of the honest insensibility of the folk consciousness. For that sensitiveness, that touchiness, if one likes, our history has induced in us, he had but little feeling : the "harrow of sorrow" is a common phrase in Irish poetry, and a harrow reduces to fineness. As for our religious consciousness, he was not quite unaware of it, it is true ; was sometimes even touched by it—if also, at other times, estranged—but certainly he never became initiate of it. Knowing of this dullness of his to what is ever almost too alert, too quick, in our people's consciousness, we are able to conceive that he could honestly think the audience would enjoy the play even as he himself would enjoy it if another pen had written it. And his bearing in the theatre during the first performance falls in with this view of him. He is said to have remarked that it would be necessary to establish a society for the preservation of Irish humour. For humour he had an Anglo-Irish stomach, which, remembering Swift, and Lever, and Lover, and Maginn, and Prout, and George Birmingham, and Sean O'Casey, and Somerville and Ross, and St. John Ervine, and Dr. Gogarty, one thinks must be as strong, if not as naïve, as the folk stomach in all lands. On that night some of the pressmen questioned him on the play, and he answered them that certain incidents in it were improbable, that the whole thing was extravaganza. This admission his admirers at the time regarded as calamitous ; and Synge himself in a short and very curious letter to the Press immediately withdrew it

> " *The Playboy of the Western World* is not a play with a
> ' purpose ' in the modern sense of the word, but, although
> parts of it are, or are meant to be, extravagant comedy, still
> a great deal that is in it and a great deal more that is behind
> it is perfectly serious when looked at in a certain light. This is
> often the case, I think, with comedy, and no one is quite
> sure to-day whether Shylock or Alceste should be played
> seriously or not. There are, it may be hinted, several sides
> to *The Playboy*." [1]

This is an honest letter. An artist makes a play and afterwards analyses his own impulses in doing so ; when Synge wrote this letter he was only beginning the analysing process. Far more illuminating, however, is this passage in a personal letter of his to a friend, written about the same time :

> " It isn't quite accurate to say, I think, that the thing is
> a generalization from a single case. If the idea had occurred
> to me I could and would just as readily have written the

[1] *John Millington Synge*, by M. Bourgeois.

> thing, as it stands, without the Lynchehaun case or the
> Aran case. My story—*in its essence* ("essence" underlined
> four times) is probable given the psychic state of the locality.
> I used the cases afterwards to controvert critics who said it
> was *impossible*." [1]

Extravaganza, of course, was not the right word. Dionysiac
would have served him better, meaning by that word the
serving of the irresponsible spirit of the natural man.
Between extravaganzaic and Dionysiac there is a difference,
but not a world of difference : if one adds sufficient
champagne, so fizzing up the mixture, one thinks the Dionysiac becomes straightway extravaganza ; and *The Playboy* is
drenched in poteen, which is, of course, the champagne of
the Western World. We therefore cannot hold that his
admission that the play was extravaganza makes any great
difference. His view not only of art, but of life, was
naturalistic ; he had no subtler philosophy ; the daemon
within us must be served, as even Martin Doul and Mary
Doul, illiterates though they are, come to understand through
the very teaching of life itself. What have we in *The Playboy* ?
Christy Mahon haphazardly becoming conscious that by
serving the daemon within him he has become 'master of all
fights from now.' Except his *Riders to the Sea*, Synge's
entire work is an apology for the daemonic in life. Not for
a moment do we think he intended *The Playboy* as a satire
on the people of the West. Rather is it his tribute to them,
his thank offering that, among them, the daemonic had
liberty to strike out, to caper on the sands, to tumble about,
even outrageously. This was for him the real spirit of the
place, its psychic state. But one had to search it out. "Yet
it is only in the intonation of a few sentences or some old
fragment of melody that I catch the real spirit of the island,
for in general the men sit together and talk with endless
iteration of the tides and fish, and of the price of kelp in
Connemara." [2] Those who rail against *The Playboy* take it
as Synge's picture of life in the West, a satirical picture.

[1] *John Millington Synge*, by M. Bourgeois.
[2] *The Aran Islands.* (i.)

Prosaic themselves they want the *endless iteration*, whereas what Synge offers them is really the flash in the eyes of a young fisherman singing a passionate Irish love-song in the Irish manner, which is to say, with an intense concentration on the matter sung and no thought at all of the vulgar exploitation either of his own voice or his own personality. Were Synge to deal with any other *stratum* of life, the life of his own Anglo-Irish circle for instance, or the life of Paris or London, he would equally have sought out the daemonic urge in the heart of it. He would have given us his dramatization of the psychic state of that place, as he had read it ; than which no man can do more, we, of course, understanding that no two readings of a psyche can ever be the same. In England he could take no interest, holding that life had been too whitened there to be of use to the dramatist. We may imagine he would not have found himself fully contented with any family or tribe or city or nation in the world unless that community, few or many, had, without any qualification, created the daemon within them sole arbiter of their destinies. He went sorrowing through life because no such community was to be found. He thought the lack of sophistication among the people of the West, their open-air adventurous life, their instruction at the mouth of the winds, at the strong hands of the ocean, at the eyes of the stars, their living close to the earth—that all these circumstances had fattened in their midst the roots of the golden bough of life, and kept it evergreen and flourishing. In such places life was really lived, was natural. In cities and towns it was put upon by laws and regulations as well as a multiplicity of institutions : it was strangled by them, so de-energised as to be incapable of blossoming. His choice of Mayo was therefore so much flattery of Mayo : had it contained a whole population of *Playboys* he would have hailed it as a bit of heaven itself ! His early detractors did not understand this. His wild phrases were held up to obloquy, as if he had intended them for considered pronouncements ! In reality they were his equivalent for the flashing eyes of Connacht.

Synge would distil the poetry of the place into something rich and rare ; his detractors, however, looked for glossy photographs of the people with their Sunday clothes upon their backs.

Remembering that the Dionysiac is the spirited and not the spiritual, it is patent that he whose quest it is will come roughly up against the people's religious susceptibilities, for their religious susceptibilities are the very flower of their labouring to keep the daemonic in check. The quester would have them be what they have always been trying not to be. In his headlong pursuit, Synge became altogether irresponsible ; the cheapest thing, the most regrettable thing in *The Playboy* is the quite unnecessary flinging about of holy names and religious allusions. We are not forgetting that the religious consciousness in the Irish people overflows into curious channels ; that it is to be met with in the most unexpected associations ; yet Synge not only overdoes his painting of this abundance, but overdoes it clumsily and without either cause or effect. One regrets he did not himself take the advice old Mahon gave his son, the Playboy : ' Leave troubling the Almighty God.' Of this perhaps somewhat slapdash abundance in the people's religious consciousness he probably became aware when reading their Irish poetry, but in the poetry the challenging phrases usually seem nothing less than forced from the singers. And naturally we come on them in the serious rather than in the humorous lyrics. They have always a striking effect, which is exactly what they have not when Synge makes use of them.

It must be allowed that every artist is partial towards the daemonic. It is the principle that opposes the mechanical, the theoretic ; it is the Greek mistrust of professionalism ; it is in everyman the root of honest laughter ; it is in everyman the mirror of nature, answering its moods ; it is the fount of heroism, it is the very colour of life itself—as ineffable as is the spirit of music ; wherefore, of course, artists as such, who never will rank themselves on the side of the cut and dried, are taken by it. Yet for all that, the greater artists have never shown anything but the deepest reverence for what Goethe used to call the earnest conduct of life, which, at its best when the daemon suffuses it with warmth, becomes mere chaos when the daemon overlords it with no regard to any of the other powers within us. By so much do the greater poets differ somehow from the little terrible fry of the Bohemian *cénacles*, fanatics for theories, whether they know it or not. Synge obviously fell short of the great artist. Occasionally in his essays we find honest testimony from him to the necessity for this earnest conduct of life, and Mr. Yeats tells us he insisted that an artist, as well as anybody else, should provide for his family. Apart, however, from *Riders to the Sea*, all his art is so much laudation of one especial attribute of life, the spirited, rather than of the totality of life itself, multiple spirit as it is. Obviously, for all that, it would be quite unjust to rank him with those of the artistic *cénacles* : he didn't like them ; he would have given a score of them for an Aran fisherman or a Wicklow tramp. His mind was more many-sided, therefore, than his art ; he had not learnt how to master and shape forth all that he had received into it from life. But he was always ripening, which, of course, does not mean that each successive play was better than the last. Quite honestly, he expresses in *The Playboy* his idea of Connacht ; yet one could show from his own essays that he knew and deeply felt other forces and other currents in the consciousness of the people. If he wrote *The Playboy*, he also wrote *Riders to the Sea ;* and Shaw's flippant description of him as the Playboy himself is about as wrong as it could be. He was never a Playboy, not even while Christy Mahon was tumultuous in his brain. Molière was known as the Contemplative ; and the name does not misfit John Synge by much.

Is there any reason, then, why we should take sides as between Synge and his scandalized audience ? Both were honest, both consistent. If, playing the small boy, Synge did in places throw out a phrase to make them jump in their seats, they, probably knowingly and unjustly, decided to hiss at everything in the play since they had begun the rumpus at all. The critics who in cold blood, and with forensic attitudinizing, took sides seem to us to be far more erring than either Synge or his protesting audience.

## II.

The story of *The Playboy of the Western World* is so full of twists and turns that it takes some time to tell it, not a good sign of a play. The scene is a country public house, a shebeen. It is nightfall. Pegeen is in possession. Her father, Michael James, and the neighbours are setting off to pass the night at a wake across the sands. There enters a ' queer fellow,'—a slight young man, very tired, frightened, and dirty. This is Christy Mahon whom, later, we are to know as the Playboy. Stranger as he is, they all stare at him. He hints the police may be looking for him : is it a safe house ? He tells them in covered phrases that he cannot recall any person, gentle, simple, judge or jury, did the like of him. He leads them on. Him they lead on, until at last in a sudden impulse of bravado he informs them that a week ago last Tuesday he killed his father in a quarrel. The glamour of this romantic story seizes on them all ; he is made pot-boy to the house. Michael James, the owner of the house, and the neighbours set off towards the wake, leaving Pegeen, Shawn Keogh, who is soon to marry her, and Christy Mahon behind them. Shawn Keogh, whom the Playboy has eclipsed, Pegeen soon gets rid of : then she has Christy Mahon to herself. Their pleasure in each other's company is spoiled by the entrance of Widow Quinn, whom Shawn Keogh has sent to spy on the Playboy. But her, too, Pegeen gets rid of. In the end, Pegeen leaves the Playboy for the night, going into another room. As he examines the comfortable bed she has arranged for him he soliloquizes : " Well, it's a clean bed and soft with it, and it's great luck and company

I've won me in the end of time—two fine women fighting for the likes of me—till I'm thinking this night wasn't I a foolish fellow not to kill my father in the years gone by."

The second act is merely a piece of contrivance : there is nothing inevitable about it. We see Christy next morning receiving visits from the young women of the neighbourhood, whom the romantic story, even at second hand ! we are to believe, has bewitched, just as it bewitched the men the night before. Widow Quinn subsequently enters ; and, still later, Christy's ' murdered ' father himself ! Christy, in the nick of time, hides himself, leaving Widow Quinn the task of setting his father on the wrong track as to his whereabouts, for it is in search of his son he has arrived at the shebeen.

In Act III. we have the Playboy entering into competition with the local athletes and defeating them all : we are to understand that the sudden realization of manhood, which Pegeen's infatuation for him has brought to him, enables him to do so. Victor, laden with prizes, he returns to her from the sports ; and there follows the rather famous love scene between them. Unfortunately, just as Christy is, as he himself would have said, mounted on the stars of luck, his father enters once more, spoiling everything. Pegeen turns against Christy—he is obviously a liar, he has not killed his father at all ! Maddened, Christy chases his father out, and this time, we are to understand, really kills him. Now, having made his boasting true, he expects Pegeen to receive him with open arms. But she tells him there is a great difference between a romantic story and a dirty deed in your back yard—which statement, of course, is Synge's apology for the comedy, and indeed an explanation of its idea. But the father survives this second killing also. Once more he enters, this time to drive his son home before him. Christy however is no longer the ' dirty stuttering lout,' and it is he who drives his father out before him, like a heathen slave. Pegeen too he treats with disdain. He has attained.

III.

The sources of *The Playboy* are interesting. In the *Aran Islands* we come on this passage :

> " He often tells me about a Connaught man who killed his father with the blow of a spade when he was in a passion, and then fled to this island and threw himself on the mercy of some of the natives with whom he was said to be related. They hid him in a hole—which the old man has shown me—and kept him safe for weeks, though the police came and searched for him, and he could hear their boots grinding on the stones over his head. In spite of a reward which was offered, the island was incorruptible, and after much trouble the man was safely shipped to America." [1]

Some years after the storm aroused by Synge's play, Professor Ó Máille searched out the details of the whole incident on which the play is based, and whoever wishes may now find the whole legend set out, names and all, in the Professor's book : *An Ghaoth Aniar*. Although Synge's version of the story is thus partially true, the incident itself was tragic, as one might expect, and not humorous. Reading of it in Professor Ó Máille's book, the curious thought strikes one that the man himself who, having killed his father, found refuge among the people until he escaped, may have looked on Synge's drama with his own eyes, when the Abbey company took it to America. He would then have been something more than seventy years of age.

As with Synge's other plays, not only do we find the fable itself in his note-books, but in them also we come on phrases, speeches, and records of incidents which, tightened up somewhat, we are familiar with in the play. In the play we have : " What's a single man, I ask you, eating a bit in one house and drinking a sup in another, and he with no place of his own, like an old braying jackass strayed upon the rocks ? " Here, recorded in Synge's note-book, is the same speech as it fell from the mouth of old Mourteen : " Bedad, noble person, I'm thinking it's soon you'll be getting married.

[1] *The Aran Islands.* (1.)

Listen to what I'm telling you : a man who is not married is no better than an old jackass. He goes into his sister's house, and into his brother's house ; he eats a bit in this place and a bit in another place, but he has no home for himself ; like an old jackass straying on the rocks." Such a speech one can imagine Synge as repeating to himself, with great delight, for many days after he had come upon it. In the play we have horse-racing on the sands, and in his book on Wicklow and Kerry, we have such a scene fully described. The extent to which he depended on what he had seen and heard is an indication of his distrust of what was theoretic and merely invented.

IV.

*The Playboy* is too fantastic, comes not easily enough within our common experience of life, to form part of the tradition of great comedy. Admitting that spirit is an unaccountable thing, miracle-working, that it dazzles with swift wings, drugs with unwonted perfumes, yet the falling of a whole countryside at the feet of a self-declared parricide simply on account of his gamey heart and his fine bit of talk, is an assumption to which we cannot give more than grudging acceptance. The readiness with which the people in the play swallow down what we cannot look at, antagonises us ; and this antagonism is kept alive by constant reference to the supposed crime. From our difficulty in accepting the scheme of *The Playboy*, we may learn that the scarcely possible is not half so comfortable a basis for comedy as the almost probable ; and the whole *Playboy* scheme is hardly even scarcely possible. We are all the time engaged in coercing our minds not to engage in argument against the proposition before us. Skipping this weakness we find much brain-work in the play. The point of it is the continuous upgrowth of Christy Mahon's character from nothingness to full manhood. And this 'upliftment' is due almost entirely to his meeting with Pegeen ; she, however, we are to remember, is, like the others in the shebeen, drawn to him by the glamour that the great adventure of killing his father has thrown around him. Later on of course we learn from her own lips that it is not the deed itself that wins either her, or the others, it is Christy's telling of the tale, the fine bit of talk. As on a chart we can follow the Playboy's upgrowth. He was a quiet poor fellow with no man giving him heed, he tells us ; only the dumb beasts in the fields were his friends (John Synge is remembering his own boyhood). To Pegeen he is only a soft lad ; she treats him to bread and milk ! To Widow Quinn he appears as one fitter to be saying his catechism than slaying his da. To his father he was only a dirty stuttering lout, one who spent his days fooling over little birds he had, finches and felts ; one who'd be off to hide in the sticks if he saw a red petticoat come swinging over the hill. In one place the Playboy remembers his own past, and Pegeen comforts him :

> " What call have you to be that lonesome when there's poor girls walking Mayo in their thousands now." " It's well you know," Christy answers grimly, " what call I have. It's well you know it's a lonesome thing to be passing small towns with the lights shining sideways when the night is down, or going in strange places with a dog noising before you and a dog noising behind, or drawn to the cities where you'd hear a voice kissing and talking deep love in every shadow of the ditch, and you passing on with an empty, hungry stomach failing from your heart."

Next to this passage, one of the most pleasing in the play, let us place his words when he knows he has won Pegeen's love :

> " Let you wait, to hear me talking, till we're astray in Erris, when Good Friday's by, drinking a sup from a well, and making mighty kisses with our wetted mouths, or gaming in a gap of sunshine, with yourself stretched back unto your necklace, in the flowers of the earth."
>
> Pegeen (*in a low voice, moved by his tone*) I'd be nice so, is it ?
>
> Christy (*with rapture*) If the mitred bishops seen you that time they'd be the like of the holy prophets, I'm thinking, do be straining the bars of Paradise to lay eyes on the Lady Helen of Troy, and she abroad, pacing back and forward, with a nosegay in her golden shawl."

M

Always then we are looking at the Playboy striding forward, until, at the close, when his father would assert his authority over him, crying out : " Come on now." Christy answers : " Go with you, is it ? I will then like a gallant captain with his heathen slave. Go on now and I'll see you from this day stewing my oatmeal and washing my spuds, for I'm master of all fights from now." His astonished father can but gape, exclaiming : " Glory be to God ! " Christy's upgrowth is the strong spine of meaning in the play, if we may use Mr. Galsworthy's phrase. In it, therefore, we have one more working out of the old theme that Dante knew of, that Goethe declared openly :

> The indescribable, here it is done,
> The woman soul leadeth us upwards and on.

—only, of course, the plane of the spiritual, in which the great ones were at home, has been exchanged for that of the spirited. Writing a comedy, as Synge was, some such difference was to be looked for, because comedy is, as Aristotle pointed out so long ago, the imitation of ignoble actions, an opinion that might be dwelt upon by those who write of *The Playboy* as if it should pass the same tests as a treatise on morals.

Christy Mahon himself is the only character that changes and grows ; once it is seen for what it is, the graph of his progress is so direct as not to be interesting. Synge's sense of the psyche of place was always more subtle than his sense of the psyche of any man or woman, and of his men and women Christy Mahon is one of the simplest. One easily exhausts him. It is only when he triumphs, when he drives his stormy parent like a heathen slave before him, that he becomes fit material for great drama. For Christy Mahon lacks an abundant background within himself. He is poverty-stricken where Martin Doul is opulent. And Pegeen Mike, the only other character in the play who has a leading part, is, in background, even still more poverty-stricken. Indeed her background is to be found in theatre-land rather than in the Western World. She is the commonest thing in

Synge, pert, bright-eyed, quick-witted, efficient in love-making as in bar-tending. She is the stock figure in amateur play-writing ; and amateur actors revel in her type, because they know what to do with any such. Widow Quinn is a thinner Mary Doul, she is a Mary Doul who speaks for effect This feeling is all over *The Playboy*. From the Playboy himself downwards, every person is speaking for effect, an unwonted fault with Synge. Even Michael James does it, although his speech where he gives his blessing to the young pair who, one at either side, support him while he makes it, is indeed as rich as it has a right to be. So, too, one relishes old Mahon, with his pride in the atrociousness of the wound his son inflicted on him. His ' Glory be to God ! ' at the end of all is one of the best things in the play, far truer than Christy's carefully modulated cadences.

The two of these, old Mahon and Michael James, live, each of them, openly and unashamedly the life of the natural man. They care for nobody. They drink their fill and speak their fill, while the spirit we behold assuming sway over Christy makes of him ' a likely gaffer '—' master of all fights from now.' In the book *Wicklow and West Kerry*, Synge describes the simple people from beyond Dingle as revelling in the gaudiness of a travelling circus : a wet night did not prevent them from measuring out long miles of rough mountainy roadway to witness it. The bedizenment of the *Playboy*, the scorn of half-tones, the splashes of crude reds and yellows and apple greens, the efflorescences, the flaunting of such daemon as is either callously heroic or outrageously comic—it recalls somehow the travelling circus, posters and all. Poetry, Synge held, must become brutal again to find a way out. So too, he believed, must comedy.

### v.

It is the florid diction of the play that infects our mind somewhat as might the high .colours of the circus-poster. Perhaps only those not gone far in the twenties take that diction to be quite successful. Except for the great difference in their characteristic themes, the associations that cling about them, Francis Thompson would perhaps strike us similarly ; he, as well as Synge, depended on not so much the 'little more' as 'the wasteful and ridiculous excess' to lift us beyond the prosaic. Mr. T. S. Eliot quite correctly points out that "Elizabethanism was a verbal even more than an emotional debauch" ; and Synge in *The Playboy* outdoes the Elizabethans. Those selfsame Elizabethans seem to have gradually replaced Racine, and indeed French drama in general, in his affections. His rhythms in *The Playboy* are more obtrusive, more rotund than in the earlier plays, as the incidents are more bustling—the whole aim is at excitement, tension, surprise. The excess of colour in his work we owe to his affection for the Elizabethans as we owe the daring, as also the homeliness, of his imagery to the Gaelic songs of Connacht, many of them truly folk songs. But both Elizabethans and Gaels had an instinct that told them that neither rapture nor intensity nor ecstasy ran to headlong verbalism. They knew when to rein in. They felt, and more especially the Gaelic poets felt, that the measure of intensity produced is in inverse ratio to the volume of the verbiage employed. In so far as you trick out your sentences with geegaw adjectives you diminish the effect the sentences produce : it is as if you were to wrap your hammer head about with webbing ; let the webbing be as variegated as it may, the heart is taken out of the blow struck. Gaelic equivalents are to be found for many of Synge's most characteristic phrases, more especially for such of them as refer to religion, but the Irish phrases are always far swifter in their effect, far more effective : the hammer head is bared, and strikes home hard and true.

> Mallacht Dé do'n té sin
> A bhain diom mo ghrádh.

> The curse of God on him
> Who snatched my love from me.

says the Gael, striking the nail on the head. Synge would have decorated both the curse and the beloved one, muffling the blow. There is in *The Playboy* a straining after terrible things, with not much more than a mush of colour and sweet sound resulting—a curious failure for one who would have the timber rather than the flower of poetry in his work. Adjectives, he should have known, always beat about the bush and give us time to set up defences. The Irish poets on the other hand show us no quarter, for it is not words that come hurtling against us, but the things for which the words stand—that is how it feels. With Synge, although taught of them, it is always words, words, words ; and sometimes very feeble words. We do not recollect any Gaelic original for : "Aid me for to win her, and I'll be asking God to stretch a hand to you in the hour of death, and lead you short cuts through the Meadows of Ease, and up the floor of Heaven to the Footstool of the Virgin's Son." Yet, if original there be, one may be quite certain it produces an altogether different effect. Instead of the overwhelming intensity aimed at, the passage quoted has the whine of the beggar in it, whose aim it is not to make an end. One feels the tension of the mind slackening as the words flow on and on. It is like something one would find in Sean O'Casey at his worst, or is it his best ? And there is hardly a page in *The Playboy* that is not stuffed with such long-winded figures, some of them, it is true, exhibiting the excess of his strength ; most of them, however, exhibiting nothing more than a disturbing mannerism. Now, mannerisms, as soon as we know them for such, have an uncanny power of instantly chilling the mind ; and all Synge's own interest in his puppets, his liking for them, his own innate warmth of feeling, is scarcely powerful enough to sweep us alive through those ever recurring tricks of phrase and cadence. Even while reading these word-spinnings, one suspects their efficacy as an element of dramatic technique ; in the theatre itself one cannot help wondering at their ineptitude. They become thus a double distraction. Whetting our appetites, they aim at the ultimate, and achieve nothing more than the moderate, losing half their breath in calling attention to themselves.

This desire of his to go ' beyond the beyonds ' accounts for his frequent introduction of phrases with religious allusions in them : if we are to challenge anyone let us challenge God himself ! Still less does this obvious phrase-making of his achieve when he draws upon the religious consciousness of the people. That consciousness was, as we have before explained, *terra incognita* to him : he knew it only dimly, could realize it only superficially. And if we would finally satisfy ourselves as to the truth that intensity in literature is to be achieved only by getting rid of the sense of language, getting back to the thing itself, we have only to compare his refashioning of some Irish phrase or sentence with the original. Thus Synge has : " When you'll feel my two hands stretched around you, and I squeezing kisses on your puckered lips, till I'd feel a kind of pity for the Lord God is all ages sitting lonesome in His golden chair." The original we find in the lines of the well-known *Una Bhán :*

> B'fhearr liomsa bheith ar leabaidh lei 'ga sior-phógadh
> 'Na 'mo shuidhe i bhflaitheas i g-cathaoir na Trinóide.

> I'd rather be ever kissing her on a couch
> Than to be sitting in heaven in the Chair of the Trinity.

This is not a good example to illustrate the difference between love poems in Irish and Synge's idea of them ; nobody would think of quoting the lines to illustrate any trait in these songs ; what strikes us about them in general is that whenever the nameless singers go beyond the beyonds they find themselves truly driven to it : their songs seem to have been no more made for a public than Beethoven's last quartets. Synge's phrases are literary ; from that feeling we cannot escape ; but how far from that feeling we are when we find ' Uch, Mac Muire na nGrás dom shaoradh ' (O, may the Son of Mary of the Graces save me !) in the well-known *Snowy-breasted Pearl* or when we come, in

Liam Dall Ó h-Ifearnáin's perfect lyric : *Pé i nEirinn í* on

> Cé sheolfadh Aon Mhac Dé im' líon
> Ach stór mo chléibh ?
>
> Whom did the Only Son of God direct into my net
> But my heart's treasure ?

Synge's phrases, then, seem not alone watery to us who know the originals, but very often strike us as being also absurd. Every Catholic knows that no Connacht peasant, drunk or sober or utterly lost in ecstasy, could have used them, no more than drunk or sober or gone in our five wits, we could find ourselves asserting that two and two made five. Knowledge imbibed at our mother's knees is not to be put away from us so easily ; yet to utter themselves as Synge's peasants sometimes do, such knowledge they must have forgotten ; as we ourselves must forget it, if we would accept such a phrase as :—" Oh, St. Joseph and St. Patrick and St. Brigid and St. James have mercy on me now ! " Such passages remind us that Synge's idea of the religious consciousness of the people was that of the outsider ; for in that consciousness there is a vast chasm between the attributes of the Almighty and those of the saints.

## VI.

There is a world of difference in feeling between *The Playboy* and *The Well of the Saints*. In *The Well of the Saints* we are, as it were, in a strange and distant land, yet our constant surprise is not so much the strangeness of it all as the familiarity of it all. The people, we are sure, have undergone bewitchment : they have all become a little ' natural.' They move to a slow music, processionally. Let us remind ourselves as often as we may that the whole matter is absurd, that these people are quaintly ridiculous, yet they continue to move on gravely, in a sort of stricken quietude, scarcely ever laughing and but rarely smiling, undisturbed by our presence. They sojourn in a removéd ground. They

are at a distance from us : we mistrust the clearness of our
sight. But our gazing at them, our overhearing of them,
has been an experience : we have had not only holiday but
unique holiday. Quite different is our feeling towards *The
Playboy*. For all the rather outlandish lingo and topsy
turvy evaluing of life in it, we experience far less sense of
distance, of strange voyaging. It is a bustling scene we
have happened upon : the people bounce against us : we
know them for folk who have dressed up very well indeed ;
yet we are sure we have met them before, many of them,
Pegeen most frequently of all, on the ' boards.' One tires
easily of the rough and tumble ; contrariwise, again and
again we find ourselves drawn back to those pieces of
literature where the whole event seems to be kept at a
distance from us. In such cases the writer has organized a
little world of his own. We wish to go back into it, for
something whispers us that due to our own inattention,
perhaps, we assuredly did not bring the last time we were
there as much with us as we might have done ; this time,
we delude ourselves, we shall get closer to the passionate
hearts of the citizens. How curious a thing it is that atmosphere, mood, is the most inexhaustible element in literature !
When we have satisfactorily encompassed a thought or a set
of thoughts, we find ourselves enriched for ever more ; but
to the book or play where we found them, unless it have in
it more than these thoughts, we had better not return ; if
we do so we shall find it a little cold. In those strange books,
however, where thought is but one of the elements, those
strange books that are self-centred, self-lighted, as from
within, Musset's plays, for instance, we shall always find
some new instruction, some further stimulus : they grow in
depth it seems not only with our growth, but a little more
than it, so that we once again feel that we are leaving them
incontinently, as indeed we shall leave life itself. *The
Playboy* has its own atmosphere ; as compared with *The
Well of the Saints* it is, however, a commonplace atmosphere,
commonplace even in its surprises. One easily fathoms it,

easily exhausts it ; only small passages in it entirely grip us when we return to it after voyaging elsewhere.

At first glance the play seems to be more typical of Synge than anything else he wrote. It is of course the piece that made him famous : the word ' playboy, ' has gone abroad throughout the English-speaking world ; every other day this man is described as the playboy of American politics, this other as the playboy of English letters, and so on ; while Synge himself is of course, for many, the Playboy of the Western World—that, and no more. Yet there is less of Synge's self in this play than in any other thing he wrote. He was a brooder by nature ; his mind was a wandering star, free, through want of purpose perhaps, of many orbits. When, however, that wandering star had had its orbit fixed, its path determined, with a terminus assigned, doubtless it travelled faster than before and, it may be, glowed the brighter for the speed. This brilliancy, however, if such we reckon it, hardly compensates for the more varying tints it exhibited, the choicer atmospheres it drew with it, when it wandered hither and thither, unfolding its own self, revealing its own self hail-fellow-well-met, in leisurely contact with sympathetic phenomena round about. The scheme of *The Playboy* was very definite. That very definiteness of itself, by too-hard focussing of the powers of its creator's mind, may have hindered that mind from revealing itself with such fullness as we have found it doing when it had permission to linger and, shutting its eyes, as it were, to draw riches from its own resources. The fact is, Synge never met in life either the Playboy or Pegeen Mike—neither in Aran nor in Wicklow, in Kerry nor in Mayo. He found the scheme and he created his types to suit it. And paradoxical as it may appear, because he invented them all out of his own brain, they remain apart from his own self—a thing that always happens : it would seem we must find ourselves in others if ourselves we would project on the vision of others. If we create a *Playboy*, all out of our own brain, it is as if we kneaded a homunculus between our fingers—the figure may be very dainty, very charming, but it has length and breadth, height and depth, with a birthday recorded in the annals. If, however, we meet in Wicklow, or elsewhere, a Martin Doul, and try earnestly to realize him in all his amplitude of nature—why, we lose ourselves, we use ourselves up in the effort ; there is not enough in ourselves of love, of knowledge, of experience, to encompass him ; we are conscious of lacking means fittingly to project that one affectioned figure on the consciousness of others. We may, therefore, understand how much thinner *The Playboy* is than *The Well of the Saints*. In the depth of Synge's being there was a deep-toned music : it found its provenance in the sense of loneliness, in the consciousness that beauty had but little time to stay, love itself not even so long, that old age was upon us almost before we knew, that the grave was the end of all. This undersong that was Synge's very self, breathes here and there in *The Playboy*—there is the passage already quoted where Christy tells of his lonely wanderings, with a dog noising before and a dog noising behind, beholding others deep in love, himself uncompanioned—but truly not more than a hint of his inner self is to be found in it, whereas he is everywhere in *The Well of the Saints*. *The Well of the Saints* is therefore lit from within, and is a strange region, ineffable, unique ; to travel in it is to be refreshed. *The Playboy* is contrived : we encompass the trick of it ; we can see all round it. In comparison with his other plays we may speak of it as stagey, if indeed it be almost nature itself when compared with the dramas that were being written in England, and in other English-speaking countries, at the same time.

In only one way does it show progress : it is more obviously the work of a playwright. The acts are not complete, each in itself, as in *The Well of the Saints ;* they flow over, not only inviting conjecture, but half-directing, half-waylaying it. Act I. is a good well-articulated piece of dramatic writing : it opens well, and continues well, the line of interest rising right through. Act II. has far too much padding in it. The only essential point in it is the entrance of the Playboy's father, and one does not understand why this entry could not have been kept back until Act III. thus reducing the play to two acts. Act III. is a good, bustling act, alive from beginning to end, even if a little repetitious. It is full of matter : the sports on the sands, the return of Michael James from the wake, the real wonder of old Mahon that his son could achieve such heights of manhood, the love scene between Christy and Pegeen, the turning of the tables on the father, the swift ending. However much we may sigh for the aloofness of *The Well of the Saints*, *The Playboy* has more of the feel of legitimate drama in it, no slight recompense.

One quality, which is the very seal of creative genius, it shares with *The Well of the Saints*, as indeed with all his plays, it is homogeneous : all the men and women in it, even if none of them be as rich tempered as he or she might be, draw sustenance from the same impulse of creation : their little vessels of being have all been filled at the same fount, wherever in the Western World that fount may be. They differ from each other, each remaining the whole time harmonious with himself, yet all tread upon the same enchanted ground and are true children of it. Perhaps the Playboy's speech at the very end of the first act, where he half regrets not having killed his father long ago, is the only blunder in the play. It is the only passage in which the Playboy is truly a playboy, consciously rogue. In the real sense of the term, a playboy lives by roguery, is conscious of it, is conscious too that to the initiated his roguery is an open book ; is one moreover who enjoys not only his own roguery, but the sensations, half-looked for by them, that it excites in the initiated. Christy Mahon is no such playboy. If his words at the end of Act I. really give us his very self, if he is truly a rogue, he cannot but behave quite differently from what he does all through Act II. and Act III. A real playboy would not allow himself to be tied up by the simple Mayo men ; he would, one thinks, rather have got them to tie up his father. Christy Mahon is an innocent rather than a rogue; and the play in which he is the chief figure is, therefore, not a piece of picaresque drama.

*The Playboy of the Western World* is a gaudy reckless spectacle; yet it was no small magic that raised it from the rather drab and meagre scheme of life of one of our poorest seaboards. In hidden places, and with the most crazy gear, the peasants there distil that potent spirit poteen which, Synge tells us, sends a shock of joy to the blood. No more, no less than that, did he ever wish this handful of living people to do for us

# CHAPTER X.

## "DEIRDRE OF THE SORROWS"

### I.

DURING the past hundred years from the great story of Deirdre has sprung a vast quantity of closet drama, which, of all sorts of literature, is certainly the least readable. Closet drama is bookishness ; and if it be wrong, as surely it is, to transmute immemorial classics, all of which live enduringly not so much through their perfection of form as through their grip on the human heart, into mere bookishness, the wrong is at its worst when it is a Gaelic classic that is so transmuted, for the excellence of such lies entirely in the biting reality of the men and women who move within them. Tradition in literature, a settled style, gives a chance to the weak writer to express himself with some clearness and without meanness ; it helps him, although he be unconscious of the help. But it seems to hinder the strong writer ; it restricts him, or at least he feels so as he wrestles against it ; yet in the end him also it helps. Actually it gets the best they are individually capable of from weak as from strong ; from the one, unconsciously ; from the other, only after clubbing down the wilfulnesses that are indeed a sign of his natural powers. So is it also with a classic theme, this story of Deirdre for instance. However inapt the treatment, some of the virtue of the original will be found to survive in it. The weakest writer will not drain it of all its compacted human feeling ; while the economy of the original will exert on the strong writer a restraint that is wholesome : willynilly, as he works, he is being instructed in how much he may leave out ; so that, let him indulge whatever ulterior motives he may in choosing the ancient theme, some at least of its quintessence survives, as indeed also some of the open-eyed sanity which is a note of classic art in whatever medium it exists. Further, we may recollect that the weak writer in choosing a classic theme, sets out, paradoxically, to accomplish a more difficult task than the strong writer who does so ; for, whether he adverts to it or not, he undertakes no less a task than the gilding of refined gold. A.E's *Deirdre* is an example, but Tennyson's *Idylls* is of course likely to be the most typical example for many years in the English language. Cézanne is reported to have said : ' Look at that cloud ; I would like to be able to paint that. Now Monet, he could do it. He has the muscles.' Weak writers may be very genuine in their desire to paint such bright clouds as Deirdre, but they unfortunately lack the muscles. The strong writers err differently. They roughen the features of whatever they choose from old time. The Elizabethans, strong with the strength of their *milieu*, did so ; and, true once more to his kinship with them, so did Synge as he worked upon his classic theme. Indeed he worked with a certain share of savagery.

We have said he threw it into a folklore mould. It is truer to say he threw it into a peasant mould. In Irish very many recensions of the story exist : and some of them have much folklore quality in them. Synge would most probably have read the version published, with translation, by the Society for the Preservation of the Irish Language. This recension was made by Andrew MacCurtin, of Co. Clare, in 1740. It is full of folklore colour. Individually the heroes go out to the fray, and they slay, some of them, one hundred and fifty, and others three hundred of the enemy. Synge himself was set against sophisticated literature, but for the superhuman, as for the inhuman, he had no feeling. Spirit he loved, naïveté he loved, but it should be rustic rather than romantic or fairy-like. In Dr. Hyde's *Literary History of Ireland* there is, however, a version of Deirdre which, very full in other ways, does not contain such incidents. One thinks that it was this version Synge mostly used.[1] If so,

1 Of course he might also have used Lady Gregory's version. It is to be had in her *Cuchulain of Muirthemne*, which was first published in 1902.

it is not too much to say that he went about his work with a certain savagery. In this version Deirdre is a princess, nurtured and educated as such. So, too, the King is a true king, and the sons of Usna true princes. In MacCurtin's telling, Conchubor's household consists of 1,665 persons. But Synge's Conchubor comes and goes accompanied by only one or two companions. And in Synge, king and prince, princess and common drudge, soldier and spy—they all speak not so much the one language as the one dialect, giving us the thought that of schooling they never have had any except what came from their own tumultuous hearts. Synge therefore roughened the tale, acting surely more wisely than those who watered the hot blood that is in all Irish tellings of it. This is the first thing we have to remember when considering this play. Yet although a strong writer, as we may know from this one characteristic, the old tale did not fail to chasten his wilfulnesses a good deal. The ' dawn of day ' is in it, as also the ' fall of night '; one has, however, to seek them out. Synge was perhaps ripe for such chastening. He had aimed at being a ' lord of language,' but there was other stuff all the time within him, protesting against such an ideal. And the literature of early Irish, as distinguished from the folk song literature of the seventeenth and eighteenth centuries, was exactly the right school to nourish within him those protesting elements which the glamour of Elizabethan English had suppressed. The ancient literature must really, one thinks, have released for him his deeper self. If his version of Deirdre makes all other versions of it seem pale and weak, there surely was some of the bleakness and intensity that we find always present in Irish literature at its best, already within himself. *Riders to the Sea* foretold this play of *Deirdre of the Sorrows*.

How Synge induced a peasant feeling in a story of kings and princes has been already hinted at. Of the household of 1,665 souls we hear nothing. The King enters and departs with one or two companions. When he is about his slaughtering of the Sons of Usna he has soldiers at his command, hidden in the trees ; but not many soldiers are required to kill three men. Conchubor, it is true, refers to himself as the King of Ulster, in language, however, that comes out of a peasant's hut and not from a palace. Synge, and how fortunately, never aims at local colour or historical colour, which in his case could not be anything except half-digested fragments of archaeological lore. With him there is no scene in the King's palace. His own mind, intent on the impulsive current in the old tale, shows itself in all this economy of material, though of course, the exigencies of the Abbey stage may also have directed him towards it. Between those exigencies, his own build of mind, that is, his distaste for bookishness, for the merely literary, and his feeling for the natural as opposed to the sophisticated in human life, we have in *Deirdre of the Sorrows*, despite occasional references to thrones and queens, as surely a piece of peasant drama as *The Shadow of the Glen*. On the whole one is thankful, thankful to find an old theme giving birth to something truly vital ; yet for all that, one cannot refrain from asking questions. One asks, for instance, whether Conchubor's kingship has nothing to do with the tragedy—not so much with its happening as with the atmosphere which it should naturally induce in the mind ? Conchubor, in Synge's play, says : " I'm a ripe man and in great love, and yet, Deirdre, I'm the King of Ulster." More significantly he says : " Make your lamentation a short while if you will, but it isn't long till a day'll come when you begin pitying a man is old and desolate, and High King also." Yet as we view the drama, Conchubor's kingship is never in our minds, it adds neither poignancy to his sufferings nor amplitude to the action ; it is no active principle in the play. Synge, intentionally or otherwise, through his methods, has taken all pains to annul the large effects that troop with majesty. And surely it is no human weakness in us that notices not only the omission of them but the effort to eliminate them. Such consideration adds point to Hegel's definition of fine art. " Fine art," he says, " is the free and adequate embodiment of the idea in a form appropriate to the idea itself." But, of course, if Conchubor's kingship has nothing to do with the idea, then Hegel's words do not apply ; and one thinks that in spite of Conchubor's occasional reference to himself as King, Synge's play is, as its name implies, the story of Deirdre, and not the story of Conchubor. Yet one cannot help feeling, and it is our one dissatisfaction with the play, that Synge unduly restricted the scope of consciousness within us to which the story by its own natural powers must make appeal. Synge himself in such references as we have quoted to Conchubor's kingship, invited us to open up, as if for fertilization, whole regions of our minds, only later to disappoint us, only later to tempt us to say that Synge after all was Synge, though perhaps, more wisely, we should rather say that Synge was not yet the Synge that was to be, if only he were to live.

## II.

The quintessence of the original tale for us moderns is not the prophecy that Deirdre would bring sorrow to Ulster, but the love of Conchubor for Deirdre, and the love of Deirdre for Naisi. And it was with this quintessence that Synge chose to deal. He worked so earnestly in this spirit, gave himself so whole-heartedly to what was eternally human in the legend, that he may be counted as one of that small band of writers who began the movement to restore the note of intensity to English literature. Perhaps it is only readers of Irish literature, or readers of Dante, or of Villon, who become aware of the scarcity of this note in English literature since the sixteenth century. The point is worth dwelling on if we would realize the place of this drama in modern English playwriting. Here is Mr. Padraic Colum's translation of an Irish poem :

> O woman, shapely as the swan,
> On your account I shall not die.
> The men you've slain, a trivial clan,
> Were less than I.

I ask me shall I die for thee .
For blossom-teeth and scarlet lips ?
And shall that delicate swan shape
Bring me eclipse ?

Well shaped the breasts and smooth the skin,
The cheeks are fair, the tresses free ;
And yet I shall not suffer death,
God over me.

Those even brows, that hair like gold,
Those languorous tones, that virgin way,
The flowing limbs, the rounded heel,
Slight men betray.

Thy spirit keen through radiant mien,
Thy shining throat and smiling eye,
Thy little palm, thy side like foam,
I cannot die.

O woman, shapely as the swan,
In a cunning house hard-reared was I,
O bosom white, O well-shaped palm,
I shall not die.

This is a good translation, almost word for word, losing, for all that, something of the intensity of the original.[1]  It is worth while to hear Mr. Chesterton's remarks on it : " Take for example Mr. Colum's stern and simple rendering of the bitter old Irish verses—O Woman Shapely as the Swan. Like Fitzgerald's *Omar* and all good translations, it leaves one wondering whether the original was so good ; but to an Englishman the note is not only unique, but almost hostile. It is the hardness of the real Irishman which has been so skilfully hidden under the softness of the stage Irishman. The words are ages old I believe ; they come out of the ancient Ireland of cairns and fallen kings ; and yet the words might have been spoken by one of Bernard Shaw's modern heroes to one of his modern heroines.  The curt, bleak words, the haughty heathen spirit, are certainly as

1 The original is to be found in *Dánta Grádha, An Anthology of Irish Love Poetry* (A.D. 1350-1750).  Collected and Edited by Prof. T. F. O'Rahilly.

remote as anything can be from the luxuriant humility of Francis Thompson." [1]

Mr. Chesterton is both right and wrong. He is right when he says the note is unique, that is, in English literature since the Renaissance. And it is true that Mr. Shaw might have put the sentiments into the mouth of one of his characters—but how differently phrased. Why, if Mr. Shaw could handle words in the Irish way we should all take pains to remember not only what his people say, but the actual words they use, a thing we never do. Mr. Chesterton is, however, quite wrong when he discovers in the poem a haughty heathen spirit. What we find in its mode is the very spirit of all Christian art : one has only to look at the sculptures of the Middle Ages to know this. But again he is right when he chooses Francis Thompson as an opposite ; wrong, however, when he chooses him as a Christian opposite, for Francis Thompson's poetics are pagan and not Christian. The chiefest note in Christian art is intensity, a note Thompson never uses. It is also the chiefest note in Irish literature. That note in English literature suffered eclipse when the Renaissance, with its grandiose attitude, its conscious dignity, its magnificence, overwhelmed it. The Renaissance induced in English a scorn of the homely, a scorn of the words in which the homely expresses itself, that is, household words. Now it is a curious thing that it is not possible to eliminate the household words from the literary modes of a language without eliminating the note of intensity from them ; for intensity can be expressed only in household words. The literary man cannot help reading a very special and salutary meaning into St. Teresa's saying that God moves among the pots and pans. It has been remarked that Shakespeare falls back on pure English in his most intense passages ; but has it been remarked that he had to do so ? Or that every other poet has done the same ? For one cannot be both literary and intense. Only homely words bring the objects for which they stand, present to the sense, to borrow Mr. Desmond

1 Introduction to *Eyes of Youth*, a collection of lyrics by various writers.

MacCarthy's phrase. And it is the sense of *thing*, achieved only by the annihilation of the sense of *word*, that pierces the mind to its depths. It is as if a thing can wound us, while a word can not. When Mr. Desmond MacCarthy wanted to illustrate his phrase he turned to Synge's *Playboy*, the most *quasi*-literary of all his plays, but he would, of course, have found better illustration in *Deirdre of the Sorrows*.

It is Synge's recapture of this note of intensity that makes his early death entirely regrettable.[1] Entirely regrettable from the Irish point of view, for if Irish life differs from English life, and it differs everyway, that difference is due to a quality of intenseness in Irish mind, there racially or else induced by whole centuries of suffering, for the expression of which, current modes of English literature offer but little opportunity. Had Synge lived,—but to say this is to bring us to a more personal point of view. His mastery of this note in certain passages in *Deirdre of the Sorrows* marks the end of his first phase, or rather of what would, had he lived, come to be regarded as his first phase. It would also have marked the beginning of his next phase : *Deirdre of the Sorrows* would have been the first of a number of plays more serious than those he had previously written (and if we keep this play in mind we feel how shallow was his own interpretation of that word *Serious*) for the note of intensity is not ever achieved by triflers or by those who are merely clever. We have remarked on the foolishness of Mr. Howe's saying that Synge had dealt with all that is essential in life, so that had he lived, though he might certainly have added to the number of his plays, he would not have added to the range of his dramaturgy. In a few years, Mr. Howe would persuade us, he had, presumably, emptied the whole human gamut of surprises. The fact is, of course, that all his characters live happily in the one plane—a rough and tumble plane usually, and always unsophisticated—all happily, we

1 Mr. W. B. Yeats has schooled himself since Synge's death in the use of this note ; and he alone has really mastered it. Whether there is in the themes he chooses a seriousness fundamental enough to demand its use is another question.

say, except those in *Deirdre of the Sorrows*. They, unlike
the others, we feel have been rather savagely thrust into that
plane and, not without some stress, kept within it. An
increased seriousness in the man himself would have, one
by one, discovered other planes of existence, for their name
is myriad. It is this play of *Deirdre* then, with examples of
this note of intensity so frequent in it, that makes us aware
how great a loss he was, whether from the purely personal
or the purely Irish point of view.

Naturally it is towards the end of the drama where the
tragedy is being consummated that we find the better
examples of this note of intensity. " Let you not break the
thing I've set my life on, and you giving yourself up to sorrow,
when it's joy and sorrow do burn out like straw blazing in
an east wind." . . . . " It was a clean death was your
share, Naisi ; and it is not I will quit your head, when it's
many a dark night among the snipe and plover that you and
I were whispering together." . . . . " I will not go
away when there is no light in the heavens, and no flower
on the earth under them, but is saying to me that it is Naisi
who is gone for ever." . . . . " Let you go back to
your arms, Conchubor, and councils, for in this place you
are an old man and a fool only." . . . . " Draw a little
back with the squabbling of fools when I am broken up with
misery." . . . . " I have put away sorrow like a shoe
that is worn out and muddy, for it is I have had a life that
will be envied by great companies." . . . . " It is not
a small thing to be rid of grey hairs and the loosening of
the teeth."

These passages, which illustrate the bleakness of spirit that
is in the whole play, are surely very far removed from the
luxuriant verbiage of *The Playboy*. The words in them, it
may be noted, are, for the most part, monosyllabic, and
always homely ; and one is right in describing them as
examples of intensity in literature, for, in all cases, it is the
feeling behind the words and not the words themselves that
seems to invade the mind. A passage that is literary fails

to do this. It is about to affect us, and then something happens : we begin to linger on the individual words, or on the images, or the rhythms, we are in some way or another taken by the surface charm of the presentation, and the feeling that had begun to colour our minds is dissipated ; such traces of it as seem to get through are thin and ineffectual. Where there are literary passages in *Deirdre of the Sorrows*, and there are such, we feel that they have not attained final form, that, had their writer lived longer, he would have stripped them until they too harmonized with the general spirit of curtness that is in the whole play. " Deirdre's no thought of getting old or wearied ; it's that puts wonder in her ways, and she with spirits would keep bravery and laughter in a town with plague." . . . . " I've had dread, I tell you, dread winter and summer, and the autumn and the springtime, even when there's a bird in every bush making his own stir till the fall of night ; but this talk's brought me ease, and I see we're as happy as the leaves on the young trees, and we'll be so ever and always, though we'd live the age of the eagle and the salmon and the crow of Britain." We take meaning out of such words, nevertheless our minds do not yield to them, do not empty themselves of personality before the imperiousness of them, which is indeed what seems to happen when we come on a real example of intensity. All such passages as these in this play we feel had not attained final form when the pen fell from the writer's fingers.

Where Synge's other plays are lyric, *Deirdre of the Sorrows* is intense, and intensity should be the chief note in tragedy. The dramatist was triumphing over the lyric poet. Indeed it is only in *Deirdre of the Sorrows* that Synge is purely dramatist. Here is a passage :

*Loud knocking on door at the right.*

Lavarcham (*startled*). Who is that ?

Naisi (*outside*). Naisi, and his brothers.

Lavarcham. We are lonely women. What is it you're wanting in the blackness of the night ?

Naisi.  We met a young girl in the woods who told us we might shelter this place if the rivers rose on the pathways and the floods gathered from the butt of the hills.

*Old woman clasps her hands in horror.*

Lavarcham (*with great alarm*).  You cannot come in. . . . There is no one let in here, and no young girl with us.

Naisi.  Let us in from the great storm.  Let us in and we will go further when the cloud will rise.

Lavarcham.  Go round east to the shed and you'll have shelter.  You cannot come in.

Naisi (*knocking loudly*).  Open the door or we will burst it.  (*The door is shaken*).

Old Woman (*in a timid whisper*).  Let them in, and keep Deirdre in her room to-night.

Ainnle and Ardan (*outside*).  Open ! Open !

Lavarcham (*to Old Woman*).  Go in and keep her.

Old Woman.  I couldn't keep her.  I've no hold on her.  Go in yourself and I will free the door.

Lavarcham.  I must stay and turn them out.  (*She pulls her hair and cloak over her face*).  Go in and keep her.

Old Woman.  The Gods help us.

*She runs into the inner room.*

Voices.  Open !

Lavarcham (*opening the door*).  Come in then and ill-luck if you'll have it so.

*Naisi and Ainnle and Ardan come in and look round with astonishment.*

Naisi.  It's a rich man has this place, and no herd at all.

Lavarcham (*sitting down with her head half covered*).  It is not, and you'd best be going quickly.

Naisi (*hilariously, shaking rain from his clothes*).  When we've had the pick of luck finding princely comfort in the darkness of the night !  Some rich man of Ulster should come here and he chasing in the woods.  May we drink ? (*He takes up flask*).  Whose wine is this that we may drink his health ?

Lavarcham.  It's no one's that you've call to know.

Naisi.  Your own health then and length of life.  (*Pouring out wine for the three.  They drink*).

The influence of the stage is palpable in this.  Synge writes like any other dramatist born to the business.  The excitement, the hurry, the dread in the scene express themselves in the form of every sentence; the scene therefore acts itself. Even apart from the context it is good drama; in its place it is, however, still better, for while it enriches with added significance the scene that has gone before, it is itself, at the same time, enriched and deepened by that previous scene. To give some idea of it: Conchubor has astonished Deirdre by telling her that she is to go with him to Emain. With much entreaty she has obtained of him a short respite. When he is gone her suppressed spirit breaks free, and she prepares to admit the lover she has herself chosen:

Deirdre. Are the stepping-stones flooding, Lavarcham? Will the night be stormy in the hills?

Lavarcham (*looking at her curiously*). The stepping-stones are flooding, surely, and the night will be the worst, I'm thinking, we've seen these years gone by.

Deirdre (*tearing open the press and pulling out clothes and tapestries*). Lay these mats and hangings by the windows, and at the tables for our feet, and take out the skillets of silver, and the golden cups we have, and our two flasks of wine.

Lavarcham. What ails you?

Deirdre (*gathering up a dress*). Lay them out quickly, Lavarcham, we've no call dawdling this night. Lay them out quickly; I'm going into the room to put on the rich dresses and jewels have been sent from Emain.

Lavarcham. Putting on dresses at this hour, and it dark and drenching with the weight of rain! Are you away in your head?

Deirdre (*gathering her things together with an outburst of excitement*). I will dress like Emer in Dundealgan, or Maeve in her house in Connaught. If Conchubor'll make me a queen, I'll have the right of a queen who is a master, taking her own choice and making a stir to the edges of the seas. . . . . Lay out your mats and hangings where I can stand this night and look about me. Lay out the skins of the rams of Connaught and of the goats of the west. I will not be a child or plaything; I'll put on my robes that are the richest, for I will not be brought down to Emain as Cuchulain brings his horse to the yoke, or Conall Cearnach puts his shield upon his arm; and maybe from this day I will turn the men of Ireland like a wind blowing on the heath.

Here, as in the other scene quoted, we have no sentences that stifle the actor's voice. They speak themselves, so audibly indeed that, as we read them, we seem to hear them. The texture is dramatic, not lyric. Chekhov and other moderns seem to deny that there is such a pattern as carries drama in itself, in its face, so to speak. It is as if they said that drama is without a genius of its own. Yet Chekhov left very definite and very valuable advice as to the pattern of the short story—this is how it must be written, just because it is a short story, and not a novel, nor an essay. It is hard to understand how one branch of literary art can have a genius of its own, an inner principle due to its very nature, that informs all its elements, and another branch of it have no such innate virtue. A play that commends itself to actors as such, does not seriously violate the inner principle of drama, however stultified it may be by other shortcomings such as lack of wit, lack of taste, weak intelligence, or dull imagination. *Deirdre of the Sorrows* commends itself to actors as such ; and would still further commend itself, had its creator lived longer.

### III.

Unity is a constant excellence in Synge : there is no play of his that is not harmoniously developed from one root ; in *Deirdre of the Sorrows* that development is, all the time, dramatically conceived. The *Leitmotif* of Old Age, like a sombre steadying chord, recurs in all parts of that development. Synge was a sickly man, soon to die. It is customary with us gratuitously to imagine that such a one dwells rather on the tragedy of premature death—death that callously cuts off beauty and genius at their prime, than on the far-off and slow fading out of spirit and love which follows on the passing of many years. But is it so ? It may be that the weakly, taught subconsciously of their own bodies, cannot brook the idea of any further diminution of vitality by the clumsy and passionless onslaught of the slow years. But instead of wondering if invalids think more frequently of death or of old age, perhaps it were wiser to think of Synge the passionate lover of beauty, rather than of Synge the invalid, as having written this and indeed all his plays. Of Synge's contemporaries, Padraig Pearse was most akin to him in genius. They both were marked with that characteristic that Goethe took notice of in genuine poets, hearts over-flowing with emotion. How acutely such lovers of beauty feel the inevitableness of decay is brought home to us by recollecting that Padraig Pearse, awaiting execution, with only a few hours to live, let his mind go back to the simple things that had stirred him—peasants in the west reaping their mountainy fields, rabbits coming from their burrows in the cool of evening, barefoot children playing in the streets of little towns in Connacht—and recalls them only to remember that they all must wither and pass away :

> And then my heart hath told me :
> These will pass,
> Will pass and change, will die and be no more,
> Things bright and green, things young and happy ;
> And I have gone upon my way
> Sorrowful.

The *Leitmotif* in the original tale of Deirdre is of course the prophecy that gave her her name, the meaning of which is Alarm. Synge was no Greek ; he could not give himself to anything so metaphysical as prophecy. That original *Leitmotif* was particular, concerning Deirdre alone. As an active principle in the play, he replaced it by one that was, in his eyes, common to the human race : the horror of old age, the decay of love consequent on the passing of youth ; replaced it, therefore, by something whose utterance gave him, the scorner of metaphysics, the passionate lover of beauty, some modicum of personal relief : " Isn't it a small thing is foretold about the ruin of ourselves, Naisi, when all men have age coming and great ruin in the end." The voice is the voice of Deirdre, but it is Synge's own heart that beats in the message, as also is the case when Deirdre finds herself

" wondering all times is it a game worth playing, living on until you're dried and old, and our joy is gone for ever." This *Leitmotif* serves to unify the various parts in one common mood, it is a recurring chord ; but it serves also in other ways. It aids both Deirdre and Naisi individually to consent to return to Emain from Scotland, thus forwarding the action : " It may be I will not have Naisi growing an old man in Alban with an old woman at his side, and young girls pointing out and saying : ' that is Deirdre and Naisi had great beauty in their youth.' " It is this *Leitmotif* that, moreover, throws about the ending of the play an air of exaltation and victory, for here the chord is resolved, and instead of ' old, old,' we come on the word ' young ' ringing out again and again triumphantly. Above the grave wherein Naisi and his brothers have been laid, Deirdre raises her voice : " It's you three will not see age or death coming—you that were my company when the fires on the hill-tops were put out and the stars were our friends only." And a little later she stays Conchubor with a gesture : " Draw a little back from Naisi, who is young for ever." Still later the words already quoted : " It is not a small thing to be rid of grey hairs and the loosening of the teeth."

The sterling quality in parts of this play is due to the overwhelming appeal the subject matter made to what was most vital in Synge's own being. The horror of decay was always present with him, as also was a keen delight in beauty that was bright, wilful, and daring. Queens of tragedy that were marmorean, that moved about as if burdened with their own fame, he could not but gibe at. Deirdre was none such, she was one to appeal to all that was most essentially himself. He loved her ' little ways,' her wilfulness, as much as he loved her wild beauty. But indeed the whole story laid its spell upon him, so that when he uses words and phrases from the original, they may as well have come straight from his own heart : he had become attuned to many strains in the Gaelic mode. " It's a lonesome thing to be away from Ireland always." . . . . . " Let you come this day, for there's no place but Ireland where the Gael can have peace always." . . . . " When I was a young man we'd have given a lifetime to be in Ireland a score of weeks." Most of the place names he leaves as he found them in the Irish, scornful of what the Sasanach would make of them : Emain Macha, Glen Masain, Glen da Ruadh, Glen Laoi, Slieve Fuadh, though one is surprised to find him dull, once in a while, to the magical ' little more ' that often heightens them in Deirdre's lament. *His* Deirdre cries out : " Woods of Cuan, woods of Cuan, dear country of the east ! " But the Irish Deirdre cries out :

> Coil Cuana ón ! Coill Cuana
> I bhfuilid na huiscidhe fuara,
> Aoibhinn do bhios-sa an tan
> Do bhí Naoise i n-oirthear Alban.

> Woods of Cuan, O woods of Cuan,
> In which are the cold waters,
> Joyous indeed was I
> When Naisi was in the east of Alban.

How did he miss that second line, which creates for us those particular woods ? [1]

Irish literature is pre-eminently the literature of place names : Deirdre's lament, in the original, is a litany of them ; in Irish literature the love of Ireland overflows ; Ireland is everywhere in it, just as Greece is everywhere in Greek literature ; while Deirdre, of course, was not only a figure in Irish literature, but a figure in Irish consciousness. It is not, however, the place names in Synge's *Deirdre of the Sorrows*, nor that overflow of feeling for Ireland that is in it, nor the Gaelic theme, nor all of these together, that make it one of the most Irish of his plays ; it is rather that core of hardness in it, the ' curt, bleak words,' the temper of the writing, that does so. And the focal point in that temper

---

[1] It is right to say that this line is not found in many versions of the lament.

is the final parting between Deirdre and Naisi. So intense is their love for each other that the thought of death is far less terrifying to them than the fear that the dragging years may chill the ardour of it ; yet how in the end do they take farewell of each other ? In bitter and mocking words ! Naisi's brothers, Ainnle and Ardan, outside, cry for help :

Deirdre (*clinging to Naisi*). There is no battle . . . . Do not leave me, Naisi.

Naisi. I must go to them.

Deirdre (*beseechingly*). Do not leave me, Naisi. Let us creep up in the darkness behind the grave. If there's a battle, maybe the strange fighters will be destroyed, when Ainnle and Ardan are against them. (*Cries heard*).

Naisi (*wildly*). I hear Ardan crying out. Do not hold me from my brothers.

Deirdre. Do not leave me, Naisi. Do not leave me broken and alone.

Naisi. I cannot leave my brothers when it is I who have defied the king.

Deirdre. I will go with you.

Naisi. You cannot come. Do not hold me from the fight.

*He throws her aside almost roughly.*

Deirdre (*with restraint*). Go to your brothers. For seven years you have been kindly, but the hardness of death has come between us.

Naisi (*looking at her aghast*). And you'll have me meet death with a hard word from your lips in my ear ?

*Deirdre.* We've had a dream, but this night has waked us surely. In a little while we've lived too long, Naisi, and isn't it a poor thing we should miss the safety of the grave, and we trampling its edge ?

Ainnle (*behind*). Naisi, Naisi, we are attacked and ruined !

Deirdre. Let you go where they are calling. (*She looks at him for an instant coldly*). Have you no shame loitering and talking, and a cruel death facing Ainnle and Ardan in the woods ?

*Naisi* (*frantic*). They'll not get a death that's cruel, and they with men alone. It's women that have loved are cruel only ; and if I went on living from this day I'd be putting a curse on the lot of them I'd meet walking in the east or west, putting a curse on the sun that gave them beauty, and on the madder and the stone-crop put red upon their cloaks.

Deirdre (*bitterly*). I'm well pleased there's no one in this place to make a story that Naisi was a laughing-stock the night he died.

Naisi. There'd not be many'd make a story, for that mockery is in your eyes this night will spot the face of Emain with a plague of pitted graves. (*He goes out*).

Conchubor (*outside*). That is Naisi. Strike him !

The passage in its own place in the drama is still more significant, for, following swiftly and suddenly on a moment of blessed relief, in which Deirdre has almost brought about reconciliation between Conchubor and Naisi, its stringent poignancy has been prepared for by a breath of sweetness and hope. No tenderness of lyrical farewelling could so move us to pity : we feel the intensity of their union in the violence of its snapping.

The play thus develops harmoniously from one germ. In all its parts there is correspondence. The theme ; the *Leitmotif* beneath it ; the language ; the characterization ; this farewell—they all are unified in feeling. Here and there we come on patches which are loose and untidy—the speech of Naisi in the extract just made, for instance : " They'll not get a death ; " but we may be certain that such patches had not received the final touches.

### IV.

Of the various people in the play Mr. E. A. Boyd pertinently remarks : " There is an untamed fierceness in these people which marks them at once as belonging to that race of unspoiled children of nature whom Synge loved to study." [1] This 'untamed fierceness' is, perhaps, to be equated with

1 *Ireland's Literary Renaissance*, by E. A. Boyd.

Mr. Colum's ' vivid personality.' Vivid personality obviously is better expressed in such phrasing, in such diction, as we have in *Deirdre of the Sorrows* than in the lyrical linked sweetnesses of *The Playboy*; and this is why *Deirdre of the Sorrows* is the more sterling piece of work of the two. Thought and style are more closely wedded. To Deirdre herself Synge gave his whole heart. How could he help loving one who did nothing by halves ? In his vision she must have been a consuming flame. " Fools and kings and scholars are all one in a story with her like," says Lavarcham : it is her way of saying : ' Where she comes, the winds must stir.' How else could Synge think of her except as one whose only business was to love and to be loved ? How natural for her to shrink from the thought of old age : " Isn't it a better thing to be following on to a near death, than to be bending the head down, and dragging with the feet, and seeing one day a blight showing upon love where it is sweet and tender ? " she says herself, and Lavarcham, who knows her best of all, says of her : " Who'd check her like was made to have her pleasure only ? " She therefore is no tragedy queen, for such are uplifted by ideals ; unlike them she flings out, tosses her head, speaks mockingly. As in the old saga, she is the huntress : it is she who entices Naisi to her, whatever his own thought may be. Yet the clay in her is finer, one feels, than in any of the other women Synge created in the mood that spirit alone is what takes men captive. Over against her, Naisi is dull and slow. He speaks more ' Synge ' than any other character in the piece : "And it is you who go around in the woods making the thrushes bear a grudge against the heavens for the sweetness of your voice singing,"—words that leave but little mark in our minds ; what we notice is the poor actor's struggle to fit them all into his mouthful of breath. To Conchubor, the aged king, who will have Deirdre for himself, although he fears from the beginning that she will escape him, Synge gave far more affection. Indeed in Conchubor, who, knowing himself for king, master of his people's destinies, fears, for all that, he'll miss Deirdre in the end, who also speaks of the wildness and confusion in his own mind—in him, Synge, if he only knew it, had happened on the only type of human being that can move men to the depths of their being—the character that is divided in his own mind. In Mr. Galsworthy's *Strife* master is so evenly matched against man, and man against master, that stalemate is the outcome of their tragic contending : two positives negative each other. Now, to look on at such strife is to be moved ; but we are moved in quite a different way, in a higher plane surely, when such tragic contention arises from two positives clashing together within the one poor human soul. Strife or tension is not the secret of tragic drama, but the fact that strife or tension or disaster is where it ought not to be ; for we are not moved to pity by any other consideration. So is it with Oedipus, with Lear, with Othello, Hamlet, Tess. Synge did not work out the drama that is in Conchubor's self. He could not, for he had not philosophised enough. In the story of Deirdre the king is the most tragic figure : his will is the active principle that issues in wreckage. This, in Synge's play, Conchubor does not seem to realize. But one does not recall any treatment of the story where he is not placed in wrong attitudes, just because his will is not treated as the active principle. Owen, that curious figure in *Deirdre of the Sorrows*, is Synge's own only addition to the legend : there is no Owen in the original. It is said he intended to create some such figure as we might find among Shakespeare's fools. One wonders if this experiment gave him any doubts as to his wisdom in making king, queen, soldier, spy, and servant all speak the same dialect ? One wonders how, cleaving to his methods, he could ever succeed in making Owen stand sufficiently apart from the others properly to act the part of chorus. The chorus must stand a little apart, for aware of the beginning and end simultaneously with the event itself, it takes its station naturally in a more removed ground. Its nature is a thing apart from the nature of the characters proper to the drama.

v.

We have seen how much more dramatic the phrasing in *Deirdre of the Sorrows* is than that in *The Playboy*. So too the lay-out of the work is more skilful and better proportioned. The first act has the economy and the swift impulse, as also the balance, of a movement in a good sonata. The King brings gifts to the secret place where Deirdre is ' gathering new life ' to herself with no thought except for her own pleasure and her own beauty. She is filled with terror when he tells her she is to come to him in Emain in two days or three. When he goes away, she brings all her thoughts to one firm resolution. The night turns to rain and storm, the worst that has ever been ; and Deirdre changes too. We have seen her only as a girl of the woods, a herder of geese. Now, we see her assume the princess : for the first time, we understand, she bids the attendants bring forth the gifts the King has sent to her from time to time. At her bidding they decorate the chamber with the rich stuffs that have come from him, and the floor with the sumptuous skins. She herself leaving them at their own task retires to divest herself of her homespun gowns, to reclothe herself with the garments from the King's palace. In the midst of this excitement, quite unwonted in the hut, we understand, there comes masterful hammering at the door. Those outside will not be stayed. Naisi and his two brothers enter. They find costly cloths and skins, They discover the King's seal on the precious goblets they are drinking from. Into the midst of all this wonder and surprise Deirdre, clad as a princess, makes her entry. There follow love-making and marriage, while the rain falls heavily outside, through which, we remember, the King is, in wild confusion of mind, making dejectedly for Emain. Here is good drama that sets the mind travelling forward in high expectancy. From the start we have been led from surprise to surprise, which is the very essence of play-writing. Conchubor is surprised, on entering, to discover that Deirdre is abroad in the woods, and alone. He is surprised to discover that she is quite unmoved by the rich gifts he has been bestowing on her. Deirdre is surprised at the sudden command to go to Emain in a day or two. Lavarcham is surprised at the great change that comes over her. In the bustle of spreading skins on the floor and cloths upon the walls there comes the disturbing demand for entry. Naisi and his brothers are surprised at what they find before them. Then Deirdre, whom they had seen previously as a girl herding geese or gathering twigs for the fire, enters to them, clothed like a queen. We go, then, from surprise to surprise, and every scene in the act is a *scène à faire*. Act II. is not so effectively arranged. There is scarcely an inevitable *scène à faire* in it. There is, however, one grateful touch of simple ritual. It is where Deirdre overhears Naisi confess to Fergus that he has had misgivings that he might one day grow weary of Deirdre's voice and that Deirdre herself might perceive his weariness. This stage direction follows : *Deirdre drops the horn of wine and crouches down where she is.* An efficient producer would probably direct her to crouch down before she spills the wine, for the boards of a stage, when things are dropped on them, very snappishly proclaim themselves for boards and nothing else, breaking up the strongest mood. But Deirdre's silent in-gathering of Naisi's words, her crouching down, her spilling of the wine she was bringing the others—it is such a picture as one might find on a Grecian vase. As for Act III., Mr. Padraic Colum tells us that when Synge informed him that he intended to show an open grave on the stage, he argued against it. But one does not imagine that Padraic Colum, having read or seen the act, would argue against it, for one finds it to be the key of the whole act. It focuses the feeling, it explains the hard bare phrasing, it heightens the exaltation in which the play ends. It sanctions one of the best passages in the play : " I'll say so near that grave we seem three lonesome people, and by a new made grave there's no man will keep brooding on a woman's lips, or on the man he hates." The handling of the matter in this act is also quite dramatic.

In *Deirdre of the Sorrows* we find everywhere a ripened artistry ; we find also a more serious outlook ; on any more subtle insight into human motives we, however, do not come ; yet we feel that that refinement would not much longer be denied to one whose nature was earnest and not flashy or clever. But then he died.

# CHAPTER XI.

## " POEMS AND TRANSLATIONS "

TO be examined there now remains only his slender book of *Poems and Translations*.

His poems number about a score, and they are all short, most of them lyrics of eight or twelve lines. In the preface of two short pages we find a riper man than in the poems themselves; indeed in all his prefaces his prose is more nervous and varied than it is in his prose poems or essays. This preface, as we already know, is a protest against such poetry as is artificial—the town-writing of the eighteenth century is his own way of putting it—as also against that kind of poetry that is inhuman, such as we find in Shelley and Coleridge. We are therefore prepared for that *Volkston*, the roots of life rather than its blossoms, that we find permeating the book, in the translations as well as in the original poems. Where we do not find that *Volkston*, we may conclude that those pages were written before he had clarified his own ideas on literature and poetry.

His poems do not enshrine any moment of deep feeling in enduring form. Strangely enough the John Synge we come upon in them seems a softer and less integral being than the John Synge who wrote the plays. There are certain men who cannot write openly about their own selves. They are the writers who naturally will shape out sooner or later into classic and reticent forms what is deepest in themselves; they are the writers who the more they try to keep themselves out of their work the more they weave themselves into its every mesh. In those poems Synge sometimes writes openly of himself, and achieves little or nothing. We surely

are not glad to come upon such lines as these in a writer
we like :

> My arms are round you, and I lean
> Against you, while the lark
> Sings over us, and golden lights, and green
> Shadows are on your bark.
>
> There'll come a season when you'll stretch
> Black boards to cover me ;
> Then in Mount Jerome I will lie, poor wretch,
> With worms eternally.

One does not say that such a thought is not material for
poetry, for, since all poets are miracle workers, who will
circumscribe what they are to attempt ?   One says, however,
that the thought is not bettered in its utterance.  If we
rid ourselves of all memory of the second verse, there
remains a rather charming quatrain, such as one with a
feeling for words might keep turning on his tongue ; that
second stanza however simply disintegrates what the first
creates in the mind ; yet that stanza seems to be the *raison
d'être* of the poem.  The relaxed temper, the weakness of
grip, that we find here we find also in many other pages of the
book.  This want of success is really due, not to any lack
of poetry in the man himself, but to his want of skill in poetic
form.  He had not taken at all the same pains with it as
with the texture of prose.

If we had no other hints from himself as to his own build
of mind we must welcome and treasure such a Wordsworthian
echo as this :

> I knew the stars, the flowers, and the birds,
> The grey and wintry sides of many glens,
> And did but half remember human words,
> In converse with the mountains, moors, and fens.

So also we must treasure *The Passing of the Shee*, where he
opposes A.E's feeling for the "plumed yet skinny Shee"
with his own liking for a bout of poaching with Red Dan
Philly's bitch.  Such poems, however, do not reinforce the

idea of him we gather from his work in prose ; and where poetry does not reinforce it disintegrates. His best snatch of lyric music is his *Beg-Innish*.

> Bring Kateen-Beug and Maurya Jude
> To dance in Beg-Innish,
> And when the lads (they're in Dunquin)
> Have sold their crabs and fish,
> Wave fawny shawls and call them in,
> And call the little girls who spin,
> And seven weavers from Dunquin,
> To dance in Beg-Innish.
>
> I'll play you jigs, and Maurice Kean,
> Where nets are laid to dry,
> I've silken strings would draw a dance
> From girls are lame or shy ;
> Four strings I've brought from Spain and France
> To make your long men skip and prance,
> Till stars look out to see the dance
> Where nets are laid to dry.
>
> We'll have no priest or peeler in
> To dance in Beg-Innish ;
> But we'll have drink from M'riarty Jim
> Rowed round while gannets fish,
> A keg with porter to the brim,
> That every lad may have his whim,
> Till we up with sails with M'riarty Jim
> And sail from Beg-Innish.

Here there is not perfection, it is true, but a swiftness, a happy spontaneity and brightness break upon us as might a breath from the western sea itself where the island lies. It is not a mere exercise in verse, as so many of the others seem to be ; it has its own world alive within it : we are thankful to experience that world, happier for having done so.

Most of the translations also one feels to be exercises rather than final achievements. One may not quite agree with him that poetry cannot be translated ; but one may well be certain that poetry cannot be translated into prose ; which

is what he attempted. Here are some lines from Villon
(Ballade que feit Villon à la requeste de sa mère) :

> Femme je suis povrette et ancienne,
> Qui riens ne sçay, oncques lettre ne leuz ;
> Au monstier voy dont suis parroissienne,
> Paradis painct, où sont harpes et luz,
> Et ung enfer où damnez sont boulluz ;
> L'ung me faict paour, l'autre joye et liesse.
> La joye avoir fais-moy, haulte Deesse,
> A qui pecheurs doivent tous recourir,
> Comblez de foy, sans faincte ne paresse.
> En ceste foy je vueil vivre et mourir.

> I'm a poor aged woman, was never at school,
> and is no scholar with letters, but I've
> seen pictures in the chapel with Paradise
> on one side, and harps and pipes in it,
> and the place on the other side, where sinners
> do be boiled in torment ; the one gave me great
> joy, the other a great fright and scaring ; let me
> have the good place, Mother of God, and it's
> in your faith I'll live always.

The difference between these is a matter of texture ; and
this we see more clearly if we compare any bit of his *Old
Woman's Lamentations* with the original. He translates from
Villon's *Les Regrets de la Belle Heaulmière :*

> Or il est mort, passé trente ans,
> Et je remains vieille, chenue.
> Quand je pense, las ! au bon temps,
> Quelle fus, quelle devenue,
> Quand me regarde toute nue,
> Et je me voy si tres changée,
> Povre, seiche, maigre, menue,
> Je suis presque toute enragée.

> The man I had a love for—a great rascal would
> kick me in the gutter—is dead thirty years and
> over it, and it is I am left behind, grey and aged.
> When I do be minding the good days I had, minding
> what I was one time, and what it is I'm come
> to, and when I do look on my own self, poor and dry,
> and pinched together, it wouldn't be much would
> set me raging in the streets.

One can only say that verse translations made by writers with but little of Synge's genius in them give a better idea of the original. The fact is that in poetry the form itself is an active element ; in prose, even how good, the form itself must never be asked to play as important a part. To ask it to do so is to ask it to outrage its own nature. We do not say that such prose as Synge here writes does all that prose can be expected to do ; it does not ; it has, at the same time, the homeliness that is one of the notes of all pre-Renaissance art, yet we do not see how prose could accomplish, in any hands, such miracles as Villon did in his verse, Villon, who, like so many other mediæval artists, throws off a *tour de force* without seeming to know he is doing so. Synge's prose in these translations is too relaxed : the spirit that is within the content does not enliven the body that would convey that content to our minds.

Of the content it is right to speak, for it was always for the sake of the subject matter Synge chose such passages as he did. All the translations he made, whether from Petrarch or Villon, deal with the profound and common interests of life. They are in themselves a sufficient answer to those critics who aver that he was merely ' artistic,' merely bizarre, for in no case does he seem to have selected for translation such passages as exhibit craftmanship rather than matter. He was too serious to have such an outlook in literature.

# CHAPTER XII.

## CONCLUSION

### I.

THE creations of Synge's genius have now passed by, as in a frieze. They were all peasants, even if a few of them carried crowns upon their heads. When they laughed, the laugh was loud and coarse, as befitted their background, a country public-house or a tinker's ditch ; when they sorrowed, the sorrow was unrestrained and wild : the glens were there to receive it. The land in which these peasants lived, through which they made their way, was barren of all except the homeliest and the simplest economies of life. From trafficking their dreams were so far apart, their needs were so few, they could do without institutions or codes of laws or schemes of government. They were neither buying nor selling ; their intercourse was chiefly with Life and Love and Death. Somehow, even when their laugh was loudest, we knew them to be travelling that road of which the old Greek wrote : ' You cannot miss it though you shut your eyes.' This they also knew themselves, yet it was not this thought that made them cry out, but their fear that their human hearts would dry up and shrink, and their limbs totter and fail, before the end was come. Such of them as were beautiful were reckless ; and those that were grotesque were not conscious of it. They never took thought of that beauty which ' lies in no secret of proportion.' The rapture of self-sacrifice, the quality of mercy, the joy of reconciliation, the relief of forgiveness, they knew nothing of ; strangely enough, for all of us, however circumscribed our days may have been, have experienced such revelations. None of these revelations however recurred to our memories while our ears were

233

stretched and our eyes opened to what was afoot among those excited and excitable men and women. It was only afterwards we thought that our own experience of life humdrum and drab as it may have been, was for all that, rounder and fuller than theirs. Those men and women were strange, because they were a little lopsided ; none the less, their companionship brought an unwonted delight ; we relished the warmth of their hearts, their bright eyes, their reckless and astounding tongues. We cannot but think the outflow of spirit from them went a little to our heads : we could not help making a free day of it while with them. And they led us far away from the stifling streets of cities and dull towns ; we went with them over the hillsides, into mountainy glens, across the bogs with their wild myrtle and flowers ; we reached the sea itself. Returning, the world about us appeared piteously drab and slow.

We think that those who refused to share our traffic with them are to be pitied, for surely we all have need, at times, of respite from the intricate pattern of our days, we all require draughts of swift courage and high spirits ; and it is always good to partake in a way of life that is simple, yet deep ; slow, yet stately with rhythm ; different from ours, not broken up, as ours is, with the hissing and snapping of opinions, but enlarged in the presence of wide skies, of great storms, of the rallying and dispersal of fogs and mists. To share in such wayfaring gives not everything ; still it gives very much. As a company these men and women live out such transfigured schemes of life as literature knows of. And therefore to look upon them transforms us, even if not deeply, rather than teaches us in the letter. It is our eyes they affect rather than our brain. We see differently ; we begin to question if there be not something of despair in the heart of our day in, day out, complacency. The vision of them, so bright, so fierce with spirit, shakes us a little ; and that is good. Even Terence Mac Swiney, who himself was such a living example of that kind of beauty those people never dreamed of was not unaware of the adventurous spirit that literature demands : his words are : " If we put a play before the people, it must be with a hope of arresting attention, striking their imagination, giving them a grip of reality, and filling them with a joy in life ! " He was not enamoured of certain of Synge's plays, but he saw that his work was rich in those qualities that literature cannot do without. And of course only for those qualities in it Synge's work could not give us this respite from the vexing criss-cross of daily life. These plays are so unified in mood, so solid in texture, that they come, like a four-square reality, between us and the world that we would, for the nonce, be rid of. Other books of a flashier type, designed solely for such a purpose, in this do not succeed, for the reason that they have no body in them. We never whole-heartedly enter into them at all : all the time, airs and sensations of the old world we would leave, cling about us, so that at the best we receive from them only such questionable repairment of spirit as we might from a drug-induced slumber. The fitting praise of Synge's work is that the comedy in it enables us, not unprofitably, to forget the flatness of our daily lives ; while what is tragic in it genuinely enlarges the spirit.

## II.

We may be certain that Synge would never have written plays with such quality in them only for his having, humbly, gone into the cabins of the poor, only for his having, in the flesh, as one might say, experienced patriotism. That western world into which he plunged lies out in the sea, in ' an incomparable mist,' like Moy Mell itself, the islanders not less rare than their dwelling place ; yet Synge came to feel that all he saw in that strange world—the crazy sea-craft, the hardy men and beasts, the meagre crops, the tumultuous rocks, had, on account of what was happening within his own soul, fledged themselves with a more than natural magic that set him thinking new thoughts—thoughts more moving than any that had come to him in the famous lands he had travelled far to contemplate. We speak lightly of the genius of place ; but who except those who have intimately come to know and to love some one spot of earth, can form any idea of what the phrase means ? Synge was doubly blest, for he came to know not only a place, but a nation ; and fortunately for us was artist as well as lover. Artist-like he reports truly. We understand therefore the warmth that is in his work. That warmth comes only into the work of a writer for whom both place and people are one, the one unthinkable except in terms of the other, for he experiences reality. Hardy is an example, a writer with whom Synge, of course, has much in common. His work, like Hardy's, is opposed to that great mass of literature which is in fashion to-day, which names itself 'international,' using a word that in the connection is hard to understand. 'Russia can do without us, but none of us can do without Russia,' wrote Turgenev, but with this opinion those internationalists do not agree. With great success, of a sort, and certainly with great profits to themselves, they do without their *patria* as much as ever they can. Practising strange inhibitions, they write for the stranger : he is first in their thoughts. To speak to mankind at large they deny themselves the pleasure of gossiping with their neighbours ; they aim at the essence of things, but they acquire and bring with them only the greatest common measure of them, which is certainly not the same. Like all others who go in for mass production what they produce is a very Robot for efficiency : it goes out into the world conquering many lands, so thoroughly, so swiftly, that we wonder if we have not all along been over-rating the great gift of Life. That way of writing which produces best sellers not only in one but in half the countries of the civilized world, sanctioned as it seems to be not so much by its filling of a need, as by the annihilation of distance which modern transport methods as well as wireless have brought about, one asks where it is to end ? One is left wondering, for the world has never seen the like. Mr. Shaw writes a play and it is produced for the first time in a different language a thousand or more miles away. Literature designed for such ends can be nothing but brain. Collaboration with Man may help in its creation, but not collaboration with men, and it is in men that the Human Spirit resides. What can such work have in common, say, with the literature of the Greeks, for whom Greece was everything, for whom tradition meant so much, for whose work there was a prepared atmosphere, not a mere set of opinions, but the aura that exhales from compacted faiths in which multiple opinions have lost themselves ages before ? In old Greece there was harmony : the folk consciousness, the land itself, the traditions, the modes of the literature, the personality of the writer—all were but different aspects of Greece ; without any one of them Greece was not so entirely itself. There could scarcely have been a turn of speech, scarcely a word, in the language, that did not carry a content over and above the ostensible meaning. And it is by virtue of this further content that literature is literature, is ineffably meaningful, like music.

Synge's work is almost as old-fashioned as that of Periclean Greece. Indeed, as already hinted, it may be that as he fashioned it he mentally saw it staged before a Western audience, joyously thinking how this or that would strike the natives of the islands or the Kerry seaboard. The colour in his work, the warmth, derives of course from this feeling of his towards every aspect of the matter he was dealing with. And is it possible that such a natural way of working has become demoded ; that writers no more are to avail themselves of the half-thoughts, of the colour that is in memoried words, of the pieties the ages weave into the very texture of life, of the almost unchanging idiom of the fireside, the workshop, the ship, the field—the unchanging idiom that remains beneath the inflow of new names, always conquering those new names ? The best books in every language contain a far greater number of those unbookish words than the weak books, it is the use of them that tests a creative writer ; and it is by such testing that we note how slack is the creative impulse in the Internationalists. The fewer these words in a piece of literature the more translatable it is, the more easily will it make its way from tongue to tongue, from land to land ; and the more easily also will it shame-facedly slip away after a short time into the eternal silence. There seems to be no new way in literature. But indeed not only are the ancients and their methods opposed to the Internationalists, but the *Zeitgeist*—the term must be a child of their own—is also against them. Their ideal is, or should be, one tongue for the whole world ; yet we know that instead of diminishing, the number of efficient languages on the surface of the earth is increasing, so that we are farther off than ever from such a consummation. Languages here and there are dying, it is true ; but we know for certain that within Soviet Russia alone there are about one hundred tongues spoken, and that many of these, for the first time, have lately had their grammar systems organised, are, for the first time being written down. The same spirit is in the East. A language which becomes conscious of itself as an implement of thought as well as an implement of daily traffic is of course sufficient recompense for the death of many local dialects. But indeed so strong a factor has nationalism now become in the modern world that to write of dying languages is to write of what *was* happening rather than of what *is* happening. In wireless, mankind has discovered for itself a speaking trumpet that carries round the world ; yet, crassly enough, mankind insists on using it for extending Babel across the globe ! To hear of any country, however small, as claiming a wavelength of its own, is to know that that people has become language proud.

When we take such a view of the present-day world, we may feel that the almost sudden death which overtakes so many of those international ' masterpieces ' may not be entirely due to their own intrinsically weakling hearts. Perhaps after all they do *not* answer to the real needs of our time. To have nationalism ruling the world is to have the natural pieties—of which Greek literature is full to overflowing—organised to stand in the way of International literature, just as languages do, languages themselves also being natural pieties. So that Synge's work wrought out in the ancient and natural way, may be destined to exert on the world's literature such influence as work of a classical nature cannot help doing. With that phrase, classical nature, we must content ourselves. We must not speak of his plays simply as classics; the claim would be too great; one thinks that his elimination of so much of the spiritual left a certain narrowness in them within which the human spirit cannot abidingly find sustenance or ease. If universality be felt as wanting to his creations, therein is the cause. His people, except those in *Riders to the Sea*, are inclined to be naturalistic rather than human, for it is human to practice inhibitions for the sake of ideas, to curb appetite by traditions, dreams, faiths well or ill-founded (if so we may put the matter under its most general aspect). Synge's characters are incomplete, inasmuch as they lie outside this universal scheme of life. It is in this way they are freakish, and not in the poetry talk they indulge in nor in their want of practicality in human affairs.

If this blemish in his work be due to an inactive sense of the spiritual in himself, how much greater that blemish must have shown itself had he never come to feel for any community as he did actually come to feel for Aran and the islanders? Everywhere the peasant lives in the consciousness of the other world; his is undoubtedly a realm not only of natural but supernatural pieties; and Synge's *Riders to the Sea* and his essays, of themselves, tell us, as we have seen, that the islanders in Aran are no different from the peasants everywhere else. Synge himself was more than once stirred, even disturbed, by the thought of the difference between his own consciousness and theirs. Nowhere else, we may take it, had he so nearly attained to a lively sense of the spiritual as he did on certain occasions in these islands,—such a sense of the spiritual as might have enabled him to create pieces of literature classic not only in energy, sanity, and fullness, but also in spirituality, which of itself demands a more subtle energy, a rarer sanity, a vaster fullness. It is therefore not without cause that it is in the drama most closely adhering to the islands that we find his most classic work. ' Is fuirist fuinne i n-aice na mine,' runs the Irish proverb : ' Kneading is easy where the meal's at hand.' The meal was to hand in these islands where the people's age-long trafficking with a range of thoughts beyond the needs of nature had induced in them a dignity and settled peace that Synge not only noted but envied. Yet the feeling thus awakened in him became only in the slightest degree an active principle in his æsthetic. Had it more fully done so, his work must have come at least somewhat nearer to the permanent and universal standard, for that feeling is rooted in the heart of man. At the same time his work must have still further separated itself from those international books and plays that minister to a craving for sensation rather than to the thirst for truth. But even as it is his plays are worlds apart from the writings of the Internationalists, and it is his discovery of Aran that accounts for that difference. That is to say, he practised collaboration in a way far more comprehensive than his own theory of it.

### III.

If his going to the folk meant so much for Synge why did not, why do not the other Anglo-Irish writers act similarly ? It has been already remarked that he alone of them did so with any thoroughness, learning the language of the people and suffering the inconveniences of their meagre way of living. But it is only the outsider asks such a question. A writer is, as well as everybody else, a member of a community ; and in Ireland the whole social tradition, as practised and preached, is against the native quality of things, is provincial. If one is reared on an alien porridge one does not take kindly to the native grain. Synge's class have always been reared on an alien porridge ; and the remaining class, though reared on the native meal, begin to discern as they grow up that if they are to succeed 'in the world' they had better do as the rest : they even deny their origin and change their names. Provincialism in Ireland is so thick, so omnipresent, that its lineaments are difficult to scan ; we have never known the native quality with which we might contrast it ; at that native quality we can but guess, our guessing helped out by old Irish tunes, old Irish stones, old Irish poems, as well as the look in the eyes of the people when they are moved. But even if we entirely lacked such touchstones we could guess that provincialism is everywhere in our midst, from the fact that Ireland—the Ireland that counts—is practically sterile in the arts. To what else except provincialism are we to ascribe the whole topsy-turvydom of Irish life ? Naturally (or is it unnaturally ?) it is our cities and towns that are most provincial. Perhaps ninety per cent. of the companies visiting the Irish theatres are English : they perform plays, revues, etc.,—all obviously written for quite a different people. Our press, for the most part, is made up of junks of news and comments written up by English agencies for the English people. If one has any thought for Irish nationhood a bookseller's window in Dublin or Cork is a sad sight. There may be hundreds of books in it ; not even one dozen of them will have been written for Ireland or about Ireland. I have often examined such a window and failed to find in it even one book dealing with our own life. Year after year the sale of English dailies and weeklies increases in our midst, so that it can be accepted that the vast bulk of our reading matter is overwhelmingly English not only in language, but in thought, feeling, outlook. In our cities and towns Literary Societies may sometimes be discovered ; if one examines their programmes, noting that not even ten per cent. of the lectures delivered, of the papers discussed, will concern themselves with our own affairs, our outlook, our past, may not one conclude that these societies ought justly to be described as Societies for the Promotion of Provincialism ? Many of our higher schools and colleges instead of setting themselves with all their might, for mere sanity's sake, against so topsy-turvy a scheme of things, yield to it, seem even to revel in it, if one is to judge them either by the atmosphere within them, or by the annals they very foolishly publish, by their prize-day celebrations, or the yearly feasting of their Old Boys' Associations. Naturally resulting from such a way of life we find among all classes in the country, but especially among the professional classes, an ignorance of Ireland, of all things really native that is not only appalling but incredible. Such culture as exists among them, since it is not indigenous, can hardly be spoken of as culture at all, for genuine culture could not abide the hegemony of an alien social tradition, could not but rebel against an economy of life so poor-spirited as not even to desire to express itself. One remembers the Germany of the eighteenth century, how Goethe wrote of it : ". . . . the development of the higher classes by other moral influences and foreign literature, despite the great advantage which we have derived therefrom, has nevertheless hindered the Germans as Germans, from developing themselves at an earlier stage." [1] Yet it was not Goethe, of course, but Lessing who did a man's part in giving the German nation confidence in itself and in its star. It was he who taught the German people, as Madame de Stael tells us, that there was such a thing as ' un goût national, une grâce naturelle ' ; teaching them with such sturdiness, such success, that when he had finished ' on osa se dire Allemand en Allemagne.' [2] Ireland's present condition, as will be understood from what has been said, is incomparably worse than Germany's ever was ; and not one but a whole battalion of Lessings would be needed to establish a normal state of mind among us. One can but predicate not one Lessing nor a succession of them, but rather a succession of nationalistic movements, rising and falling, each dissolving into a period of reaction, of provincialism, yet each for all that leaving the nation a little more sturdy, a little more normal, a little less provincial than before.

[1] *Literary Sansculottism* (1795).
[2] *De l'Allemagne.*

# CONCLUSION

Only for the fact that there was a nationalistic movement in the land when Synge returned to Ireland he would never have come to write *Riders to the Sea*, no matter how often he visited the Aran Islands nor how long he stayed in them. His success is testimony to the necessity for such movements in every country situated as ours, that is, unprotected against the overflow of a stronger and richer neighbouring tradition. How otherwise is that continuous overflow to be resisted one may ask ; and then if one shrinks, as one may indeed well shrink, from the prospect of a series of nationalistic movements, each and everyone of them using up a large amount of national energy in mere propaganda, one may begin to understand why Ireland is set on having a language of its own, not only as an indigenous medium of expression, but as a wall of defence.

To take a full view of Synge's work is to be convinced of those conclusions. Unless we learn to know ourselves, to stand on our own feet, we shall never achieve self-expression. Unless a writer sink himself in the heart of his own people, he will never, let his own gifts be what they may, accomplish work of such a nature as permanently satisfies the human spirit.

# APPENDIX

## (I) THE WORKS OF JOHN M. SYNGE

1897-9  Contributions to " Kottabos," " New Ireland Review,"
    " Daily Express," (Dublin).

1900    Contributions to London " Speaker."

1901-4  Contributions to New York " Gael."
    *The Last Fortress of the Celt*, April, 1901.
    *An Autumn Night in the Hills*, April, 1903.
    *A Dream of Inishmaan*, March, 1904.

1903    *In the Shadow of the Glen.* First performance, October 8th,
    at the Molesworth Hall, Dublin.

1904    *Riders to the Sea.* First performance, February 25th, at
    the Molesworth Hall, Dublin.

1905    Contributions to " Manchester Guardian."
    *In the Congested District.*

1905    *The Well of the Saints.* First performance, February 4th,
    at the Abbey Theatre, Dublin.

1906-7  Contributions to " Shanachie."
    *The Vagrants of Wicklow.*
    *The People of the Glens.*
    *In West Kerry.*
    *In West Kerry : The Blasket Islands.*
    *In West Kerry : Puck Fair.*

1907    *The Playboy of the Western World.* First performance,
    January 26th, at the Abbey Theatre, Dublin.

1907    *The Aran Islands.*

1909    *Poems and Translations.*

1909    *The Tinker's Wedding.* First performance, November 11th,
    at His Majesty's Theatre, London. (The Afternoon
    Theatre).

1910    *Deirdre of the Sorrows.* First performance, January 13th,
    at the Abbey Theatre, Dublin.

# (II) GENERAL WORKS

A. E., D. P. MORAN, GEORGE MOORE, DOUGLAS HYDE, STANDISH O'GRADY, W. B. YEATS, *Ideals in Ireland.* 1901.

BICKLEY, FRANCIS, *J. M. Synge and the Irish Dramatic Movement.* 1912.

BOURGEOIS, MAURICE, *John Millington Synge and the Irish Theatre.* 1913.

BOYD, ERNEST A., *Ireland's Literary Renaissance.* 1923.
   *Appreciations and Depreciations.* 1917.
   *The Contemporary Drama of Ireland.* 1918.

BROOKE, STOPFORD A. and ROLLESTON, T. W., *Treasury of Irish Poetry in the English Tongue.* 1900.

COLUM, PADRAIC, *The Road Round Ireland.* 1926.

FLOOD, J. M., *Life of Chevalier Wogan.*

GREGORY, LADY, *Cuchulain of Muirthemne.* 1902.
   *Our Irish Theatre.* 1913.

GWYNN, STEPHEN, *Irish Books and Irish People.* 1919.

HOWE, P. P., *J. M. Synge : A Critical Study.* 1912.

HYDE, DOUGLAS, *Beside the Fire.* 1890.
   *Love Songs of Connacht.* 1893.
   *Literary History of Ireland.* 1899.

KRANS, HORATIO SHEAFE, *Irish Life in Irish Fiction.*
   *W. B. Yeats and the Irish Literary Revival.* 1905.

KRIEGER, HANS, *John Millington Synge : Ein dichter der keltischen renaissance.* 1916.

LAW, HUGH, *Anglo-Irish Literature.* 1926.

LYND, ROBERT, *Old and New Masters.* 1919.

MacDONAGH, THOMAS, *Literature in Ireland.* 1916.

MAIR, G. H., *English Literature : Modern.* (Home University Series).

MALONE, ANDREW E. (L. P. Byrne), *The Irish Drama.* 1929.

MASEFIELD, JOHN, *Article : ' Synge, John Millington,'* in Dictionary of National Biography.

MIRSKY, D. S., *Contemporary Russian Literature.* 1926.

O'GRADY, STANDISH, *Selections from S. O'G.* Ed. by E. A. Boyd.

O'RAHILLY, T. F., *Dánta Grádha.* 1926.

246

# APPENDIX

Ó MÁILLE, T., *An Ghaoth Aniar*.

REID, FORREST, *W. B. Yeats.* 1915.

ROBINSON, LENNOX, *A Young Man from the South.* 1917.

TÉRY, SIMONE, *L'île des bardes : notes sur la littérature irlandaise contemporaine.* 1915.

WEST, REBECCA, *The Strange Necessity*.

WEYGANDT, CORNELIUS, *Irish Plays and Playwrights.* 1913.

YEATS, W. B., *Autobiographies.* 1926.
   *Essays—*
   *Preface to the First Edition of the " Well of the Saints."*
   *Preface to the First Edition of John M. Synge's " Poems and Translations."*
   *John M. Synge and the Ireland of his Time.* 1924.
   *Plays and Controversies.* (The Irish Dramatic Movement). 1923.

P. 112
Thoreau

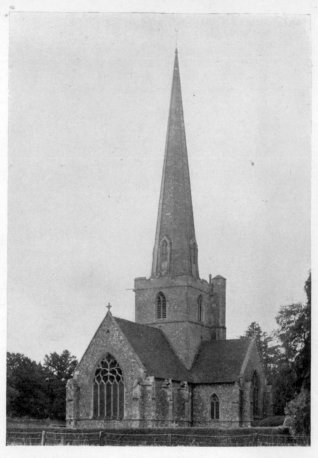

Shottesbroke, Berks., rebuilt by Sir William Trussell in 1337, possibly
on the foundations of a cruciform Norman church.   From the NE.

# THE PARISH CHURCH

## ITS ARCHITECTURE
## AND ANTIQUITIES

By
E A. GREENING LAMBORN

OXFORD
AT THE CLARENDON PRESS
LONDON: HUMPHREY MILFORD
1929

' This was the occasion which first engaged me in inquiries and searches after papers and records which might any way relate to my church and parish. When I had once begun to be thus inquisitive, the slow discoveries which I gradually made did not so much satisfy my mind, as they did incite it to more impatient desires.'—WHITE KENNETT, Preface to *Parochial Antiquities*.

*Second impression*

PRINTED IN GREAT BRITAIN AT THE UNIVERSITY PRESS OXFORD
BY JOHN JOHNSON PRINTER TO THE UNIVERSITY

# PREFACE

'When your children shall ask their fathers in time to come saying " What mean these stones ? " then ye shall answer. . . .'

THE most precious inheritance of the English is their poetry and their parish churches. These are our unique possessions, our peculiar treasures; and no Englishman can take a just pride in his race and country who has not learned to appreciate and love them.

The parish church is hallowed not merely by its purpose but by its age-old associations. Thirty genera-. tions have worked upon its fabric and revealed in their work their needs in this life and their ideas of another; it has been associated not merely with the great crises of their lives, with baptism, marriage, and burial, but with the daily round, the common task, the common amusements; its bells measured out their days and called them to work and rest as well as to prayer; it was their school in childhood, their club-room in adult life, the centre of their social no less than of their religious activities; they could no more have envisaged a life without the church than a child could bear to imagine existence without its mother.

To be insensible to the mute appeal of a building so rich in human pathos is to lose an emotional stimulus, to forgo a spiritual experience, and to neglect an opportunity to enrich our own personalities by developing our powers of imaginative sympathy. For 'whatever withdraws us from the power of our senses, whatever makes the past, the distant, or the future, predominate over the present, advances us in the dignity of thinking beings. Far from me, and from my friends, be such frigid philosophy as may conduct us indifferent and unmoved over any ground which has been dignified by wisdom, bravery, or virtue. That man is little to be envied whose patriotism would not gain force upon the plain of Marathon, or whose piety would not grow warmer among the ruins of Iona.' An Englishman need not have gone so far afield for his illustrations; he could have found them in his own parish—if he had known its history as well as that of Greece.

The purpose of this little book is to reveal the wealth of interest, historical and artistic, that is to be found in an ancient parish church; to help the reader to follow the stages of its growth and to understand the motives and the methods by which that growth was determined; to make significant the features and fittings that are no longer in familiar use; and to fulfil the wistful longings of the dead by making their memorials a part of the active consciousness of the living.

All this can be done better by illustrations than by verbal description: the best book on architecture is a picture-book; and this, by the good will of the publishers, is illustrated with such liberality that it may be so described. One great advantage of the line blocks which constitute the majority of the illustrations is that they submit to the scrutiny of a reading-glass or lens, and this help to their study is strongly recommended. So, too, is the use of the index.

I have to thank my friend Mr. F. E. Howard for counsel and criticism, and Mr. J. R. H. Weaver for the photograph of Earls Barton.

LITTLEMORE.                                    E. A. G. L.

*All Saints' Day,* 1928.

# CONTENTS

# LIST OF ILLUSTRATIONS

# I. THE PLAN

BEDE AND GILDAS tell us of Christians in Britain during the Roman Occupation, of their persecution under the Emperor Diocletian, and of the building and rebuilding of Christian churches throughout Roman-Britain. Both wrote several centuries after the event—Bede in 731, Gildas probably about 564; but the former, at least, relied on documents copied for him at Rome as well as on tradition; and vestiges of two churches of Roman date remain to confirm their testimony.

The most important of these are the foundations of a church uncovered when the site of the Roman city of Calleva (Silchester, Hants) was excavated in the nineties. Its plan, like those of Romano-Christian churches still extant in Italy and Syria, has some features in common with the basilicas or public halls of Roman cities which were formerly supposed to have served as models for the early Christian architects. Although this, and a more recent theory, which derives it from the domestic hall where the early Christian household would have assembled for worship, are now discredited the plan is usually called the basilican. Whatever its origin its essential features are a semicircular apse for the altar and its priests, and a rectangular hall (usually with a portico at the end) for the congregation; the one is still represented by the chancel, the other by the nave (Fig. 1). But indeed this twofold division may at first have been unpremeditated. It is suggested by Mr. G. Gilbert Scott that the earliest

Christian church was simply a small rectangular chamber, representing the room in a disciple's house in which the converts of the first and second centuries used to meet, having a window over the altar at one end and a doorway at the other. Examples of this primitive plan still exist in Ireland,[1] the most perfect being the oratory at Dingle. The congregation probably assembled outside the shrine; in any case but few could enter. The next step therefore was to add a second small room for the altar, entered by a doorway through the end wall, and to admit the congregation to the original chamber. Thus a primitive nave and chancel were formed; but the latter was a rectangle, not an apse; and the plan contained, what the basilican did not, the germ of a chancel arch in the doorway between the two chambers—though the word chancel itself is derived from the screens (Latin *cancelli*) that enclosed a space in front of the apse which served as a choir for the singers. This earlier plan was eventually to determine the lay-out of churches great and small throughout the Middle Ages in Great Britain.

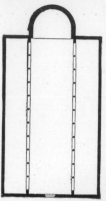

Fig. 1. Plan of a basilica, with semicircular apse for the altar and rectangular hall for worshippers. A space in front of the apse would be railed off for the choir.

[1] The foundations of others exist in Cornwall. Many small Welsh churches retain their early plan though their fabrics have been rebuilt at later periods.

It is possible that it was represented in Roman Britain by the existing chancel of the church of St. Martin at Canterbury, 'built' as Bede records 'whilst the Romans were still in the island', and afterwards

FIG. 2. An Anglo-Saxon church, Corhampton, on the Celtic plan of rectangular nave and chancel, showing pilaster strips and long-and-short work characteristic of the eleventh century. Cf. Pls. II, V.

used as an oratory by Bertha, the Christian wife of Ethelbert of Kent. Part of its walls are of Roman brick, and the foundations, at least, of Romano-British workmanship.

If Bede and Gildas can be trusted these churches were but two out of many; no traces of others, however, have survived the Anglo-Saxon invasion. But of churches built by the English after their conversion there are numerous vestiges throughout the country.

The plan of the majority of these is the double rectangle of the primitive type common in Ireland; and this has therefore been called the Celtic plan. Some authorities, however, now hold that, like the basilican, it came directly from the Continent, as the masons who built the earliest Anglo-Saxon churches certainly did. Of churches on the basilican plan reintroduced by Augustine, Brixworth is the earliest and Wing the latest and most complete example now remaining, though foundations and ruins of others exist—mostly in the neighbourhood of Canterbury. But of churches of the Celtic type there are many more early examples, of which Escomb, Jarrow, Monkwearmouth, Corbridge, Repton, Bradford on Avon and Britford are among the most interesting. The far more numerous churches of the late Anglo-Saxon period are all originally of the rectangular, aisle-less type. Coln Rogers is the most perfect example. (Pl. II.)

The first addition made to the plan was a porch protecting the entrance; Monkwearmouth has a good example. After the Danish inroads a western tower superseded the porch, being sometimes, as at Monkwearmouth, built over it, and besides fulfilling the same function, housed the bells and served as a landmark and possibly as a refuge. The design of the Saxon tower was quite unlike any of later date; it had no buttresses nor stair-turret, its area was always small, and its proportions were tall and slim, quite different from those of Norman towers which were usually but two cubes high and often less.

Next, porch-like projections were built out north and south of the nave, the walls of which were pierced with archways opening into them, as in the early church at Britford near Salisbury and at Bradford-on-Avon. But as the western entrance remained the principal, if not the only, one during the Saxon period, these lateral chambers were probably used as chapels to contain the two side altars that must otherwise have stood in the nave on either side of the chancel arch. They seem to have suggested to the later Saxon builders the idea of a central tower with chapels opening out of it to north and south, which is found at Dover Castle and at Breamore, Hants.

Some Saxon churches like the early basilicas at Rome had crypts below the altar, which were perhaps symbolical of the catacombs in which the fathers of the Church were buried, and which were used to safeguard the holy relics that every church aspired to possess. Round the crypt ran a processional pathway, entered by two openings in the nave floor, from which the worshippers in making the circuit could view and venerate the relics. Hexham has the earliest, and Wing the most complete example.

The Normans had their own ideas of church building, and they destroyed a large number of earlier churches in order to replace them by new ones. They favoured the central tower, and they were skilful enough to build it not upon walls pierced with openings in the Saxon manner but upon piers and arches. They also reintroduced the apse of the basilican plan, though they built, too, many chancels of the rectangular type, but much wider in proportion to their length and height than the Saxon churches were—a typical Saxon chancel suggests the proportions of a grave. But their great contribution to English church-planning was the addition of aisles to the nave of the large church—the small

# DESCRIPTION OF PLATE II

The long-and-short work of the pilaster-strips and of the quoins at the angle of the nave shows that the walls are of the eleventh century. Lancet-lights replaced the original windows [1] in the thirteenth century and were themselves superseded in the nave by the present windows in the fifteenth century, when the low-arched priest's door was inserted in the chancel wall, destroying the lower part of a pilaster-strip.

[1] Except one in the north wall of the chancel, which has rebated jambs showing that it was fitted with a shutter and not glazed—for glass in Anglo-Saxon times was very rare.

II. COLN ROGERS, GLOS. FROM THE SOUTH

one continued to be built on the simple Celtic plan throughout the Middle Ages, except that the western entrance was superseded by doorways north and south of the nave and was reserved for processional purposes only.

All the larger basilican churches of the Continent had aisles, for as they were roofed with timber it was not possible to get beams long enough to span a church of considerable breadth; two rows of arches were therefore built down the length of the building, and upon these walls were raised, standing as it were upon legs, to support the roof over the middle portion; the sides were then covered by lean-to roofs resting upon the outer and leaning against the inner, arch-borne walls which were pierced by high window-openings to lessen the weight upon the arches no less than to admit light. The Saxon architects had sometimes attempted the same thing, but Wing and Brixworth are the only remaining examples of their success in accomplishing it, and at Brixworth the aisles have been destroyed.

But the Norman aisle was not only a device to facilitate the roofing of a wide nave; it was designed also to provide a path for processions round the building, and a means by which worshippers could reach any part of the church without disturbing those already in their places.

The addition of an aisle was also at once seen to be obviously the readiest means of enlarging an existing church by piercing its nave walls with arches and building lower walls parallel with them to carry a lean-to roof. So many Saxon churches on the Celtic plan were extended laterally in this way. Bibury, Glos., and Avebury, Wilts., are notable examples (Pl. V).

The central tower offered another means of increasing the size of a church and providing space for side altars in transepts built to north and south of it. This produced the cruciform plan which became the rule in all large churches—though after the twelfth century the western tower again became general in the smaller ones. By piercing the eastern walls of the transepts chapels could be built out parallel with the chancel, and this was often done, e.g. at Uffington and Cholsey, Berks.; for to provide an altar and an endowment for a priest to say masses at it was the surest means of securing the soul's welfare after death; and therefore all who could afford it were ready to enlarge their parish church at any available point.

Developments of ritual in the thirteenth century led to a general movement for the enlargement of the chancels so as to provide more space for the choir and for ceremonial processions. The obvious plan was to extend the church eastwards by building a new sanctuary and using the original chancel for a choir, but often at the same time the chancel walls were pierced and aisles or chapels built north or south, each with its side altar at which masses could be said for the souls of the founders, who were not only individual rich men but guilds or, as we should now call them, clubs or associations of traders or craftsmen organized for the welfare of their members in the next world as well as in this one. Sometimes a vestry would be built; but this, too, as its piscina remains to show, was also a chapel with its altar. By the end of the Middle Ages most parish churches, in addition to the High Altar at the east end, had half a dozen side altars in various chapels at which masses were daily said.

But by the end of the Middle Ages, when a church was to be built or rebuilt its designers planned it so as to exhibit to full advantage the great screen between nave and chancel which had then become the most imposing object in the building. They therefore eschewed a central tower and even the chancel arch, and, instead of building transepts, carried the nave aisles eastward to overlap the chancel. The plan thus finally arrived at is therefore practically a reversion to that of the early basilica except that a square sanctuary takes the place of the apse. In such a church the chapels are not excrescences each under its own roof but are enclosures like great pews [1] formed by screening off a bay of an aisle. The screens have been destroyed in most churches but have left their traces on the caps and bases of the columns cut to receive the ends of their beams.

At the time of the Reformation therefore the builder's ideal plan was practically identical with our own: it was that of a great rectangular hall with a small eastward projection. But the aims which led him to it were very different from ours; we need a large auditorium from every part of which the preacher and the priest at prayer can be heard and seen; his aim was to ensure that from every point in the church the screen with its Rood and loft for organs and singers, the High Altar and some at least of the side altars should be in full view. For from the sixth century to the sixteenth a church was primarily a shelter for altars; and going

[1] After the Reformation many of them were actually used as pews by the descendants of their founders and thus provided models for the horse-box pews of the Jacobean squires.

to church meant seeing and hearing the Sacrifice of the Mass, and being reminded of the Event it commemorated.

## II. THE ROOF

BUT IN our climate, at least, a shelter means more than the enclosing walls with the lay-out of which we have so far been concerned. The parts of a church have not only to be screened but covered. The most obvious and the earliest method is to rest a roof upon the walls as the lid rests upon a box. But while walls can be built of any kind of stone the space between them can only be thus bridged by stones of a length difficult to handle and even more difficult to procure. In Egypt the thing was done, but elsewhere the builders had to fall back upon a wooden lid,[1] since timber could more readily be obtained in lengths of adequate span.

Merely to lay planks from wall to wall, however, would produce a flat roof upon which rain would collect. The lid was therefore constructed as a rigid rectangular framework with sloping sides, prevented from 'spreading' or altering its shape by means of horizontal tie-beams keeping its long sides parallel. The long sides, 'the wall-plates', of this framework, rested upon the flat tops of the walls; its sloping sides, the rafters, were covered externally with thatch, tiles,

---

[1] A good many Anglo-Saxon churches were built entirely of wood. Thus Dunstan 'apud Magaveldam (Mayfield) sicut in aliis hospitiorum suorum locis, ligneam ecclesiam fabricavit'; and Bede records the building of churches 'non de lapide, sed de robore secto'—of split oaks. An example of the early eleventh century still exists at Greensted, Essex.

shingles, or in the later Middle Ages, sheets of lead, and internally with boards. It lay as a dead weight upon the walls—so long as its tie-beams held, and received from them support along the whole length of its wall-plates.[1] Its weakness was the liability of timber to decay and, still more, its inflammability.

It was the second weakness that led the builders from the earliest times to seek a means of constructing a stone roof or at least an inner shell of stone to lessen the risks from fire—from heaven in the form of lightning, from men in time of war. The first step towards the solution of their problem was taken when some early inventive genius, of an unknown race and country, devised a means of bridging the head of a doorway, not by spanning it with a long stone or beam, but by fitting stones together in a curve where their mutual pressure kept them from falling out of their places.

But an arch has no great advantage over a lintel unless the space to be bridged is a wide one; and then its construction presents two serious difficulties, the need to provide first a great timber framework or centring on which to support the voussoirs (arch-stones) until all are in place, and secondly an adequate abutment to prevent the arch from flattening out by pushing aside its supports. The danger can be illustrated simply and effectively by bending a cane and placing it between two books on a table; unless the books are fairly heavy the cane will push them farther apart in the effort to straighten out. More books laid upon the others will

---

[1] After the invention of the Gothic buttress roofs were often constructed of timber arches so as to dispense with tie-beams, which are very costly except for narrow spans.

check this tendency; [1] but pressure upon the top of the curve will set them moving again until a weight equal to it is placed at the ends of the cane.

The arch therefore presented the early builders with more serious problems than it solved; and though it was known and used in many lands for centuries before the Christian era it was employed only in small openings or below the ground level where the surrounding earth provided an immovable abutment.

The Roman engineers of the second century B. C. were the first to devise a system of building in which the arch with perfect stability and safety took the place of beam and lintel in every part of the structure, and above all, in the roof. They realized, for example, that if two equal arches spring from a common point their thrusts are neutralized and converted into a dead weight, and that therefore the mass of the support at this point is immaterial, so long as it is solid enough to resist compression. And so they carried their aqueducts across country for scores of miles upon hundreds of arches, the thrusts of each being met by those of its fellows on either side of it. Thus arch fought arch all down the line, the thrusts of the end ones being annihilated by a solid weight of masonry.

But the most important invention of the Roman architect was the cross vault, which is indeed the most far-reaching discovery that has been made in the history of architecture. It came as the result of experimenting with arched tunnels or barrel vaults (which are simply

[1] The same thing could be done by tying the ends of the cane together, and in modern architecture this is sometimes done with the feet of arches by using iron tie-rods.

long archways) intersecting at right angles; and it showed that any square space could be roofed by sections of a barrel vault, carried upon arches springing from its corners, and therefore that any rectangular area might,

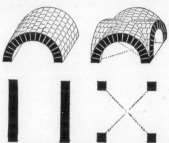

Fig. 3. Barrel or tunnel vault and cross or groined vault formed by the intersection of two tunnels. The lines of intersection are known as groins. Cf. Fig. 5.

by division into squares, be roofed by a series of cross vaults supported by columns at their corners (Fig. 3).

The cross, or quadripartite vault is the essential feature alike of Roman architecture and of that imitation of it which was developed by the barbarians of western Europe and is known as Romanesque. It may be objected that among all our examples of Saxon Romanesque there is not a single vaulted building above ground, and that the great majority of Norman Romanesque churches are also without vaults. Nevertheless, the ideal of every medieval architect was a vaulted building; wherever the skill, and the centring, was available, as in the case of monasteries and cathedrals, this ideal was achieved with more or less completeness; and the parochial builders who could not raise a vault

yet copied the arches whose essential function is to
support one, though lintels in doorways and window-
heads would have served their purpose equally well.

So it happens that not the cross vault but its semi-

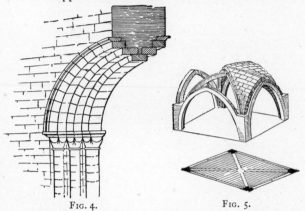

FIG. 4.                              FIG. 5.

FIG. 4. Showing Norman method of constructing an arch in successive
rings or orders, each supported by a shaft recessed in the jambs.
FIG. 5. Gothic vault, built up on a skeleton of pointed arches of varying
span but equal height.

circular arch is the mark by which most of our Romanesque work is distinguished.

The Saxon arches are nearest to the Roman model;
sometimes indeed as at Escomb they are actually Roman
work rebuilt in a new position; always (except in
windows where a splay is necessary to allow the light
to spread) they are cut straight through the wall like
a tunnel, in the Roman manner (Pl. V b). The Norman
method was very different: to save centring they built
their arches in successive rings one above another, each

wider than the last, using centring only for the first and narrowest, upon which the others were built up (Figs. 4, 6); and they usually set nook-shafts in the jambs to support each ring or 'order' of the arch.[1] This recessing gave their arches a richly elaborate effect which was increased by decorative carving on the edges of the orders and by ornamenting the caps of the nook-shafts with scallops (Figs. 29, 31) or even with naturalistic carving of birds and beasts. So the Norman architect, like Wordsworth's Happy Warrior, 'turned his necessity to glorious gain'.

This effort to economize centring, in days when all shaping must be done by hand and by means of the axe alone, had still more important results: it led the late eleventh-century builders to experiment in making a cross vault not as in the Roman manner with complete centring but by constructing a skeleton of arches, like the ribs of an umbrella, and then filling in the webs between them one by one, using for each the same set of centring (Figs. 5, 7). The device, perhaps invented to ceil the aisles at Durham in 1095, so simplified the construction of cross vaults that scores of Norman towers and square chancels are to this day provided with stone ceilings, and every Norman cathedral and abbey church has its aisles vaulted by this means.

This method also revealed very clearly the important

[1] One or two late Saxon churches, e.g. Hadstock, Essex, have rude shafts in the door-jambs. These belong to the Confessor's reign and are crude reflections of the work of his Norman masons at Westminster where from about 1055 he was building an abbey church on the model of that at Jumièges. The very interesting door at Hadstock, with its ironwork, is contemporary, and is thus the oldest piece of carpentry in England.

fact that the thrusts of a cross vault were concentrated
at the angles from which the skeleton arches sprang, and
that if adequate abutment were provided at these points

Fig. 6. Porchester church, twelfth century, showing Norman windows
and door and shallow buttresses at the angles of nave and transept.

the rest of the walling might be built light and thin
without risk to stability and with a great saving of
material. So the buttress came into visible existence, in
Norman work a pilaster (Figs. 6, 8 and Pls. III, VI), a
mere thickening of the wall at a point where pressure was

concentrated, but afterwards a projecting mass of masonry designed to relieve the walls of their original function of supporting the roof and so to convert them simply into screens against the weather, which might be, and in fact eventually became, great sheets of painted glass.

With the emergence of the buttress as the essential factor in the stability of the building, the Norman style passed into the Gothic, the earliest development of which was named by those who would appear to have studied only English examples, the Early English Style.

## III. THE BUTTRESS

BY THOSE who observe merely the details and not the constructive principles of a building Gothic is supposed to be any system of architecture that employs the pointed arch. But the pointed arch was used quite early in Norman work, and the round one persisted all through the Gothic period, though of course the one was exceptional before and the other after the reign of Henry II.

The pointed arch, like the round, was of prehistoric origin—indeed the first man who improvised a rude compass to strike a round arch must, by the intersection of equal arcs, have struck pointed ones too (Fig. 54)—but it had been neglected for centuries after its invention. It is probable that crusaders observed it in Saracenic building and realized its value in solving the great problem of Romanesque architecture, how to construct a high vault above an aisled nave. This had been found practically impossible by means of round arches alone, for, as the nave was wider than the aisle, its bays, the area defined by the aisle pillars, were oblong, and therefore could not be roofed by square

cross vaults, which require four arches of equal height.
Semicircular arches can of course rise to only half their

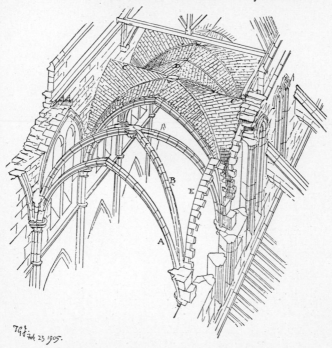

FIG. 7. Construction of a Gothic high vault over an aisled nave by means
of a skeleton of arches supported by flying buttresses. Note lean-to
timber roof of aisle and tie-beam roof over nave vault.

span: the crowns of the narrow side arches would therefore fall far below those of the wide transverse ones
across the nave. A pointed arch, however, can be

brought to a height independent of its span; by making the narrow arches lofty and sinking the wide ones all could be brought to the same level in the crown of the vault (Figs. 5, 7). And thus the pointed arch solved the great problem of the Romanesque builders and in so doing improved their system out of existence.

For, as is the way with problems, the solution confronted the builders with a fresh one: how to maintain the stability of their new construction? The nave walls could not be thickened at the points where the arch-thrusts were received, for they were themselves carried upon the row of arches below them. Some unknown architect of France, where the pointed vault earliest developed, hit upon the plan of building a tall buttress outside the aisle wall, opposite the point where the high-vault thrusts were concentrated, and transmitting them to it by means of a bar of stone, as a bulging wall is shored up by a prop—except that the flying buttress, as the bar is called, takes off not from the ground but from the summit of a tall mass of masonry (Fig. 7).

The early Gothic buttresses, like the flat Norman pilasters from which they had developed, tended to be wide in proportion to their projection (Figs. 6, 8, 9). Throughout the Gothic period their depth increased until in the fifteenth century it was often double or treble their width, for this shape is obviously the most effective in resisting outward thrusts, and also increases the area of wall available for windows (Figs. 10, 11, 47). Since the essential quality in a buttress is weight the pinnacle was soon invented to increase its mass and at the same time to throw off the wet and beautify the sky-line of the building.

It is not impossible that in the pinnacle we may see
the germ of that most impressive of all Gothic inven-

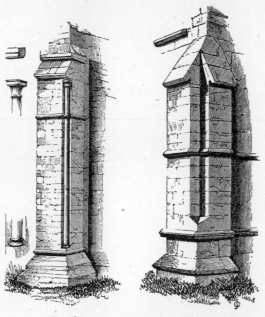

FIG. 8.                    FIG. 9.

FIG. 8. Late Norman corner buttress with angle shaft having cap with
        square abacus and water-holding base. *c.* 1160.
FIG. 9. Early Gothic coupled buttress of slight projection. *c.* 1200.

tions, the spire; which, both structurally and artistically, is merely a logical development of the pinnacle,
and appears almost simultaneously with it, as if the one

device had suggested the other.[1] Structurally its function

 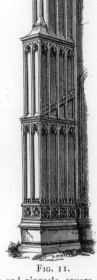

Fig. 10.                    Fig. 11.

FIG. 10. Decorated buttress with niche and pinnacle, square on plan.
*c.* 1330. Cf. Pl. VIII.
FIG. 11. Perpendicular buttress of deep projection with panelled surface
and of several stages. *c.* 1450. Cf. Fig. 47.

is to weight the tower against the thrusts of the arches
that abut upon it; its weight is set in balance against

    [1] The usually accepted origin of the spire is in the pyramidal
roof of the Romanesque towers.

that of the walls carried by the arches. Artistically it at once enriches the sky-line of the building, serves as a point round which its parts group themselves, and emphasizes the monumental character of the structure as a building raised not merely for the service but for the glory of God.

The earliest spires of the thirteenth century were of the broach type, four of their faces rising from the outer edges of the tower walls; later examples usually spring from the inner edges of the walls, thus leaving room for a parapeted walk round the base from which ladders may be run up or cradles slung when repairs are necessary. Obviously, too, this device simplified the building of a spire, since the necessary scaffolding could be set up on the top of the tower walls instead of being built up all the way from the ground level (Frontispiece).

A good many of our Norman towers, e.g. Castor and Cassington, have been given an upper stage, to serve as the base of a spire, by the architects of the thirteenth and fourteenth centuries (Pl. IV).

The early Gothic buttress of slight projection was of uniform depth, like a flat, bold pilaster; but as its depth increased it was built in diminishing stages, two or three in the thirteenth century, three or four in the fourteenth, and even more in the fifteenth. Each stage sloped sharply into the next so that the rain might be thrown off and prevented from soaking into the stone-work. The earlier buttresses were set in pairs at the angles of the building, but after the thirteenth century they are often built diagonally at the corner, so that only one is needed (Figs. 9, 13, Pl. VIII).

Parish churches are seldom provided with vaults, for

the setting out, in spite of the simplified method of skeleton arches, required considerable skill and experience. Moreover in the climate of western Europe a vault requires protection from the weather on its

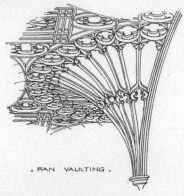

. FAN VAULTING .

Fig. 12. Cone of fan-tracery vault, showing lierne ribs. *c.* 1450.

external face, and therefore timber roofs were still necessary. Few parishes could afford the luxury of a duplicate roof. But the cathedrals could, and in them the skeletal method continued to develop until in the fourteenth century the vault became a net-work of light arches bridged across by lierne ribs so that the filling-in could be done with flat stones without centring; and then the vaulting of a porch or chapel presented little difficulty even to the village masons. The junction of the arch-ribs was greatly simplified by the invention of the boss, a block of stone into which their ends fitted, which gave scope to the carver as well as convenience to the mason (Fig. 7).

Finally, in the latter half of the fourteenth century the invention of fan-vaulting, in which sections of an incurved cone or 'trumpet' are poised against each other, enabled the builder to construct a vault by fitting its panels together without any skeleton of arches, though ribs, structurally useless, were still cut upon the sections of the cone, for the enrichment of the surface and to suggest the lines of pressure (Fig. 12).

The fan-vault with its thin, light panelling exercised little thrust, and so would have enabled the builders to reduce the projection of the enormous and numerous buttresses which are so prominent a feature in early Gothic that looking at some of our cathedrals one can hardly see the church for its supports.[1] Yet the new invention did not become really popular until the Reformation and the end of Gothic were in sight; and it never became a common feature in parish churches except in porches and towers.

## IV. THE WINDOWS AND DOORWAYS

BUT IF the high vault was rare in the parish church its concomitants, the pointed arch and the buttress, soon became universal; for though in the absence of a vault neither is indispensable yet the one allowed of far greater variety in the proportions of doorways and windows, and the other enabled walls to be constructed more strongly with less material.[2]

[1] It must be remembered, however, that to monastic builders the interior effect was the great thing aimed at.

[2] Buttresses also enabled the builder to dispense with tie-beams in the construction of the roof, by resisting the thrusts of timber arches.

The arch most commonly used in the first century of Gothic, that is from the time of Richard to that of Edward I, the Early English period, was of an acutely

FIG. 13. Stanton Harcourt church, showing Early English lancet windows with hood-moulds, and coupled buttresses, *c.* 1220 ; and a central Norman tower with a fourteenth-century upper stage.

pointed form, its radius being seldom less than its span and sometimes much greater. It gave the windows the long, narrow shape of lancets, and in order that these might admit adequate light they were widely splayed internally and set fairly close together in the walls (Figs. 13, 14). In gable ends they were usually grouped

in pairs or triplets with a little arched projecting ridge of
stone above them, a string-course or hood-mould, to
throw off the wet; quite early in the thirteenth century

FIG. 14. Lancet window, splayed internally, with hood-mould or dripstone above the arch and string-course below. *c.* 1220.

it became the practice to pierce the triangular spaces
between the hood-mould and the lancet heads with
circular openings (Fig. 16). This was the origin of
tracery, a pattern-work of openings in the head of a

window. By the middle of the century the early 'plate-tracery' of pierced openings had been completely super-seded by a new method of constructing a single arched

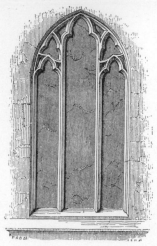

opening, filling its head with a pattern of curved stone bars, and dividing its lower part vertically into lancet lights by means of long stone mul-lions (Fig. 15). Before the end of the century the single lancet had been abandoned alto-gether in favour of the traceried window, and often the small openings in earlier buildings were enlarged so that the new tracery might be inserted. With the lancet went the acutely pointed arch. The most popular form was now equilateral; but

FIG. 15. Early bar-tracery of simple geometrical design. *c.* 1260.

width was obtained in many windows by giving the heads a segmental curve. In the middle of the fourteenth century the four-centred arch was transferred from the fan-vault to which it was essential into the heads of the windows, where it remained until the end (Fig. 47).

The early tracery was of a simple geometrical form, consisting mainly of quatrefoiled circles and trefoiled triangles above a pair or triplet of mullioned lancet lights (Figs. 17, 51, Pl. VII). But during the time of the first

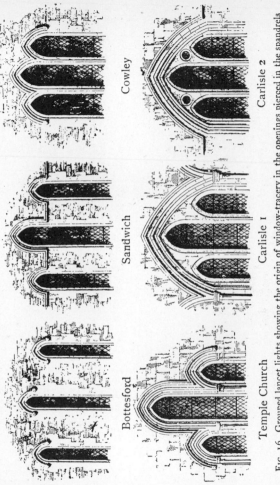

Cowley

Sandwich

Bottesford

Carlisle 2

Carlisle 1

Temple Church

FIG. 16. Grouped lancet lights showing the origin of window-tracery in the openings pierced in the spandrels between the window-heads and the hood-mould.

two Edwards windows increased greatly in size and tracery in complexity, the openings assuming a variety of shapes and sizes that must have presented grave diffi-

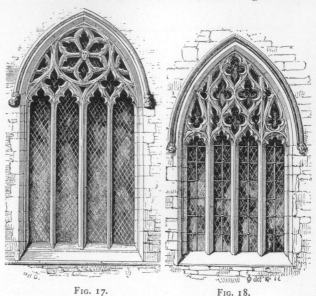

Fig. 17.     Fig. 18.

Fig. 17. Decorated or curvilinear tracery of geometrical type. *c.* 1300.

Fig. 18. Decorated tracery, 'flowing' type, *c.* 1360. Two of the mullions run up to the head of the arch in the manner characteristic of the succeeding style.

culties to the glazier who had to fill them with pictures in coloured glass (Figs. 18, 19, 20, Pls. VI, VIII). Early in the reign of Edward III a reaction set in, well illustrated at Gloucester in the reconstruction of the choir begun in

1337, for which the glaziers were at least partly responsible; and by the end of the reign the Decorated or curvilinear tracery was everywhere giving place to the Perpen-

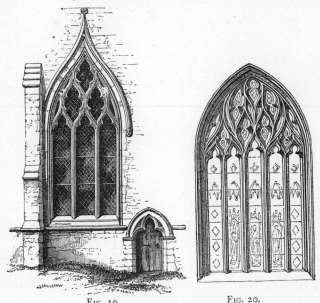

FIG. 19.                    FIG. 20.

FIG. 19. Decorated flowing tracery of the pattern known as reticulated. *c.* 1340.

FIG. 20. Late Decorated tracery of flamboyant type, *c.* 1360. In France this persisted during the English Perpendicular period.

dicular or rectilinear form, in which the main mullions often ran straight through from the sill to the arch, and shorter vertical and horizontal bars divided the head into panels conveniently shaped to receive a stained glass portrait (Fig. 21). At the same time, by the general adoption of the four-centred arch, window heads widened and their haunches rose until little curve was left in their

Fig. 21. Perpendicular or rectilinear tracery, in which the vertical line predominates. *c.* 1400. The wide, shallow casement moulding running round the arch and jambs is characteristic of the style.

arches, and many were simply lintels supported by the mullions (Pls. III, VI). So at the beginning of the fifteenth century the typical window had, as Ruskin scornfully said, the form of a gridiron. Nevertheless it was perfectly adapted to its purpose of composing a picture in coloured glass; it is only when its glass is gone that it loses by con-

trast with the varied curves of Decorated tracery; and
even so, what it lacks in variety of line it gains in variety
of gradation and subordination of the thickness of its
framework, from the heavy weight-bearing mullions to
the slight vertical members of the upper lights.

It is often argued nowadays that only in France did
Gothic reach its full development, because only there
did the vaulted roof which brought it into existence give
significance to the details by its presence in every building. It is true that most of our parish churches, unlike
those of France, lack the stone ceiling which is the
*raison d'être* of most of their details; but it is also true
that the invention of the fan-vault, which is the final
and perfect solution of the vaulting problem and the
logical conclusion of all the earlier experiments, was
reached in England alone; and that the Perpendicular
window which is equally the inevitable conclusion of
a system of screen-walls and buttresses is also a purely
English development. For Gothic is essentially a system
which substitutes the buttress for the wall; it is indeed
nothing else than the construction of a stone lantern;
and the window extending from one buttress to the next
is the form proper to it. But such a window must be
designed to resist an enormous wind-pressure, and
therefore its principal mullions must be firmly held at
either end and must be stayed and strengthened by
transoms crossing from jamb to jamb. We are not such
an illogical people as we sometimes suppose.

It is only the raw amateur, ignorant of constructive
technique, who supposes that because Perpendicular
detail has not the naïvety, naturalness, and variety of
earlier work it must be a decadent stage of Gothic. For

Gothic construction was progressive to the last, and was never more alive and vigorous than when it was suddenly interrupted by the Reformation.

FIG. 22. Early English doorway, *c.* 1220, showing deeply shadowed mouldings and detached jamb-shafts with foliaged caps supporting the orders of the arch. Cf. Figs. 38, 51. The basement-course shows that the wall is later than the doorway, and thus that the aisle has been widened.

Doorways changed less than windows throughout the Gothic period, but their shapes followed a similar course, the acutely arched head of the thirteenth century sinking through the fourteenth to the wide, flat arch characteristic of the fifteenth. For a century or more they continued to be recessed in orders in the Norman manner, often with nook-shafts (Fig. 22); but in the fourteenth century half-columns carved on the jambs took the place of the shafts which, in the next century, dis-

Fig. 23. Perpendicular doorway, *c.* 1425. The head is set in a square frame or label, panels are sunk in the spandrels, the mouldings are shallow and angular, the casement hollow is repeated between the suites of mouldings, and the bases of the engaged shafts are of the pedestal type.

appeared altogether except in large and elaborate doorways (Figs. 23, 53).

The typical Perpendicular door may be at once recognized by having its flat-arched head set in a square hood-mould or 'label', the corners of which are filled with quatrefoiled sunk circles or with shields of arms, with which, too, the labels often end (Fig. 23, Pls. III, IV).

A similar change took place in the chancel arch which in early Gothic as in Norman work has often shafts in the jambs to carry the orders of the arch, and in the Decorated period a half-column, while in Perpendicular the arch is either omitted or, being hidden by the screen and rood, has usually neither mouldings nor columns.

In the nave arcades some traces of the Norman invention of the recessed arch remained until the end; but as walls became thinner the device ceased to have any practical value in economizing centring. The orders are therefore more clearly marked in Norman and early Gothic than in later arcades.

It should be remembered that at all periods the readiest plan of supporting the arch was a simple cylindrical or hexagonal column with a cap upon which the orders stopped; and in the simpler churches this arrangement was universally adopted as a substitute for the more logical compound pier.

# V. THE IMITATIVE STYLES

THE REFORMATION put an end to church-building for almost two centuries, until the growth of towns made necessary the creation of new parishes. Our old parish churches are therefore almost entirely a legacy of the Middle Ages. But occasionally it was found necessary in the eighteenth century to rebuild a village church, and there are even a few examples of seventeenth-century date, the most notable being that at Staunton Harold, Leicestershire, built by a squire who, as an inscription over the entrance records, 'did this best of things in the worst of times and hoped them in the most calamitous'—the date is 1653. The work so exactly

FIG. 24. Nuneham. An eighteenth-century church, 1764, in the Classic or Palladian style, with dome and pediment supported by Ionic columns.

FIG. 25. All Saints, Oxford, c. 1710. Designed by Aldrich in the Classic style; showing Corinthian columns, a balustrade, and projecting keystones in the heads of the arches.

reproduces the style of the fifteenth century that but for the mouldings, which show the influence of Renaissance models, it would be difficult to believe that the

## DESCRIPTION OF PLATE III

The 'CR' in the pediment of the porch refers to Charles I, in whose reign the church was rebuilt. But the flat buttress with the short length of string-course above it shows that the west wall at least was rebuilt on a Norman base. The windows and strings are of late Gothic type, but the porch, though contemporary, is of pure Renaissance style with classic pediment and mouldings and elliptical arch in the doorway. Elliptical curves distinguish classic from Gothic mouldings.

(The font is contemporary with and confirms the evidence of the buttress.)

III. SHRIVENHAM, BERKS. WEST WALL

inscription refers to the whole building. But, as other examples show—St. John's Church, Leeds, Carlton Husthwaite, Yorks., Welland, Hanley, and Water Eaton—the Gothic tradition was still very much alive even in the seventeenth century (Pl. III).

The building of St. Paul's after the Great Fire, if it did not kill it, at least put it to sleep. Wren's work, based ultimately on the Roman temples and basilicas, became the model for the eighteenth-century church-builder; and so the parish church of that date may be instantly recognized by its apse, its small dome, and its columns, Doric, Ionic, or Corinthian, crude imitations, *longo intervallo*, of those which supported the roof of the Greek temple (Fig. 24). Or, if it is too modest to possess any of these things, its round unrecessed arches will exhibit in their crowns the wedge-shaped, boldly projecting keystone. And only the altar furniture will distinguish it from the nonconformist chapel next door (Fig. 25).

By the middle of the century, when Hartwell and Tetbury were rebuilt, the Gothic imitation had begun; but it had little scope to manifest itself until the growth of the factory system made the provision of new town churches an urgent necessity in the second quarter of the nineteenth century. Then it broke out like an epidemic, and its results are with us yet; not only in hideous new churches in sordid streets but, worse still, in incongruous and unnecessary additions and alterations to old churches that had survived the zeal of the Puritan and the neglect of the pluralist to fall victim to the stupidity of the restorer, who supposed that workmen who had lost not merely the religion of the Middle Age but its traditions of craftsmanship, and above all its freedom of each man to do his job in his own way, could reproduce at the command of an architect, who could not handle a tool, the visible manifestation of the medieval spirit, the English parish church.

## VI. ORNAMENT

FOR THOSE visitors to our ancient churches who wish to know no more of the history of a building than the dates of its various parts the mouldings and enrichments of the arch and column afford the safest and easiest guide.

The Anglo-Saxons used few mouldings, for they rarely attempted to build columns, and so the great majority of their arches are in doorways and chancels; these are usually very small and being without orders afford little surface for mouldings; their shape is outlined by thin slabs set edgeways into the wall, with their narrow, square edges boldly projecting to form a frame running continuously round arch and jambs (Pl. V b). They spring from enormously massive impost stones which seldom have their lower edges chamfered off to form a slanting surface as in Norman work, but are usually relieved by two pairs of parallel grooved lines running horizontally round them. These parallel grooves are found in pairs also upon the baluster shafts, which stand on the centre of the sill (and are therefore sometimes called mid-wall shafts) to support the double arches of Anglo-Saxon belfry windows (Figs. 26, 27). (Other windows, intended to be glazed or perhaps closed by horn lattices, are set back deeply into the wall in late Saxon churches or, in the few early examples, the jambs are rebated for shutters, and tend to converge upwards. Windows with triangular heads occur at Deerhurst, Barton on Humber, and Herringfleet, and circular windows at Avebury, Bibury, and in East Anglia.)

The faces of Anglo-Saxon towers (all of which

FIG. 26. A belfry window of Anglo-Saxon type, eleventh century. The arches are unrecessed, their imposts are massive and square, and the mid-wall shaft is baluster-shaped.

probably belong to the tenth and eleventh centuries) and of the contemporary walls, e.g. in the almost unaltered church of Coln Rogers (Pl. II), are relieved by narrow bands of dressed stone, pilaster-strips, which, like the quoins, are formed of 'long-and-short work' in which large, squared stones with their longer axes vertical alternate with smaller ones laid flat (Fig. 27). Neither of these features occurs in the earlier work (which is often to be distinguished by the presence of Roman materials reused); they are, however, characteristic of the Rhenish churches of Germany, from which they were probably derived; for the Danish occupation of the French coast had cut us off from Gallic influences and led our architects to seek their models elsewhere. But though these details came by way of Germany their ultimate origin is in the Romanesque style of the Lombardic churches of Italy, and the pilaster-strips, like the Norman pilaster buttress, may even be traced to those of Roman buildings.

It may be noted in passing that while the Saxon often

FIG. 27. Tower of Anglo-Saxon type, St. Michael's, Oxford, eleventh century, showing windows with baluster-shafts, and long-and-short work in the angle-stones or quoins. Cf. Fig. 2 and Pl. II.

used Roman materials the Norman employed the Roman method of building walls and columns with an enormous core of rubble faced with squared stones. But as Norman mortar was usually very bad his work had not the stability of the far slighter Saxon walling, especially

that of the early period; and so a great many Norman
towers fell within a century or two of their building
and often brought down the rest of the structure with

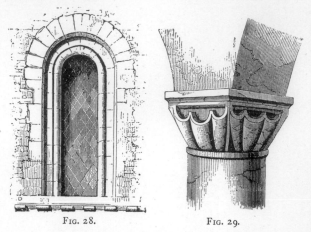

Fɪɢ. 28.                    Fɪɢ. 29.

Fɪɢ. 28.  Norman window, *c.* 1120, showing bold semicircular torus
moulding on arch and jambs, with billet ornament below.
Fɪɢ. 29.  Norman scalloped cap, *c.* 1140, with square, tile-like abacus.

them.  Yet the credit for the best masonry of Anglo-
Saxon date ought perhaps to be given to the foreigners
who, as Bede tells us, were brought into the country
by Benedict Biscop and Nectan, King of the Picts, to
construct churches of more architectural dignity than
the local masons could achieve.

The Normans also employed few mouldings—the
chamfer with a quirk or groove above it (Fig. 30) being
the chief, but their enrichments were numerous and
varied.  By far the commonest was the chevron or

FIG. 30. The quirk and chamfer, the most typical Norman moulding on the imposts of arches. Cf. Figs. 29, 31.

FIG. 31. The chancel arch, Headington, *c.* 1120, showing chamfered hood-mould, torus moulding, chevron ornament, star-pattern on chamfered imposts, and nook-shafts with cushion-caps, and flattened roll at base.

zigzag (Figs. 6, 31) which in various forms ran round the arches of doorways, windows, chancels and nave arcades, and, occasionally, as a string-course round

Fig. 33.

Fig. 32.                              Fig. 34.

Fig. 32. The keel-moulding, characteristic of the Transition period, 1160–90. Cf. Fig. 36.

Fig. 33. The water-holding base of early thirteenth-century work.

Fig. 34. The dog-tooth ornament and the mask corbel, both characteristic of Early English Gothic.

the walls both inside and out; more often, however, the string was a heavy semicircular projection (Fig. 28); and when it ran round an arch it was sometimes cabled, like a thick rope, or enriched with beak-heads—cats' or owls' faces with beaks that curved over the semicircular moulding. Round pellets, billets oblong and cylindrical (Fig. 28), and, in early work a four-pointed star, in late

Fig. 35. Late Norman bases, *c.* 1180, with flattened roll and spur of foliage.

Fig. 36. Transitional cap, *c.* 1190, with keel-moulding springing from the square Norman abacus, which is supported by crude stiff-stalked Gothic foliage.

work an ornament like a jew's harp with recurving ends, were frequently used. The dripstone or hood-mould round the arch often terminated in monstrous dragon-heads like those of crocodiles, sometimes found also in the ornamental ironwork on the door itself. Usually the caps of shafts and columns were also carved. The abacus or flat stone from which the arch sprang was almost invariably square, in the Roman manner, with its lower edge chamfered off. The cap (Figs. 29, 31) upon which it rested was usually a cube of stone with its lower corners rounded like a bowl to fit the circular shaft; often it was scalloped with truncated cones (Fig. 29), and sometimes it was carved with figures of knights or with hawks or salamanders. The Norman delighted in carving, and sometimes filled in the arched head or 'tympanum' of a doorway with a great stone on which to carve figures in bas relief. These though always crude and grotesque are also spirited and interesting. They include fabulous monsters, e.g. centaurs with bows, scenes from the Lives of Saints, our Lord in Glory, the Harrowing of Hell, St. George and the Dragon, and many subjects that cannot now be identified. It should, however, be remarked that this ornate style was developed on both sides of the Channel after the Conquest. The early Norman work of the Confessor's time, at Jumièges and Westminster for example, and probably in more English churches than we can date, was severe and plain, differing from Anglo-Saxon mainly by the employment of the recessed arch with its nook-shaft and the device of the rubble-cored wall and column.

The bases of Norman columns are square, low, and usually insignificant. The insertion of the circular pier or column is covered by a flattened roll-moulding running round its foot (Fig. 35). The Gothic builders improved away the square plinth, for it was obstructive and dangerous to shins; they sliced off its angles to make an octagon, or they rounded it to correspond with the capital above. It is worthy of note that the form of the base is the surest of all guides to the date of the work, 'so characteristic, so constant, and so easily discriminated as regards plan, projection, height, and profile'. With the pointed arch came in the keel moulding (Figs. 32, 36) and the dogtooth enrichment (Fig. 34), both characteristic of the lancet stage of Early English Gothic, as well as of the period of transition between Norman and Gothic. On the caps crude foliage, curiously developed from the scallops,[1] in an effort to imitate French copies of Corinthian capitals, curled into knobs under the corners of the still square abacus, and a 'water-holding' hollow at the base of the column (Figs. 33, 37), are other

Fig. 37. Transitional pier, *c.* 1200, with square Norman abacus and pellet pattern on cap, combined with volutes of Gothic foliage and water-holding base.

[1] The development of the scallop-capital from Norman to Early English would provide an interesting subject for a thesis.

marks by which Transition work may be easily recognized. They will often be found associated with round arches, for conservative builders continued to use that form well into the thirteenth century if they had no

Fig. 38. Early English cap, *c.* 1220, with rounded abacus deeply undercut
and stiff-stalked foliage.

'vaulting ambitions'. The form of the arch is no safe guide to date in Norman and early Gothic work.

All these features were improved away by the next generation over which Henry III, the great patron of the arts, was king. The heavy keel-moulding was lightened and deeply undercut and grouped in suites to run round the arches, emphasizing by dark shadows their soaring lines; the abacus too was undercut, and was rounded so that it had neither corners nor square edges;[1]

[1] The hexagon, afterwards common, occurs rarely. The French retained the classic square abacus, perhaps because it was a more logical form, for it clearly differentiated the load from its support. Even in Early English work this was still emphasized, to some extent, by the deep band of shadow in the undercutting of the abacus (Fig. 38).

the bell-shaped capital was carved with lobed foliage that
rose stiffly to support the abacus and then drooped over
in curling fronds (Fig. 38), and the water-holding base,
which collected dust, was superseded by a taller one with
convex moulding. Strings and
hood-moulds were also undercut and the latter often ended
on small corbels or projecting
blocks carved to look like a
buckle when seen from the front
and like a mask or face when
viewed sideways (Fig. 34). Like
the deeply undercut moulding
and the stiff-stalked foliage it
is an unmistakable mark of the
Early English period.

FIG. 39. Mouldings of the
Decorated period, fourteenth
century, the quarter-round
and the ogee, with fillets
between. (The quarter-round
was revived in the domestic
Gothic of Elizabeth and the
Stuarts.)

The increase of light from
the growing windows began
to affect the forms of the
mouldings by the end of the
thirteenth century. They grew steadily broader, and
shallower, for contrasts of applied colour, not of light
and shade, were now aimed at. In the fourteenth
century a quarter-round was universal, a concave quarter
between two convex ones (Figs. 39, 40) being most usual;
often a fillet, a narrow projecting band, was cut on the
convex moulding; sometimes the concavity was filled
with a line of ball-flowers, an ornament which had
superseded the dog-tooth and which appears to have
been derived from the globular bells of horse-trappings
and dogs'-collars, though possibly from the buds of the
yellow water-lily (Fig. 41). In rich churches the elabo-

rately carved caps of shafts and columns have foliage
faithfully copied from nature, the leaves of briony, oak,
and maple and vine twined round them in a wreath.
It was this richly elaborate carving that led the Gothic

FIG. 40.                                    FIG. 41.

FIG. 40. A Decorated cap, c. 1350, showing the quarter-round moulding.
Cf. Fig. 46.
FIG. 41. The ball-flower ornament characteristic of the Decorated work
of the early fourteenth century.

revivalist Rickman to invent the term Decorated to
describe the Edwardian style; but it is really characteristic only of the greater churches; few parishes could
afford the services of a carver equal to work of this kind,
and so most fourteenth-century caps are simply moulded
(Figs. 40, 46). It must be said, too, that beautiful as
the naturalistic foliage is, it does not, like the thirteenth-
century stalked foliage, express support of the abacus;
it is mere ornamentation without constructive suggestion, and is thus a weakness in design.

In the middle of the century a wavy or ogee curve
(Figs. 19, 43) spread from the window tracery to the
mouldings of the arches. A shallow double ogee, resem-

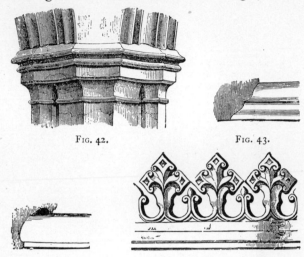

FIG. 42.                                    FIG. 43.

FIG. 44.                    FIG. 45.

FIG. 42. A Perpendicular cap, *c.* 1450, showing shallow, angular mould-
ings and the fluted shaft characteristic of the fifteenth century.
FIG. 43. The double ogee, the commonest Perpendicular moulding
except Fig. 44, the casement moulding.
FIG. 45. Tudor flower, the most characteristic Perpendicular ornament.
Cf. Fig. 58.

bling the curves made by the pages of a book opened near
the middle, was very popular all through the following
century (Fig. 43). But the characteristic and unmistakable moulding of the Perpendicular style was the
casement, a wide shallow hollow that ran round the

window-frame inside and out, and indeed round every arch and down every jamb in the building, and was often continued down the columns from the arches of the nave arcades (Figs. 42, 44, 58, 61).

The commonest of Perpendicular ornaments were the battlement and the Tudor flower, which was also an ornamental form of the battlement; these were employed in long horizontal suites, on the transoms of windows and on the tops of screens (Figs. 45, 58). Foliage of a square and lifeless kind was sometimes cut on caps by the mason, but carving had for the most part passed into the hands of the carpenter by the end of the fourteenth century. For this was the beginning of the great age of church woodwork. One important effect of the introduction of benches was the need to raise the height of all bases in order that they might not be hidden. So the typical Perpendicular base (Fig. 23) is a tall pedestal, with its mouldings oversailing the plain polygonal foot, in which, though the pews may be gone, the traces of holes cut to receive their joists will still be visible. In the richer churches the walls also

FIG. 46. A Decorated pier, *c.* 1350, showing the quarter-round moulding on the cap.

stand upon a base-course having a projecting moulding to throw the wet clear of the foundations (Figs. 23, 47).

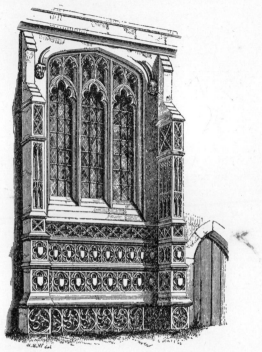

FIG. 47. Perpendicular tracery and panelling, *c.* 1450. The window with four-centred arch fills the whole space between the buttresses, which are thin and deep and of several stages.

A frequent feature in Perpendicular work is the reproduction, in sunk panels on the wall-surface, of the rectilinear tracery of the windows. On buttresses particularly this ornamentation is very common (Fig. 47).

## VII. THE ORIGIN OF THE PARISH CHURCH

WITH THESE general and introductory observations in mind, the reader will now be in a position to examine a typical parish church with the object of ascertaining the history of its development and noting the various traces of bygone customs which make every ancient church an illuminating historical record.

The first churches in England were built for the use of the monastic settlements from which the work of conversion was carried on. Most of our early examples, therefore, Jarrow, Monkwearmouth, Brixworth, Corbridge and Wing, though now parish churches were not so originally; and the same may be said of those of which portions remain at Canterbury, Ripon, Hexham, and Repton, and of most of those described in early monastic chronicles, at Peterborough, Abingdon, Glastonbury, York, Malmesbury, and other centres from which the Gospel was spread. The parish church did not, and in the social conditions could not, come into existence until the local chieftain had accepted the new faith. Our earliest existing parish church is Escomb, and even that was probably built by a monk and bishop, Wilfred, who happened to be also a 'squire' of many manors, of which Escomb seems to have been one.

It is possible, therefore, that the parish graveyard is sometimes older than the church, and the churchyard

FIG. 48. Cross of Anglo-Saxon workmanship showing
interlaced pattern derived from Celtic models.

cross than either; for it, or its predecessor, would be
set up by the missionaries as a sign for their converts, and
round it the Christian cemetery would grow (Fig. 48).
When a church came to be built it was set up on the
northern side of the enclosure so that the shadow might
not fall on the graves. That is why the church is never
central in an old graveyard, while the cross generally
is. A few churches, mainly in the north, still possess
crosses of Anglo-Saxon date, though these are now
usually preserved inside the building. They may be
known by the curious and elaborate patterns of interlaced strapwork cut in low relief upon their shafts (Fig.
48). The sole remaining vestige of Anglo-Saxon Abingdon is a fragment of such a cross built into a rubble wall
in Winsmore Lane, Ock Street, 'to instruct the pensive
beholders with an exemplary frailty'.

The parish was originally the estate of the converted
chieftain. As he had been accustomed to provide a place
of worship and a priest for his pagan followers so now
he built a church for the new worship, and probably
translated the priest from the old benefice to the new.
Still more probably he utilized the site of the old ceremonies to build his temple for the new rites; there is
evidence for believing that a great number of our ancient
churches stand upon sites which had immemorial human,
and perhaps religious, associations even at the time of
their foundation. Some are founded upon the ruins of
dolmens and stone circles; many are built within the
lines of prehistoric earthworks, or have ancient mounds
and barrows closely adjacent to them; and most are
shadowed by yew-trees that, if not older than themselves, are almost certainly sprung from those planted

on the site by primitive man, and are perhaps vestiges of the groves in which he worshipped. For, *pace* Mr. Kipling, 'yew that is old in churchyard mould' bred no mighty bows in England: it was too knotty. Bow staves were imported from Spain; and the only practical use of the churchyard yew was to garnish the church at Easter and provide the substitute for palm branches in the annual procession round the churchyard.

By 673 when Archbishop Theodore summoned a Church Council at Hertford there were secular priests enough in England to make organization necessary. The sub-kingdoms had become sees, each with its bishop acting as chaplain and adviser to the king; and at least the greater landholders had similarly their priests who served as their chaplains and ministered to the dwellers on their estates. That he should provide a church and a priest to serve it was now expected of every thegn or 'squire', and a manorial estate became also an ecclesiastical parish. As large holdings became subdivided new parishes with their churches came into being, particularly in the Norman period. The growth of towns too, even before the Conquest, made subdivision of parishes necessary; and the churches of these urban parishes would no doubt be provided largely by the townsmen themselves, who, in this as in other matters, took the first step towards democracy by associating to secure independence of their lords.

The characteristics by which the work of a particular period is recognized, and by means of which we are enabled to date approximately any building at sight, have been gradually discriminated after a century's study of dated examples and of the documents recording their foundation. A hundred years ago the round-arched Norman churches were believed to belong to Anglo-Saxon times and were spoken of as Saxon; but since then the discovery, for example, of an inscribed stone in the porch at Jarrow recording the dedication of the church on April 23, A. D. 684, and the examination of eleventh-century records at Durham which refer to contemporary building work there, have enabled us to say: work with details like those at Jarrow (or Monk-wearmouth or Hexham or Ripon, all of which are dated by Bede or some contemporary chronicler) are early Anglo-Saxon; work like that at Durham is mid-Norman. So with the criteria of Gothic; contemporary records tell us of the new building of Westminster Abbey in 1245, and from this, checked by similarly dated examples, we are justified in assigning any traceried window of the Westminster type to the middle of the thirteenth century. So that though documents relating to the building of parish churches are but rarely found their approximate dates present little difficulty.

But even parish churches of the later Middle Ages sometimes have their records. Some, like Thame, Oxon., still possess churchwardens' accounts recording the costs of building transepts in the middle of the fifteenth century; in others the monument of the founder remains, as at Lambourn, Berks., and Wymington, Beds., with an inscription describing him as 'fundator cantarie Sce Marie istius capelle' or as 'qui istam ecclesiam de novo construxit', with the date in each instance; on some, like Lavenham in Suffolk, a dated memorial inscription runs round the parapet; and in many others a coat of arms in stained glass or in carving enables us to identify the builder and so to date the fabric. The heraldry in Gipping Church, Suffolk, for example, shows that it was built by Sir James Tyrell, who, as we learn from Holinshed, contrived the murder of the Princes in the Tower, and was afterwards executed by Henry VII. The actual designers of our parish churches remain for the most part anonymous. The popular notion that the local craftsmen designed the work as well as executed it can be true of only the humblest buildings. The architects of several of the cathedrals are known from the fabric rolls (i.e. the building accounts) and other documentary records: they were neither monks nor masons, though it is probable that a part of their training had been done in the workshop; they had a social status and an income which made their position in no way inferior to that of their modern successors.

That men of this class were sometimes responsible for the building of parish churches is proved by existing records. The bursar's accounts at New College, for instance, record the expenses of rebuilding the chancel of Adderbury Church, of which the College was patron, in the early fifteenth century; the architect in charge of the work is referred to by name, Richard Winchcombe, the artist who was employed by the University to build the Divinity School, which he did not live to complete. The details of the two buildings show a close correspondence; but precisely similar details in the fifteenth-century work in the neighbouring churches of Bloxham and Broughton prove as conclusively as documents that these parishes also took the opportunity to secure Winchcombe's services in designing and supervising additions to their churches. There can be no doubt that all our finer parish churches were similarly built from designs furnished by men whose experience was far wider than that of any artisan. These men, however, were certainly not ecclesiastics like William of Wykeham, whose services to architecture were merely those of an enlightened and munificent patron; they were professional architects who had devoted their lives to the study and practice of their art. William of Wykeham would have no more supposed himself competent to execute their functions than would the present Bishop of Winchester. Where he differed from his modern successors was in knowing a good architect from a bad one. His reputation as a practising architect is a baseless myth.

Little better than a myth too is the popular belief that the finer parish churches are due to the monastic impropriators. Of some churches built in the early Middle Ages when monasticism was at its best this may be true; but a monastery always tended to regard a dependent parish as a source of income rather than as an object of benevolence.

The tithes collected from the parishioners had been originally levied for the relief of the poor and the upkeep of the chancel, and not for the maintenance of the priest, who was at first merely the collector and administrator; later on he was allowed to retain a share of the proceeds to augment his income from other sources, his glebe, fees, and free-will offerings. But when a church was given to a monastery by the lord of the manor the tithes passed with it, together with the responsibility for the repair of the chancel and the provision of the daily services. The monastery then, as a rule, appointed a vicar, granting him the right to collect the tithes of certain specified farm-produce for his stipend, but retaining for its own purposes the greater tithes, i.e. of corn. Out of this income the monastery kept the chancel in repair; but, as monastic finances were generally ill-managed, the monks seldom had money to spare for any but the bare minimum of what was necessary. Indeed there is evidence that churches were allowed to go to ruin in order that the whole of their tithes should lapse to the monastery responsible for them; but there is little or no evidence, after the thirteenth century, of any monastic zeal for parochial church-building. And so it is not uncommon to find in an impropriated church a noble nave rebuilt by the parishioners, with a small, poor chancel, witness to the neglect of the monastic rectors.

# VIII. MATERIALS

THOUGH certain criteria of date, such as mouldings, enrichments, window-tracery, and the prevailing form of arch were constant throughout England, there is still at all dates a great variety in the churches of different districts; a fifteenth-century church in East Anglia, for example, is a very different building from one of the same date in north Oxfordshire, though both have the rectilinear tracery, the angular mouldings, and the pedestal bases which mark the Perpendicular period.

These differences are due to various causes, historical, economic, geological—the last, perhaps, being most important.

The builders of our great abbey churches had resources that made them independent of local conditions; if good building stone was not locally available they could, and did, import it. Thus in Norman times vast quantities of free-stone were brought from the quarries at Caen; the comparatively small dimensions of the cubes in Norman ashlar are due to the difficulties of transporting large blocks. In the thirteenth century the dark marble of Purbeck was sent all over England in the form of shafts and caps to carry the orders of recessed arches and provide that contrast of colouring which was the ideal of the time, as may be seen in the light and shade of the deeply-cut mouldings of the Early English style (Fig. 51); and in the later Middle Ages the deficiency of building-stone in the eastern counties was supplied even in parish churches, by the importation of bricks from the Netherlands, described in the churchwardens' accounts as 'Flaundres tyles'.

But all but a few parishes had to cut their coat according to their cloth and make the best of their local materials. The result was to stimulate resourcefulness and to produce local ingenuities of the highest architectural interest and charm.

Our best native building material is the oolitic limestone of which a broad band stretches diagonally across the country from Somerset, through Gloucester, Wiltshire, Oxon., Northants. and Lincoln to Yorkshire. Along this line therefore are found the noblest churches, the towers of Somerset, the spires of Lincoln and Northants., the statuary and foliage of Wells, Salisbury, Lincoln, and Southwell, and the fine detail of the innumerable parish churches for which they served as models. In every age this advantage is manifest—in the Anglo-Saxon work at Bradford, Avebury, Bibury, Barnack, Wittering, and Earls Barton, for example, no less than in the late Perpendicular towers of Cricklade and Magdalen College, and that crowning glory of Gothic, the steeple at Louth.

But the stoneless fenland is almost equally rich in fine churches, for its numerous waterways made the transport of building material a comparatively easy matter.

The west had its quarries of warm red sandstone; but this, though beautiful in colour, is soon eroded by wind and rain and is therefore a poor material for mouldings and sculpture on the exterior of a building On the other hand the granite of Cornwall though durable is too dour and intractable for fine carving; and the flint of the chalk districts, in Berkshire, Sussex, and East Anglia, cannot be carved at all. In these last districts therefore the necessary free-stone for quoins and tracery had to be imported and was therefore used with the utmost economy. So the builders often dispensed with quoins in their towers by making them circular; when the wool-trade had enriched the chalk-lands, in the late fourteenth and fifteenth century, an upper stage of imported ashlar was added to many an early round tower, e.g. at Shefford and Welford in Berks., Acle, Norfolk, and Mutford, Suffolk. Vaults, of course, were out of the question, as were shingles for roofing, and so many churches were covered with thatch for which, in the east, the local reeds formed an excellent material.

But, as ever in medieval construction, the necessity of

## DESCRIPTION OF PLATE IV

The corbel-table, marking the original height of the tower, shows that the building dates from the Norman period. (The font and the jambs of the chancel arch are contemporary.) The tower was heightened in the fourteenth century, when (as their arcades show) the aisles were added; their windows, however, were enlarged in the fifteenth century, when the nave walls were carried up to receive the clearstory. The porch was added early in the sixteenth century and shows Tudor brick-work (see p. 79). In the gable, which has been rebuilt, modern brick-work can be compared as to size and bond with the older type. In the upper room children were taught by the chantry priest and afterwards by the parish schoolmaster. Aubrey records that he and Hobbes 'went to schoole in Westport church' in the seventeenth century.

IV. SUTTON COURTENAY, BERKS.   SOUTH-WEST OF NAVE

the builder became his glory: the East Anglian 'flush-work', of flint panelling, is so delightful in its colour-contrasts and its ingenious mosaic pattern-work that no one beholding it regrets the absence of ashlar; and the marvellous woodcarving is quite as impressive in its way as the statuary of the free-stone churches. Sussex with her 'deep ghylls that breed huge oaks and old', developed the timber spire and bell-cote, roofed with oaken shingles, and like the other stoneless districts, produced picturesque wooden porches of massive oak framing.

It was in East Anglia too that the material of which most modern buildings are constructed first came back into use, a thousand years after the last Romano-British bricklayer had laid down his line and trowel. Slabs of sun-dried clay had been a prehistoric substitute for stone; and burnt bricks had been the popular building material of the Roman Empire—they provided the Anglo-Saxons with ready-made slabs for many early churches. But, although roof-tiles continued to be baked, bricks ceased to be made in England after the Saxon invasion until their importation from the Nether-lands (where lack of stone had led to their general use) in the late thirteenth century, suggested to the East Coast builders the advisability of developing a home supply. Hull, where the connexion of the De la Poles with the Hanse merchants had led to the early importa-tion of brick, was perhaps the first town to possess a brick-field; but Essex and Suffolk, where also the De la Poles owned the manor of Wingfield, and Norfolk, where there were large settlements of Flemings, were making bricks in the fourteenth century though they did not come into general use until the fifteenth, and even then their use remained local, particularly in church-building.

The hospital at Ewelme, Oxon., and the chapel of Holy Trinity, Hull, both built by the De la Poles, are among the noblest brick buildings in England. Most of the other brick churches are of late date, many of them belonging to the seventeenth and eighteenth centuries; for though brick became the principal material in the great house-building movement of the Tudors there was little need for new churches in the sixteenth century.

Brick, however, afforded a cheap and easy means of adding a tower to a church which had not yet got one; and so a good many parishes built or rebuilt a church tower with the new material from 1600 onwards. Brick-work of early date may be known by the smaller size of the bricks and by their richer colours and more varied shades, and even more certainly by their 'English bonding', in which rows of headers and stretchers alternate vertically. In the seventeenth century Flemish bond came into fashion, with the headers and stretchers alternating in a horizontal row (Pl. IV).

Geology also influenced architecture indirectly, through its economic consequences. The Cotswolds, for instance, not only afforded building-stone but sheep-walks; and noble buildings like the churches at Campden, Northleach, Cirencester, and Fairford, owe their splendour to the wealth created by the wool-trade—and also to the concentration of that wealth in the hands of the great capitalists who make their appearance in English industrial history with the rise of the De la Poles of Hull in the reign of Edward III. Wherever we find a specially magnificent parish church built or rebuilt after that date we shall find also that it was built out of the profits of capital by some individual manufacturer or merchant, some medieval Morris or Carnegie. Thus the Grevels rebuilt Campden, the Forteys Northleach, the Tames Fairford, and the Springs the great church of Lavenham in Suffolk.

So the iron of Sussex, smelted with charcoal from her oakwoods, explains the presence of many fine churches in a district where free-stone was rare, and explains, too, the presence in them of grave-slabs of a material not found elsewhere in England—cast iron. On the other hand, the increase of wealth which led to the vast enlargement of East Anglian churches in the Perpendicular period was due to geographical conditions: the Flemings, with their arts of weaving and brick-making, settled most numerously in those parts of England nearest to the Netherlands, which also were the parts most favourably situated to dispose of their cloth in the Continental markets.

Geography too explains some peculiarities which the Norman churches of Sussex share with those of Normandy with which her ports were once in constant communication; so the medieval alliance of Scotland with France has left its traces in the ancient Scots churches, which, for example, are usually vaulted throughout, like the French.

# IX. HOW TO STUDY THE FABRIC

HAVING BEEN originally built, as a rule, by the squire, the church usually adjoins the manor house or the farm which now represents it. Almost invariably the existing level of the graveyard is above that of the road outside; for not only do roads get worn down but as the dead were buried century after century in the same narrow field the ground steadily rose, and the later generations lie in the dust of the earlier. Only the rich were coffined; the vast majority were buried in shrouds as the rubric in the Burial Service reminds us, 'the earth shall be cast upon the *body*'; they therefore disintegrated rapidly and made room for new comers. Dr. Cox in *The Parish Registers of England* quotes an illuminating entry from the Burial Register of Poyning:

'The xviij day of April (1608) was buried John Skerry a poore man that died in the place (manor house) stable, and being brought half naked with his face bare the parson would not burye him soe but first he gave a sheete and caused him to be sacked therein and they buried him more Christian like.'

So the present level of the graveyard may be five or six feet above the sill of the church door and the path that leads to it.

The grave-stones now remaining are seldom earlier than the seventeenth century. Until the end of the eighteenth they were low and massive, their tops were cut into ogee curves, and they were decorated with skulls, crossbones, and hourglasses, or with 'swags' and volutes in the Renaissance style (Pl. VII a).

The outside of the church should always be first

3481

F

## DESCRIPTION OF PLATE V

a. The upper part of a pilaster-strip and the sill of a small window west of it show that the wall was originally the external face of an eleventh-century aisleless nave (cf. Pl. II), through which arches were cut to build an aisle towards the end of the twelfth century. (The chancel walls, with the jambs of the arch, and a double-splayed circular window, originally fitted with a grille, in the south wall of the nave, are contemporary.)

b. The unrecessed arch and heavy, uncut imposts are characteristic of Anglo-Saxon work both early and late; but the pilaster-strips and the long-and-short work indicate that the building is not earlier than the tenth century.

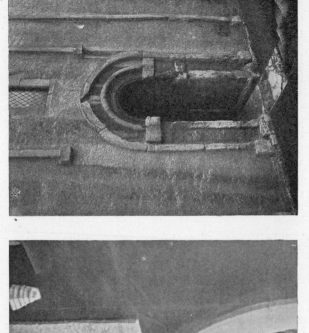

V a. BIBURY, GLOS.  NORTH WALL OF NAVE

V b. EARLS BARTON, NORTHANTS.  THE
WEST DOORWAY

examined. Sometimes a trace of long-and-short work on the jamb of a doorway or on the angle of the tower or nave, or a narrow projecting band of it in the form of a pilaster-strip on the face of a wall, may be all that is left to indicate the Anglo-Saxon origin of the building (Pl. II).

Even where a Saxon church has been completely swept away a vestige of it may remain in the form of a sundial of peculiar construction reset in the later building. On the south wall of almost every medieval church there will be found roughly scratched circles with lines 15° apart radiating from a central hole that once contained a metal pin. That the shadows on these were used as time-indicators there can be no doubt, but what times they marked and how accurately is still quite unknown; they are entirely different from the scientifically constructed dials of later times, in which the angles increase as the lines approach the horizontal. But they are also very different from the dials of the Anglo-Saxons; these marked not the hours but the 'tides' or eighth parts into which the Old English day was divided, and their circles therefore have three radii dividing their lower halves into four equal parts and marking the middle of each of the daylight tides (Fig. 49). These rays are deeply cut in wedge-shaped grooves and terminate in crosses. There is usually an additional radius, midway in the upper half-quadrant on the western side of the semicircle, marking the beginning of the first tide of the day, i.e. 7.30 a.m.

The Anglo-Saxon dials were clearly cut by skilled workmen, not scratched; but it is extremely unlikely that their makers could have discovered empirically a method of setting a gnomon so that its shadow should fall accurately on the radii all through the year. The later dial-makers may have realized that this was beyond

FIG. 49. Anglo-Saxon dial, Kirkdale, on which the shadow indicated the tides of the day, falling on the ray marked by a star at 7.30 and on the vertical ray at noon. The short, intermediate rays are unusual additions marking the beginning and end of each tide. The inscription tells that 'Orm son of Gamal bought St. Gregory's minster when it was all ruined and fallen down, and he caused it to be made new from the ground to Christ and St. Gregory in Edward's days the king and in Tosti's days the earl. This is the day's sun-marker at every tide. Hawarth made me and Brand priests'. Tosti, Harold's brother, was Earl of Northumbria 1055–65.

their powers and that an elaborately cut dial was therefore not worth the trouble it cost. They were probably content with a very rough approximation to the real time. But, since few churches are precisely orientated, even this would only have been possible if the gnomon was bent at an angle, and, moreover, an angle altered

with the varying height of the sun at different seasons.
It has been suggested that separate dials served at different times of the year, each with its gnomon at the
appropriate angle. This would explain the duplication
frequently noticed. But as there is no documentary
evidence all this must be guess-work. Meanwhile a
sculptured dial marked with the tides may be regarded
as fairly safe evidence that the church upon which it
occurs is of Anglo-Saxon work or replaces a pre-Con-
quest building.

In Anglo-Saxon times the priest was required to be
in the church for seven services daily, but after the
eleventh century three daily services were considered
sufficient in parish churches. Churchwardens' accounts
show that most parishes, at any rate in the towns,
possessed clocks in the fourteenth century. It is therefore very unusual to find a dial on a town church.

Often a doorway with zigzag or other Norman ornament will be found in the wall of a Gothic aisle; its
arch will not always be semicircular; for the builders
who reset it in their aisle may, as at Great Tew and
Bloxham, Oxon., have rebuilt it in a new form. Some
Norman doorways have been moved more than once:
when an aisle was first added to a Norman nave, and
again when the aisle was widened—for the later builders
seem to have admired the Norman carving; at Sutton
Courtenay, Berks., and in some other churches they
preserved in a side chapel the chancel arch which they
had found it necessary to replace; at Bampton and
Headington, Oxon., they even went to the trouble of
inserting a relieving arch into the wall above Norman
chancel arches that they wished to preserve (Fig. 31).

Sometimes a wide pilaster-buttress, or a line of heavy string course broken by later windows, proves that a wall is of Norman date though all its doors and windows are later insertions (Pls. III, VII). This may be revealed too by a row of carved corbels projecting to carry the eaves of the roof (Fig. 50); for the Norman plan of drainage was to make the roof wider than the building so that it sheltered the face of the wall and the foundations, like the thatch-eaves of a barn. The later builders commonly employed a parapet with a gutter inside it to collect the rain instead of allowing it to drop

Fig. 50. Upper part of north wall of nave, Cuddesdon. The flat pilaster-buttress, partly cut away, the corbel-table, and blocked windows show that this was the external wall of a late Norman nave through which arches were cut to form the present aisle in the Early English period. Cf. Pl. V.

from the eaves; openings in the parapet at intervals allowed the water to gush out through gargoyles, grotesque spouts, which shot it clear of the foundations. This arrangement also facilitated repairs since it enabled workmen to walk along the eaves; and therefore the Norman corbel table now often carries a parapet of later date (Pls. IV, VII). Dripping eaves, however, as the simpler plan, were retained in the humbler buildings, and at the date of the Renaissance were supplemented by the modern system of metal guttering. At Cumnor the line of Norman corbels is midway up the nave walls, showing that these were heightened when the fourteenth-century clearstory was inserted (Pl. VII).

Again a pair of low, shallow buttresses at the angle of the chancel, or a mask-corbel reused in the hood-mould of a Perpendicular window, may suggest that a wall has been rebuilt upon an Early English base; frequently the high-pitched 'weathering' like an inverted V on the face of a tower, above the existing nave roof, proves the original building to be Norman or early Gothic though rebuilding may have left no other trace of the fact—for early roofs, being tiled, were always of steep pitch; later ones, covered with lead, were flatter. From the weather-mould too we may learn the width of the earlier nave.

All these indications are clues to be followed up inside the building. For example, a plain tub-shaped font in a church showing long-and-short work will probably be Saxon also; Norman traces outside will similarly suggest examination of the font, and also of the chancel arch and particularly of its jambs which often remain unaltered though the arch itself has been rebuilt [1]; or when, as frequently happens, the eastern arches of the nave are different from the others, the explanation usually is that a Norman central tower has fallen or been taken down.

So a pair of angle-buttresses may be corroborated by

[1] At Bibury the early Gothic chancel arch has Saxon imposts with crude acanthus foliage from a Romano-British model.

the presence of a double piscina (Fig. 51), or by the jambs of vanished lancets at the sides of a later window as at Ramsbury, Wilts. And on the inside face of the

FIG. 51. Early English piscina, c. 1250, with geometrical tracery and deeply cut moulding. The two drains were used to receive the rinsings of the ablutions of the priest's hands and the sacred vessels before and after the Consecration of the Elements (p. 125). At a later date the ablutions of the Chalice were drunk by the celebrant.

tower there may be a gabled weathering, showing that the nave walls have been raised for the insertion of clearstory windows above the nave arcade, which proves that the bases of the walls are older than their upper portions; the clearstory in a parish church is almost invariably an addition to the original building, and is usually of the fifteenth century.

Tostock church in Suffolk affords a highly interesting opportunity for this kind of architectural detective work. As it stands it is a fifteenth-century building, complete even to its pews. Every detail suggests that it was newly built late in the Perpendicular period. Yet at the exterior face of the west end is a 'straight joint' suggesting that a flat Norman buttress has been absorbed in the present walling; and an examination of the interior reveals in the eastern wall of the nave the line of a gable above the present chancel arch and below the existing roof-line. It is therefore clear that the church was built around and above a smaller Norman building, the roof and side walls of which were then pulled down and removed; for, since daily services must be carried on while the new work was in progress, it was usual to leave the old standing until the new was ready.

When an aisle was added, for example, its wall was built and its roof put on without disturbance to the nave until all was finished; then the nave wall was pierced with arches inserted one by one, the daily services all the time going on within.

So when a chancel was lengthened, as at Iffley in the early thirteenth century, the Norman east wall was left untouched until the new sanctuary was complete; then it was taken down and the debris and scaffolding were got out through a rough archway, a 'mason's hole', left for the purpose and subsequently walled up, the traces of which are still visible (Pl. VII). This piecemeal method accounts for the fact that the parts are sometimes out of line; the chancel, for example, is often out

of alignment with the nave. The theory that this was
done intentionally to symbolize the drooping Head on
the Cross is a modern fancy.

FIG. 52. Wood Eaton. A small Early English church, *c.* 1220, with a
Perpendicular tower inserted *c.* 1450. The fall of the ground prevented
any westward extension.

The addition of an aisle to an earlier nave invariably
leaves clear traces of what has been done; the original
doorway may be reused in the new aisle wall; or above
the nave arcades there may be small blocked windows
cut into by the heads of the arches (Fig. 50); if the latter
are Early English the windows, and thus the original
walls, will be Norman or even Saxon. In that case a

## DESCRIPTION OF PLATE VI

The flat angle-buttresses show that the chancel is of late Norman date, though its windows and the deeper buttress are of the fourteenth century. The tower was added and the aisle widened (its arcade is contemporary with the angle-buttresses) in the fifteenth century, as the Perpendicular window-tracery testifies.

The ogee tracery of the south window (cf. Pl. VIII) illustrates the commonest of all fourteenth-century designs, and gives the 'repeat pattern' for the reticulated tracery of the east window.

VI. OGBOURNE ST. GEORGE, WILTS.   FROM THE SOUTH-EAST

deep respond, being part of the original wall through which the arches were cut, should be looked for at the eastern and western ends of the arcade. A deep respond, alone, is evidence that an aisleless nave preceded the existing plan.

So if an aisle has been widened its new windows will not march with the arches of the nave arcade and thus the fact is patent. And as widening implies raising the roof, the line of corbels that carried the original one may be visible below the new; or the clerestory of the old aisle may now look into the new below the present line of the roof (Fig. 50).

When the doorway is more than one bay from the west we may know that the nave has been lengthened and may expect to find the western arches different from the others. And again if the buttresses of the western tower are visible inside the church it is obvious that the tower was built clear of the nave, the walls of which were then lengthened to join up with it. In such a case there will be a 'straight joint' at the junction, i.e. the stones of the wall will not be bonded into the tower. So if a western tower has side arches these will sometimes be later than its eastern arch, showing that they were cut through the side walls when the aisles were lengthened to overlap or 'engage' the tower. When, however, a tower so engaged is later than the west wall of the church, it has clearly been inserted, not added; in such a case the explanation may be as at Wood Eaton, Oxon. (Fig. 52), that a roadway prevented any westward extension of the building. This difficulty was in some instances overcome by building the western tower upon open arches over the roadway.

While some churches have thus grown larger others have lost aisles or chapels, pulled down to save the expense of repairs. The blocked arches that opened into them may usually be traced; and their windows may have been reset in the new wall. A blocked doorway in a chancel will show that a vestry has been pulled down; sometimes a further trace of it will be found in a piscina, or a blocked squint, visible on the outer face of the wall.

# X. THE PORCH

IT IS SAID that as a rule the church stands north of the village; certainly the south door was the one commonly used, and it is often larger and more elaborate than that on the north and is usually furnished with a porch. The public notices still posted here remind us that the porch was the usual place for much civil business in the medieval parish. The coroner sat here and not in the local public house; executors made public payment of legacies; marriage banns were published, the 'I will' was said and the ring given by 'hosbonds at the chirche dore'; and those who broke their vows did penance appropriately at the place where they took them, or alternatively at the reading-desk, clad in a white sheet. Here, too, the baptismal service was begun, so that the southern entrance was sometimes called the Christening-door; through it too the parishioners passed to their graves, after being borne completely through the church from the north side.

Usually the porch had stone seats, and a stoup for holy water, though this was sometimes in a recess inside the door, on the right-hand side, conveniently for the fingers of the right hand, with which the entering worshipper crossed himself (Fig. 53). Fresh water, to which salt was added, was consecrated every Sunday; its purpose was to put the enterer in remembrance of his baptismal vows, of the Blood shed for his redemption, of the need to cleanse his soul from sin, and finally of the transitoriness of life, unstable as water. In rare instances traces exist of an altar in the porch, perhaps for the witnesses taking oath, or for sellers giving a warranty, for, as Mr. Hardy reminds us in the preface to *The Well-Beloved*, sales of property 'were carried out and covenanted in the parish church, in the face of the congregation'.

After the thirteenth century porches were frequently built with an upper room approached by a newel stair inside the church, and sometimes furnished with a fireplace and an oven, as at Northleach, where the room is obviously meant for habitation—it has candle-sconces over the fire-place. Probably this, and similar rooms occasionally found in towers, e.g. at Rycote, Oxon., were used by chantry priests both to sleep in on occasion, as, for instance, before celebrating a morrow-mass for travellers in the early morning, and also as a school for the choristers, the teaching of whom was frequently one of the conditions of the bequests on which they lived. Long after the Reformation this room was used for the same purpose; every one has heard of 'the pedant that keeps a school in a church': he had a contemporary who willed that his body should be buried 'in the lower end of the church, at the stayre foot that goeth up to my schole'. The upper room, too, contained the library and any other treasures possessed by the church, in-

Fig. 53. A Decorated doorway showing the quarter-round moulding, stoups, niches for images, and the shield of the donor. c. 1330.

cluding, sometimes, relics which were exhibited to the congregation from a high doorway opening into the nave above the south door. If, as was often the case, a watcher was employed, he too would use this room, from which most of the interior of the church could be seen. At Cirencester the great porch was built by the trade guilds, who used one of its two upper stories for their meetings.

In the porch at Wanborough, Wilts., there remains an eighteenth-century notice requiring 'all females to remove their pattens before entering the church'. When I was last there the sexton's wife was dusting it—in silk stockings and suède shoes.

## XI. THE NAVE

THE WESTERN bay of the nave was the baptistery; it was clear of benches, even when these existed elsewhere in the church, and the font stood in the centre of it: a stone desk on a nave pier, or a stone plinth projecting from its base, or a niche for the vessel containing holy oil, may still mark the original position if the font has been moved to make room for the modern pews.

Fonts usually bear in their mouldings and other ornaments unmistakable marks of their date—a few very early examples are formed of Roman altars or capitals, some are supported on Norman shafts with cushion-caps (Fig. 54), or are decorated with panels of crude Norman figure-sculpture, some have the dog-tooth and lobed foliage of the thirteenth century (Fig. 38), some the ball-flower of the fourteenth (Fig. 41), some reproduce on their panelled faces the tracery of contemporary windows (Fig. 55). But a few are simply tubs of stone without any mouldings to indicate their

date. These are sometimes Saxon, and reproduce the
form of the wooden tub in which the early convert stood
while the baptismal water was poured over him, but

FIG. 54. Norman font, *c.* 1140, with scroll-work and interlacing round
arches carried on shafts with scallop caps.

others are of transitional date, *c.* 1180, when for some
reason the form seems to have come again into fashion.
To this date also belong most of the lead fonts of which
there are about thirty still in existence. After the
Reformation wood was again, on occasion, employed
to make a font where, as at Stanford-in-the-Vale, free-
stone was not locally available.

All medieval fonts are large and deep, the older the
deeper; for immersion, as the rubric in our Prayer
Books still reminds us, was the rule. They all bear the

marks of the staple by which the lid was fastened down;
for superstitious uses of the christening water, which
remained permanently in them, led in the thirteenth

FIG. 55. Decorated font, *c.* 1340, with ball-flower ornament round the
rim, and panels showing tracery characteristic of fourteenth-century
windows.

century to an order that all fonts should be kept locked.
Their lids originally seem to have been low and plain:
the earliest, of the thirteenth century, is at Charlton,
Oxon. But in the fifteenth century, the great age of
woodwork, many or most of them were provided with
elaborate canopies of which fine examples yet exist.

The seventeenth century which provided so many of our churches with pulpits also re-covered fonts which had lost their canopies, but covers of this date are usually low and simply moulded pyramids or cones, topped by a ball or acorn.

Some churches possess two or even more fonts, for at all periods, and particularly the Norman, the builders were ready to replace an old font by a finer one; and in the eighteenth century the large medieval font was often condemned as useless and supplanted by a small marble urn on a pedestal. The archaeologists of our own age have rescued many of these discarded relics from base uses in farmyards and replaced them in the churches. Sometimes, however, their zeal, like Mr. Pickwick's, has misled them, for example at Coombe, Oxon., where a well-head, carved by an ingenious villager, has lately been placed in the church in the belief that it was an ancient font.

It should be noted that many fonts have suffered alteration: some have been transformed from the tub-shaped to the chalice-form and are thus much older than they look; some have received additional ornamentation; and many are set on bases of a date different from that of their cups. So after the Commonwealth when Charles II ordered the parishes to replace their broken fonts, many imitations of earlier work were produced which may perplex the novice.

There is some evidence for the existence of 'schools' of font-makers who specialized in this branch of masonry. Thus Buckinghamshire has a most beautiful type of font devised in the late Norman period, of which examples, evidently from the same workshop, still exist

at Dinton, Kimble, Bledlow, Aylesbury, and elsewhere.
So in Gloucestershire in the early thirteenth century
there was evidently a font-maker who specialized in
lead-work, and has left specimens of his work at
Frampton, Siston, Oxenhall, Tidenham, Lancant, and
Sandhurst, all from the same mould. There is no doubt
that other schools could be traced by the curious, just
as glass from the same workshop can be identified in
various parts of England. Thus the east window of the
chapel at North Moreton, Berks. (in which Milo de
Stapleton, of the great Yorkshire family, had licence to
found a chantry in March 1299), so closely resembles the
early fourteenth-century glass in the windows of the
nave aisles at York that it is obviously from the same
workshop. Mr. Le Couteur in *English Medieval Painted
Glass* described a figure of St. Catherine in the west
window at Cirencester which is exactly reproduced in
the east window at Oddingley, Worcestershire, and is
obviously not merely from the same workshop but from
the same cartoon. Shields of arms, the royal coat
especially, beyond all question were duplicated from one
cartoon, almost like photographs from a negative; the
Giffard shields at Buckland, Berks., for example, are
identical with the one at Baldon, Oxon., of the reign
of Edward III, and were probably made by the Oxford
firm who glazed the windows of the Latin Chapel in
the cathedral. Occasionally the actual artificer can be
identified: on the doors of some Bedfordshire churches,
Leighton Buzzard, Turvey, and Eaton Bray, the ironwork is identical with that on the tomb of Queen
Eleanor in Westminster Abbey for which 'Thomas de
Leghtone' was paid £12 in 1294. Apparently his work

in his own district had been brought to the notice of
the king.

Sepulchral monuments, too, often show in their
workmanship such close resemblances as to make it
clear that they came from the same workshop. There is,
for instance, an Elizabethan tomb at Somerton, Oxon.,
for which the contract still exists and tells us that it was
made for the executors of Thomas Fermor by the firm
of Richard and Gabriel Roiley of Burton-on-Trent.
Detail photographs taken by Mr. F. E. Howard prove
conclusively that ten or twelve similar tombs in other
counties must have come from the same workshop.
From his study of the coats of arms on the tombs
Mr. Howard was led to make the further very interesting discovery that most of the persons commemorated
were inter-connected by marriage, and hence that the
widespread business of the Roileys, like that of our
great modern firms, was based largely on the recom-
mendations of satisfied customers.

The north door is now usually blocked, but was in
constant use in the Middle Ages, both for processions,
and at funerals and christenings; it is said that it was
known as the devil's door, and that it was left open at
baptisms in order that by it the evil spirit might leave
the regenerated infant. Its blocking may therefore be
due to its association with 'superstitious uses', though
as there is no record of any general injunction ordering
its closure, the dislike of draughts may account for it.
The west door, after Norman times, was used but
rarely, e.g. at the great annual procession on Palm
Sunday.

The construction and ornament of a medieval door

will invariably be found of interest. The earlier doors, particularly, are of unique value because they afford the sole surviving examples of the skill of the most important of medieval craftsmen, the smith. In Norman and early Gothic doors the carpentry is always subsidiary to the ironwork, on which both the strength and the beauty of the door depend—the great nails, clenched on the inner side to weld together the two layers of stout planks, and the massive hinges of hammered iron, on which Time, like Æsop's viper, has gnawed in vain.

Norman hinges resemble a great sword with a crescent-shaped guard (Fig. 57); the crescent is supposed to represent a C and to refer to St. Clement, the patron of smiths; and as his emblem was an anchor, to which also the hinge bears some resemblance, there may be truth in this. But the crescent as a religious symbol is far older than Christianity, like the craft of the smith, and it has probably associations with cults long forgotten. Throughout the thirteenth century ironwork grew more and more elaborate until the outward face of the door was covered with a scroll-work of foliage resembling that on the contemporary caps (Fig. 56). When window-tracery was fully developed, in the next century, it suggested a new means of enriching the surface of doors; and so the smith gave place to the carpenter.

At first the tracery-forms with which the door was covered were sunk in the solid so that the door was panelled like a fifteenth-century font or buttress; but the more common method was to apply a traceried pattern by means of glue and nails. Plain hinges were fitted on the inner, undecorated side, and only the

handles gave the smith an opportunity to exhibit the
artistic side of his craft.  These, it may be remarked,
were intended merely for pulling-to the door, and were

Fig. 56.  Late Norman hinge.  *c.* 1180.

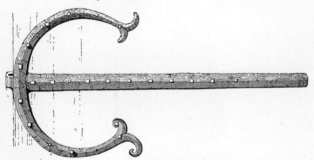

Fig. 57.  Norman hinge.  *c.* 1120.

not sanctuary-knockers; a fugitive was in safety when
he reached consecrated ground; he had no need to
cling to the door-handle.

The wood used for doors, and indeed for all other
church furniture, was oak; the stories of chestnut roofs
are sextons' tales.

## DESCRIPTION OF PLATE VII

a. The heavy string-course and the flat buttress show that the western part of the wall is Norman; the thinner string-course tells that the church was extended eastwards in the thirteenth century, when the window with simple geometrical tracery was inserted in the place of a Norman one to facilitate glazing. The blocked archway east of the buttress was a 'mason's hole' (see p. 90). The large buttress is modern. The gravestones are of eighteenth-century date.

b. The corbels projecting half-way up the wall mark the line of the original eaves and show that the lower part of the nave wall is Norman; the flat buttress, partly hidden by the white gravestone, is contemporary. The smaller clearstory window and the tall one to the west show that the walls were heightened in the middle of the fourteenth century; larger clearstory windows were inserted in the fifteenth century, when the cornice and parapet were added.

VII a. IFFLEY, OXON. SOUTH WALL OF
CHANCEL

VII b. CUMNOR, BERKS. SOUTH WALL
OF NAVE

Originally the aisles and nave were clear of all seats except a few stone benches for the infirm round the walls and, in some churches, the piers, as at Clifton Hampden, Oxon., and Sutton Bonnington, Notts. People came to church primarily to adore the Visible Presence, and to take part in the sacrifice of the Mass, 'meekly kneeling upon their knees'. The original duty of the vergers who still head our processions with their wands, was to clear a way through the congregation scattered over the nave floor. The references to seats in the earliest churchwardens' accounts suggest that they were at first provided for women only. Among the earliest pews are those at Cassington, Oxon., which show Early English mouldings of the late thirteenth century. But benches in parish churches were a rare luxury until the end of the fifteenth century when the sermon became a much more important element in the service, and the pulpit was established as a permanent part of the church furniture. It seems previously to have been a movable structure, though there is a fourteenth-century fixed pulpit at Over Winchendon, Bucks., and a large number, both of wood and stone, in Gloucestershire, of the early fifteenth century. Those of stone, being not easily removable, show that the original position of the pulpit was one bay west of the chancel arch, usually on the south side. Old pulpits are much less roomy than their modern successors; the preachers may have been smaller, or less histrionic in their oratorical methods.

The early pews, belonging as they do to the great age of English woodwork, are magnificent examples of the carpenter's art. The finest schools were in

East Anglia and the West Country. The height and depth of the seats prove that Tudor folk were considerably smaller than their descendants. On the other hand the book-ledge invariably provided suggests that the masses were neither so illiterate nor even so bookless as is popularly supposed; it is possible, however, that the ledges may have served as elbow-rests to the kneeling congregation.

Where the pews have escaped partial destruction their spacing shows that room was left at the west end for the baptistery and at the east for the side altars that, in an aisleless nave, stood against the chancel screen. But in the vast majority of churches the medieval seats were cast out in the late seventeenth century to make room for the great loose-boxes and high-backed enclosed pews in which a degenerate age sheltered itself from the draughts and from the eye of its neighbour. These, and the high galleries introduced at the same time, made expedient the elevation of the pulpit; and so the 'three decker' came into existence, with its sounding board above, close to the newly inserted ceiling of white-washed plaster that hid the carved timbers of the roof. The hour-glass stand which, though the glass itself has gone, is fixed on or near the pulpit, was introduced in the sixteenth century and became usual in the seventeenth, as we learn from churchwardens' accounts. Binfield, Berks., has one of the most interesting specimens, of wrought ironwork dated 1628, with the arms of the Smiths' and Farriers' Company.

These things excited the Gothic revivalists to a fury unequalled by that of any previous desecrators, and therefore an interior like that of Wood Eaton, Oxon.,

untouched since Stuart times, or that of Chisle-
hampton in the same county, where the church was
built and fitted in the reign of George II, is almost
as rare as one, like Fairford, little altered since the late
Middle Ages.

The free floor-space of the medieval nave was put to
many and various secular uses; it was the scene of trial
by ordeal in early times and of ecclesiastical courts later;
county courts were sometimes held in it; and if the
lord of the manor had no house in the parish he too
would hold his court here. It was also the repository
for many articles of public property: the regimental
colours still found in some parish churches remind us
that the arms and, after Tudor times, the gunpowder,
which every parish had to provide, were stored in the
church; when the room above the porch at Baldock
was opened in the last century after having been closed
and disused for generations, a large store of arms and
armour was found in it. Other churches still possess
a few 'backs and breasts' of the seventeenth century, but
as specimens of ancient armour and weapons now command a high price they have been turned into money
and will be sought for in vain.

The helmets and swords placed over the tombs of
knights and squires were almost always imitations
cheaply made for the purpose, genuine war gear being
much too expensive to be so wasted. But actual helmets
of out-of-date fashion were sometimes used as trophies.
The great helm of Sir William Barentine at Haseley,
Oxon., for instance, is a real fighting helmet. Such
genuine specimens should be safeguarded in local
museums from the risk of misappropriation; twenty

years ago in the church of Dinton, Bucks., two fifteenth-century battle helmets were lying about in an open box under the tower, and there was another on a window-ledge behind the altar at Buckland, Berks. All have now disappeared and nothing is known of their fate. They would each be worth £1,000 in the market to-day.

Stored in the church, too, was the great fire-hook with which fires were extinguished by the summary process of pulling down the burning house, which, as the ordinary cottage was of wattle and thatch, was both a necessary and a simple expedient for preventing the spread of a fire. Malmesbury and Mapledurham have early fire-engines, worked by hand-pumps; and I remember a set of leather fire-buckets, long ago embezzled, in the porch chamber at Sutton Courtenay.

The parish coffin, in which the poorer parishioners were fetched from their cottages to the churchyard, was usually stored in the church, but sometimes like the sexton's tools to-day, in a shed outside; the church-wardens' accounts of St. Alphege, London Wall, for instance, record the purchase of 'a newe coffin for the use of the P'sch v$^s$. For making of a penthouse in the church yarde for the keeping drye of the said coffen vi$^s$ viij$^d$'. Some had handles for carrying but most were laid upon the parish bier; Howden, Yorks., has a good specimen and there is another at Easingwold; Ridgewell in Essex has a medieval bier. When a body was chested, i.e. buried in a coffin, a higher burial fee was charged, perhaps because the grave was larger. An Act of Charles II for the encouragement of the woollen industry made burial in a woollen shroud compulsory, the incumbent being required to certify in the burial register that the law had been complied with at every funeral.

Leominster church still has a specimen of the ducking stool, kept by each parish for the correction of scolds and disorderly women, a chair on a pair of wheels, fixed to a long pole, in which the offender was tied and run down to the village pond. The pillory too was sometimes stored in the church, and even the stocks when these were portable; in later times they were generally fixtures on the village green. Every church too had its whip and tongs with which the appointed functionary expelled stray dogs—which were very numerous before the age of licences: 'Payde to John Whetley for Rebukyng the dogges owt off the churche xi̅ᵈ,' is a typical entry in churchwardens' accounts. In the eighteenth century the dog-whipper sometimes received additional remuneration 'for his trouble and pains in wakening sleepers in ye church and keeping children quiet'. Baslow, Derbyshire, still preserves its dog whip, and Clodock, Herefordshire, its expanding tongs. Tall, narrow cupboards recessed in the nave walls were made for the storage of the staves of crosses and banners carried in the weekly procession.

## XII. THE CHANCEL

IN ROMANESQUE architecture the nave, with its numerous secular associations, was shut off from the chancel by a wall pierced with a narrow arch, occasionally with smaller openings on either side of it as at Hinksey, Berks.; but the introduction of the loftier

pointed form led to the general use of chancel screens.
These at first were of stone as at Balking, Berks., but

Fig. 58. Southern end of screen and rood-loft, Hanborough, *c.* 1480,
showing door to rood-stair in south wall of aisle, conventional foliage and
Tudor flower on the parapet of the rood-loft, and a typical Perpendicular
respond or half-column.

Stanton Harcourt, near Oxford, has a thirteenth-century
example of oak and there are a few, for instance, at
Harwell, Berks., and Chinnor, Oxon., of fourteenth-
century date. In the fifteenth century, the golden age

3481                                    H

of wood-carving, the screen completely supplanted the chancel arch, and, with its rood, became the most striking feature of the church.

A platform, the rood-loft, was built upon it, approached by a winding stair, which, when built in the pier of a central tower, tended to weaken the whole structure. A better plan, often adopted, was to carry the screen and rood across nave and aisle, and to build the stair in a turret projecting from the outer wall (Fig. 58); occasionally an open stair was built in, or against, the inner side of the aisle wall. Though the lofts were almost all destroyed at the Reformation, the stairs with their doorways, and sometimes, as at Blewbury, Berks., their doors, remain; the door-arch, being invariably four-centred, suggests that the loft did not come into fashion until the late fourteenth century, though the presence of early piscinas in the wall above the chancel arch at Lambourne and Blewbury, Berks., Oddington, Oxon., and other churches, seems to prove that altars once existed in this elevated position, but how supported and approached is not known. The loft was often lighted by a window high up in the south wall of the nave; this, too, is almost invariably of Perpendicular date.

It is certain that before the coming of the screen and loft the rood from which both were named was in position above the chancel arch. At Bradford-on-Avon there are two carved angels in that position, who once watched the crucifix now vanished that stood between them. Set into the porch wall at Langford, Oxon., is a crucifix of Anglo-Saxon work which, it is probable, was once the rood over the eleventh-century arch of the chancel. But when the screen came in, the crucifix, with its attendant figures of St Mary and St. John, was carved in wood and set above it, backed by a painted tympanum of wood which filled the head of the arch; the roof above it also was sometimes ceiled and painted, or as at East Hendred, Berks., a canopy overhung it, which, however, may also have served as a sounding-board for the loft.

The term organ-loft, and the modern practice of placing the organ above the chancel arch, remind us that the original purpose of the rood-loft was to accommodate the organ and the soloists of the choir. At festivals the rood was decorated and numbers of candles were lit on the parapet of the loft, so that it came to be known as the candle-beam. During Lent the figures were veiled.

Pierced through the wall at the side of the chancel arch, on one or both sides, is the squint by means of which a sight of the high altar can be gained from the altar in the aisle or transept. When a chancel has been lengthened a second squint will usually be found, cut at a different angle, or the original one will show signs of enlargement. Most squints are without any ornamental treatment, but some late examples are traceried like a window, and may have been glazed. Their purpose probably was to enable the chantry priest to watch the celebration at the high altar, so as to time his own service in accordance.

On the inner side of the screen, and facing the altar, and extending also along the side walls of the chancel, were stalls for the priests taking part in the service; where they now exist all but the 'return' or eastward facing stalls are used by the choir, but in the Middle Ages there would often be chantry priests taking part in the service and assisting the incumbent. We know, from the will of a parishioner who bequeathed 'to every prest longyng to this church iii<sup>s</sup> iiii<sup>d</sup> that is to say Maister Priou<sup>r</sup> S<sup>r 1</sup> Thomas Taylour, S<sup>r</sup> Robert Thyrby, S<sup>r</sup> Thomas Schelton, S<sup>r</sup> Robert Walker', that there were at least five priests attached to Burford church in 1530.

The stalls have tip-up seats called misericords, like those of monastic and cathedral churches, and their carving is often amusing and always interesting. Neither seats nor desks were provided for the choir boys as a rule, though a few examples of seats are found, notably at Trunch, Norfolk. The earliest stalls remaining in a parish church are those at Kidlington, Oxon., of the thirteenth century; Great Budworth, Cheshire, and Hemingborough, Yorks., also have stalls of the Early English period. Fourteenth-century parochial stalls are rare, but fifteenth- and sixteenth-century examples are very common.

Below the westernmost window of the chancel, usually on the south side, but sometimes on the north, and occasionally on both, and, very rarely, in the wall near a side altar, is a smaller opening with rebated jambs showing that it was intended to be closed with a shutter, the bolt hole of which can usually be seen, though it may be concealed by the masonry that now often blocks the opening. This is the 'low side window' (Fig. 59) which continues to puzzle antiquaries in spite of the score or so of theories as to its original purpose.

---

1 'Sir', Latin *Dominus*, was the courtesy title given to priests who were not, as Masters of Arts, entitled to the style of 'Magister'.

Most of these are mere guesses without documentary
evidence to support them, and the most popular, that
the windows were leper-squints by means of which these
unfortunates who were excluded from the church could

FIG. 59. A blocked low side window, Elsfield, *c.* 1200, shewing a seat and
book-rest in the sill and eastern jamb.

get sight of the sacrament of the altar, is quite un-
tenable: they are never directed towards the altar, they
are often difficult of access from outside—at Ely for
instance, in Prior Crawden's chapel which has an under-
croft, the opening is ten feet above the ground, and at
Othery (Fig. 60) a buttress is built in front of it, through
which a second opening has been cut, and, finally, lepers
were strictly segregated in the Middle Ages, in lazar
houses provided with their own chapels and priests, as
lunatics are to-day.

## DESCRIPTION OF PLATE VIII

One small Norman window yet remains to tell that the chancel wall dates from the twelfth century. The lancet close by is the sole survivor of a row inserted in the thirteenth century, to be in turn replaced by the existing windows in the fourteenth, when the south aisle was widened and the buttresses built. (That the aisle was widened is shown by the nave arches, which are contemporary with the lancet and were cut through twelfth-century walls in which traces of Norman windows remain above them (cf. Fig. 50), and by the Early English doorway (Fig. 22) of the north aisle.) The niche on the nave gable was for the sacring bell; that in the aisle buttress for the image of a saint. The tower and clearstory are Perpendicular additions, with which, as their pitch indicates, the roofs are contemporary. (A shield of arms on a roof-corbel suggests that we owe them to the Lord Camoys, commander at Agincourt, who acquired Milton by his marriage c. 1399 and died 1419.)

VIII. GREAT MILTON, OXON. FROM THE WEST

For one theory only is there any documentary evidence; in 1281 Archbishop Peckham ordered that 'In elevatione Corporis Domini pulsetur campana in uno

Fɪɢ. 60. Low side window, Othery, *c.* 1500, obscured by a buttress through which an opening has been cut, favouring the theory that a light was set to scare spirits from the churchyard.

latere ut populares . . . seu in agris seu in domibus flectant genua', and it may be that a hand-bell was rung at these openings when there was no sacring bell in a turret on the roof above the chancel arch. In favour of the theory that the priest sat here to say his private office is the existence in some examples of a seat and, at Elsfield and Alvescot, Oxon., a book-rest (Fig. 59) in the splay of the window. The Alvescot example is specially interesting, having desks, like those of a music-lectern, at two levels, for standing and kneeling.

# XIII. THE SANCTUARY

THE SEPARATION of the sanctuary from the choir by a rail became necessary after the destruction of screens, or their gates, at the Reformation. Wren's grandfather Bishop of Norwich, in 1636, ordered that 'a rayle be made before the Communion Table reaching Crosse from the North wall to the South wall, neere one yarde in height, so thick with pillars that dogges may not gett in'. Most existing examples are of the seventeenth century, the baluster-shaped pillars of the first half, the corkscrew forms of the second (Fig. 31).

The first Christian altar was, of course, the wooden table used at the Last Supper, and there is evidence that the early Christians, like the Greek Church to-day, used altars of wood. But they also celebrated the Eucharist at the tombs of saints and martyrs, using the stone coffin-lid as an altar; and ultimately this type became universal in western Europe. In Anglo-Saxon England both wood and stone were used, and though Lanfranc issued an edict against wooden altars they were still re-tained in a few churches; and, even when made of stone, the altar-slab was sometimes raised on legs like a table and not built up in the form of a sarcophagus.

Examples of both kinds are not rare—Arundel, alone, has four, and medieval altar-slabs are quite common, though they have usually been reclaimed from other uses, having served even as floorstones, or as at Tewkesbury, to form seats in the porch. They may be known by the five crosses cut in the corners and the centre, at the spots anointed by the bishop who consecrated them with the holy oil. On the altar at Cookham, Berks., the crosses are of brass inlaid. The number is no doubt symbolical of the Five Wounds.

After the Reformation the altar was supplanted by the table, which, where Puritan theology prevailed, was of the ordinary domestic type, and, when in use, was moved[1] from the east end into the middle of the chancel —sometimes even into the nave, in order that communicants might stand, or even sit, round it in rows. Many Elizabethan examples remain and a much larger number of the Jacobean period. All have foot-rails, the purpose of which, in domestic tables, was to keep the feet clear of the often filthy, rush-strewn floor, and their legs are turned like a baluster shaft; but the earlier are the longer and lower, like the medieval altars, and their legs have great bulbous swellings like urns or melons, fluted and carved with scrolls or foliage of classic type; the later are much less elaborate, and by the end of the seventeenth century the communion table had become almost flimsy in construction. Baldon near Oxford has a Queen Anne example with a drawer, like a dressing table, now used as a writing table in the vestry. After the Restoration altars often had marble or stone tops, and many early Gothic revival altars are of stone—for instance, Ewelme, Oxon., and Christchurch, Cheltenham.

[1] The top was often detachable for convenience in moving.

The roof above the medieval altar was ceiled and painted to form a canopy. Where this remains, as at

Fig. 61. Chantry altar, *c.* 1480, with reredos and niches, from which the images are gone; showing mullions without cusping or tracery, and the casement moulding round the four-centred arch.

Hendred, Berks., there may be seen the staple or pulley from which hung the pyx, containing the reserved sacrament, covered with a veil or canopy of richly embroidered silk or linen of which a solitary example remains at Hesset in Suffolk. Three pyx canopies, emblematic of the highest use to which textiles could be put, were the medieval arms of the Drapers' company.

The great east window of stained glass, with brackets or niches for images on either side, formed the reredos to the altar, which was usually low so that there was generally room for a narrow band of carved and painted work between the altar and the sill (Fig. 61); the favourite subject was, appropriately, the twelve apostles, represented each under a canopy and holding their respective emblems. Scenes from the Passion are also frequent. After the middle of the fourteenth century reredos panels in ever increasing numbers were carved at Nottingham from alabaster quarried at Chellaston and exported to all parts of England. The figures shown on them are always dressed in the costume of Englishmen of the day, like the Greeks and Romans of the Elizabethan stage, not because the carver supposed that the High Priest's soldiers, for instance, wore plate armour, but because he was frankly ignorant of their equipment. His treatment of faces usually suggests some attempt to represent the typically Jewish nose and lips.

Sometimes a dorsal of embroidered stuff, corresponding to the altar-frontal, took the place of a reredos. Chipping Campden, Glos., has a pair of fourteenth-century date Always there were embroidered side-curtains, 'riddels', screening the altar north and south and protecting its candles from draughts; their colour, and that of the frontals, varied with the seasons of the church.

During Lent the altar was hidden by a veil hung

in front of it by means of a cord, the staples or hooks for which may often be found in the chancel walls at a height of about eight feet. Chieveley, Berks., has a beam across the sanctuary to serve this purpose; Winchendon, Bucks., has brackets on which a beam once rested.

Every altar had its drain, the piscina, usually in an arched recess in the south wall, where the rinsings of the numerous ceremonial ablutions were poured away to sink into consecrated earth. The mouldings of the arch commonly declare the date of a piscina, which is sometimes earlier than the wall in which it has been reset. During the period covered by the lifetime of Edward I it was the custom to employ two drains, apparently in order to emphasize the sacredness of rinsings from the ablution of hands or vessels that had been in contact with the consecrated elements (Fig. 51). Above the drain is a shelf, or the grooves cut for one, on which the cruets of wine and water were set out; and in the north wall opposite, or, rarely, in the east wall, is the locker in which they were kept when not in use. The door is almost always gone—there is a unique example at Drayton, Berks., complete with lock and hinges of the thirteenth century, but the bolt-hole for the lock, the staples for the hinges, and the grooves for shelves commonly remain.

In the south wall of the sanctuary are seats, sedilia, where the celebrant and his assistants sat while the Creed and Gloria were sung. They are usually the most ornate feature in the chancel, and their date is therefore easily recognizable by their mouldings. The earlier sedilia are graded at three levels, for the officiating priest and the deacon and sub-deacon who assisted him;

but as the endowment of chantries provided most churches with several clergy in full orders the later sedilia are usually on one level.

Opposite, in the north wall, may be an arched recess or an altar tomb for the Easter Sepulchre, where on the evening of Good Friday an image of Christ with the Host, together with the altar-cross, was solemnly deposited, to be watched day and night until Easter morning, when it was brought out again with high festival. Usually the Easter Sepulchre was made of wood, so that its survival is rare; but the tomb on which it was placed or the recess in which it stood, being often the grave of a parishioner who had left money for its making, may be found in a large number of churches. The example which stands under Shakespeare's monument at Stratford will be familiar to every one.

On the north wall, too, may be a stone desk at which the Gospel was read at the Mass. A movable lectern was, however, more usual, and a considerable number, both of wood and metal, still survive to support the modern Bible in the nave. Less common are choir-lecterns for music books, with desks at two levels for standing and kneeling. There is a thirteenth-century example at East Hendred, Berks.

## XIV. TOMBS AND MONUMENTS

AS THE kings of England were buried in the Abbey hard by their palace of Westminster so the lords of the manor had sepulture in the parish church. The rectors, too, were buried in their chancels. But with the rise of a middle class that privilege was shared with other benefactors, and ultimately by any parishioner who was well enough off to pay for it. Few therefore could hope

Fig. 62.                    Fig. 63.

Fig. 62. Effigy of William Longsword, 1220, showing hauberk and hose of chain mail, linen surcoat, prick-spurs, and long isosceles shield.
Fig. 63. Brass of Sir Thomas Peyton, Isleham, 1484, in Yorkist plate armour, showing glancing surfaces, heavy elbow-guards, sword slung in front, bare head, and short hair.

that their bones would lie long undisturbed by new arrivals; and in fact only those whose heirs could afford a massive tomb to mark and protect their resting-place were safe from the grave-diggers of the next generation.

Even a tomb gave but a limited immunity. Not one of Norman date remains in a parish church, and there are very few of the Early English period.

Early tombs rarely have inscriptions, but their period may be dated by their mouldings and other ornaments and by the costume of their effigies, above all by the head-dress and arrangement of the hair.

The earliest effigies are of stone or Purbeck marble, but after the thirteenth century they were also made, in ever-increasing numbers, of plates of latten imported from Cologne. These could be let into a ledger stone on the floor where a stone monument would have been in the way. The figure was cut out of the flat plate, lines representing the features and dress were engraved on it and filled in with coloured enamel, and it was then fitted into a matrix sunk to receive it in the grave-slab. The earliest existing 'brass' is that of Sir John Dabernon at Stoke Dabernon, Surrey, laid down in 1277. The engraving slowly but steadily deteriorated after the Black Death, and the figures grew ever smaller and more insignificant, until in the sixteenth century the whole effigies of a Reading alderman were cut out of the foot of a brass torn from the tomb of an early Lancastrian knight. The early brasses, like the stone effigies, were made for those who could afford to pay for good work; the later are mainly cheap substitutes provided for the new middle class.

Until the end of the fourteenth century men's hair, when visible, as in the effigies of priests and civilians, is curled and long (Figs. 76, 77); knights wear long thin moustaches and civilians beards, usually short and forked, the fashion familiar in the pictures of Chaucer. Early in

Fɪɢ. 64.                    Fɪɢ. 65.

Fɪɢ. 64. Brass of Sir John de Creke, Westley Waterless, 1327, showing
mail hauberk and chausses reinforced by plates of steel, linen cyclas cut
away in front and exposing the pointed hauberk, steel cap over mail hood,
and small heater-shaped shield.

Fɪɢ. 65. Brass of Sir John Cray, Chinnor, *c.* 1390, showing leather jupon
covering a breast-plate and short mail shirt, plate armour on legs and arms,
pointed bascinet with camail (= head-mail), sword, and dagger of mercy
in horizontal belt.

the Lancastrian period beards went out of fashion, and the hair was cut closer to the head, and in front presented a formal outline of three curves on forehead and temples somewhat suggesting a wig (Fig. 73). This fashion gave place in the middle of the century to an uglier one in which the short hair is brushed up above the forehead and ears so that effigies of this date appear to be wearing skull-caps (Fig. 63). Late in the Yorkist period it was allowed to grow long again, and was 'bobbed' at the shoulders and cut square across the forehead like a modern girl's (Figs. 67, 69). This fashion prevailed also under the early Tudors. The great majority of male effigies, however, show men in armour. This, until the beginning of the fourteenth century, was of flexible mail composed of small steel rings, and consisted of a pair of long hose reaching well above the knee, overlapped by a long, hooded shirt, the hauberk (Fig. 62). Towards the middle of the thirteenth century the hose were shortened, mail 'shorts' were substituted for their upper portions, and the knee, the most vulnerable part of a horseman, was protected by a shaped leather cap. All through the thirteenth century a long surcoat of linen, like a sleeveless night-shirt slit at the tails, was worn over the mail to protect it from moisture. The legs of effigies of this period are usually crossed, but the posture has no relation to the Crusades; it is merely an artistic device to show to advantage the lines of the figure.

In the reign of Edward II plates of steel on the arms and shins were strapped over the mail for additional protection, and the hauberk and the front of the surcoat were shortened (Fig. 64). By the middle of the century a breast-plate had been added, worn under a leather

Fig. 66. Sir Simon Felbrygge and wife, Felbrigg, 1416. He wears complete plate armour of the Lancastrian period, with gorget, cuirass, and skirt of taces with diagonal belt. She wears the crespine head-dress, close-fitting sleeves, and a mantle.

jupon, a short, sleeveless coat, in place of the linen
surcoat. The mail hood had given place to a pointed
steel cap, the bascinet, but a fringe of mail still hung
from its lower edge to protect the neck and throat.
Rowelled spurs took the place of the single-pointed
prick-spur of the surcoat period (Fig. 62), and a dagger
was added in the sword belt to dispatch a fallen enemy
(Fig. 65).

This, the camail stage, lasted until the Lancastrian
period, when mail was entirely superseded, except at
the armpits, by complete armour of plate (Fig. 66),
which grew heavier and more elaborate till in the Wars
of the Roses, 'it is a safe assertion to make that a full
suit of plate armour is the most perfect work of craftsmanship that exists'. It had shoulder-plates and elbow-
guards fluted with glancing surfaces to deflect a lance
or sword-thrust, was graduated in thickness, and lighter
on the sword-arm side so as to allow of freer movement.
This armour of proof made shields superfluous; the
presence or absence of a shield may almost be taken as
evidence that the date of an effigy is before or after the
close of the fourteenth century. From about 1450
onwards the knight's head is usually bare, and during the
Wars of the Roses his sword is slung in front instead
of at the side (Fig. 63).

In the third quarter of the century mail reappeared,
first at the throat, to replace the heavy steel gorget, and
later in the form of a skirt from the waist to a little
above the knee. Tuilles, jointed plates of steel, hung
above the skirt, were added in the Tudor period to
protect the front of the thigh (Fig. 67). The ugly
bulbous-toed sabbatons of this period are in marked

FIG. 67. Brass of William, Viscount Beaumont, Wyvenhoe, 1507, showing mail skirt with tuilles, mail gorget, round-toed sabbatons, and bobbed hair.

contrast to the long-pointed sollerets of the earlier part of the century (Figs. 63, 66, 67).

In the Yorkist and still more in the early Tudor period a tabard of arms, i.e. a kind of painted surplice with wide short sleeves, still worn by heralds, was frequently worn over the armour. Ladies usually at this date, and occasionally in earlier periods, also bore their own and their husbands' arms on their kirtles and mantles (Figs. 72, 75).

The sleeves of ladies and civilians afford a simple and trustworthy indication of their century; in the fourteenth century they were close-fitting, and often buttoned all up the forearm (Fig. 71); in the fifteenth century they were loose and baggy, and were drawn in at the wrist like a bishop's lawn sleeves (Fig. 73); in the sixteenth they had broad cuffs of fur (Fig. 75).

The effigies of ladies may be most readily and closely dated by the style of the head-dress. The earliest, of the surcoat and mail period, wear a coverchef of linen descending to the shoulders, and a wimple or gorget hiding the throat and chin, like the head-dress still worn by nuns (Fig. 74). During the camail period, the last half of the fourteenth century, the hair is shown squarely framing the forehead and cheeks and appearing to be closely confined in a sort of frilled cap, coming down over the ears, like a Victorian baby's (Fig. 71). Of this head-dress there are two varieties, in one, the 'nebuly', the frills show wavy lines, in the other, the 'zigzag', the lines run chevron-wise. Widows continued to wear 'nun's veiling'; unmarried girls at all periods wore the hair loose and flowing down the back.

Head-dresses of the fifteenth century are much more
impressive and elaborate creations. They are of gauze

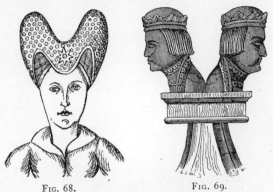

FIG. 68.                         FIG. 69.

FIG. 68. Heart-shaped head-dress, mid-fifteenth century.
FIG. 69. Bench-ends, Stanton St. John, *c.* 1500, showing hair bobbed in
early Tudor fashion.

FIG. 70. Crespine head-dress, Lancastrian period.

spread upon a wire framework, forming 'horns', either
horizontal as in the 'crespine' of early Lancastrian date
(Figs. 66, 70), or upcurved as in the 'mitre' or 'heart-
shaped' head-dress of the middle of the century (Fig. 68).

In the Yorkist period the framework grew still larger in the 'steeple' and 'butterfly' head-dresses (Fig. 72), in

FIG. 71.                    FIG. 72.

FIG. 71. The zig-zag head-dress of the mid-fourteenth century.
FIG. 72. Margaret Peyton, from a window at Long Melford, c. 1485, showing the butterfly head-dress. She bears her husband's arms on her mantle and her father's (Barnard) on her kirtle.

which the hair, brushed back from the forehead, was completely hidden.

With the Tudors the 'pedimental' or 'kennel' head-dress came into fashion, so called because it resembled, with its peaked front and side-lappets, a gable end or the front of a dog-kennel (Fig. 75). It gave place to the more becoming Paris head-dress, well-known in the pictures of Mary Queen of Scots.

It is not necessary to speak of the effigies of later periods, since their costume and dates will be recog-

Fig. 73. Fifteenth-century civilian dress, showing short hair, baggy sleeves, belt, and acutely pointed toes.

nizable from the pictures of Holbein, Van Dyck, and
later painters. Moreover they are almost invariably
accompanied by dated inscriptions in Roman lettering
and Arabic numerals.

 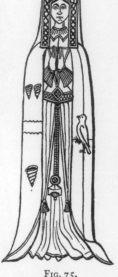

FIG. 74.                    FIG. 75.

FIG. 74. Thirteenth-century women's dress contemporary with the sur-
      coat and mail of Fig. 62, showing the gorget and veil.
FIG. 75. Brass of Elizabeth Shelley, Clapham, 1526, showing pedimental
head-dress, furred sleeves, and long chain with pomander. Her mantle
      bears the arms of Shelley and Michelgrove.

As Perpendicular work, though easily recognizable
as such, is very difficult to date within fifty years, the
details of sculptured figures are of great value in arriving

at a closer approximation. A horned head-dress on a carved corbel for example, as at Turkdean in the Cotswold, enables us to fix the date of the doorway as mid-fifteenth century; while the long, straight, squarely bobbed hair of the carved heads on the bench-ends at Stanton St. John, Oxon., shows their date to be early Tudor (Fig. 69).

From a very large number of tombs the brasses have been torn away; the indents in the matrix, however, almost always give a clue to the period. The lettering of the inscriptions, for example, until the middle of Edward III's reign, was of the kind known as Lombardic, full of curved forms; and each letter was set in an indent of its own (Fig. 77). By 1370 black-letter had come into general use (Fig. 66), every letter of which was formed of straight strokes, and the inscription was cut upon long strips of brass laid in a continuous indent. A single letter is therefore enough to determine whether a grave-slab or a fragment of stained glass is of early or later work. So the indent of a mailed coif, or of a pointed camailed bascinet or of a pedimental head-dress, will be unmistakable even though the brass itself has gone. A pair of roughly oblong indents, once containing plates engraved with kneeling figures of sons and daughters at the foot of the slab, will show it to be of the Yorkist or Tudor periods, when such representations of the survivors usually accompanied the effigies of the dead; Lancastrian examples exist, but are rare.

The language of inscriptions varies with the date and subject of the monument. For priests Latin is the invariable rule at all dates until modern times. For the laity Norman-French was usual until the Hundred

Years War led to its abandonment; the conventional inscription on grave-slabs of the thirteenth and fourteenth
centuries is

> Sire : A — : de : B — : gist : icy : Deu : de : sa : alme :
> eit : merci :
> 'Sir A. B. lies here; may God have mercy on his soul.'

Towards the end of the fourteenth century, when
black-letter superseded the Lombardic forms, Latin
became general, but gradually gave place to English
throughout the following century. The conventional
form was

> Hic jacet Dominus A. B. cujus anime propicietur Deus.
> Amen.
> 'Here lies Sir A. B. on whose soul may God have mercy.'

But the words are almost invariably abbreviated, e.g.
dn̄s, an̄e, aīe, pp̄r.

The earliest inscription in English is on a brass at
Brightwell Baldwin, Oxon., of about 1370;[1] it is also
the earliest illustration of a practice which in the next
century became popular, of supplementing the epitaph
by posthumous admonition to the living:

> 'Man com and se: how schal alle dede be: wen yow
> comes bad and bare: noth hab ven ve away fare: All ys werines
> yᵗ ve for care: Bot yᵗ ve do for godyslaf we have nothyng
> yare. Hundyr yis grave lys John yᵉ smyth: God yif hys soule
> heven grit.'

This kind of thing was afterwards supplied by the
tomb-makers, as mortuary verses are by undertakers

----

[1] English was first used in the Law Courts in 1362, and in
Parliament in 1363.

on mourning cards to-day. Stow in his *Survey* records an inscription on the tomb of John Shrow stockfish-monger in St. Michael's, Candlewick St., which is to be found also on a brass at Northleach, Glos. As a rare example of moving rhythm on a gravestone it is worth quoting.

> Farewell my frends the tyde abydeth no man
> I am departed hence and so shall ye
> But in this passage the best songe that I can
> Is requiem eternam now Jhu graunte it me
> Whan I have ended all myn adversite
> Graunte me in paradise to have a mansion
> That shed thy blode for my redemption.

Inscriptions tended to grow longer and less religious in tone all through the Tudor and Stuart periods until, in the eighteenth century, we find it asserted at the end of a long eulogy of the squire of Northleigh, Oxon., that his appearance in heaven 'exhilarabit civita-tem Dei'. But even the eighteenth century could some-times be laconic; an epitaph at Tetbury states, with a fine economy of phrasing,

> 'In a vault underneath lie several of the Saunderses; particulars the last day will disclose.'

# XV. WALL-PAINTINGS AND PAINTED GLASS

OF ALL the dismal mutations that have befallen our ancient churches the loss of their colouring is the most lamentable and the most complete. All that we now see in the most perfect church is but the frame and the background of a picture that has perished. Where, as at Fairford, the stained glass has been miraculously preserved it is only as a jewel taken out of its setting, for it was originally part of a colour-scheme that included all the interior, the walls, the splays of the windows, the pillars, the roof, the screens, even the floor, which was bright with parti-coloured tiles.

Every inch of woodwork and stone was covered with a prepared surface of gesso or plaster to which gold-leaf or paint could be applied. The smaller surfaces were treated decoratively, the larger pictorially. Above and around the chancel arch was a great picture of the Doom, showing the resurrection of the dead, the last judgement, and the fate of the just and the unjust, angels carrying some to heaven where Christ sat enthroned, and devils dragging others into the mouth of hell, represented by the open jaws of a nightmare monster. Another picture showed St. Michael weighing a soul in the balance, with our Lady standing by in prayer, and a demon trying to drag down the other scale. Elsewhere St. George fought the dragon, and the giant St. Christopher forded a stream carrying the Infant Christ—he was usually set to face the main entrance, for he was the patron of travellers and it was believed that those who looked on him were safe from death that day.

Though the Middle Ages were not so illiterate as is commonly supposed, they learned more from pictures than from books, and they certainly knew more of the Bible story than the average teacher in a modern Sunday school.

At the Reformation all this colour-work was covered

with whitewash upon which texts were inscribed in black-letter. Where the walls have not been scraped bare by later and more thorough reformers traces of colour may sometimes be seen under the wash. Among them search should be made for the twelve consecration crosses that mark the spots anointed by the bishop at the dedication ceremony when the building was first consecrated for worship. They are enclosed in circles of usually about twelve inches in diameter, and were made by striking segments of other circles with the same radius from points on the circumference of the first, in the manner familiar to every child who has played with a pair of compasses. In order that passers-by should not brush against them they were set at seven or eight feet from the floor level, a short ladder being therefore provided for the bishop to reach them at their anointing. There were twelve others on the outside walls;[1] they were sometimes of latten let into circular panels, of which an almost complete set of the early thirteenth century may be seen at Uffington, Berks., showing the rivet-holes of the vanished crosses. Other holes above or below the cross were made for the fixing of the branch to hold the candle which burnt before the cross at the time of consecration and on the anniversary of that day.

Small crosses roughly scratched or outlined in dots on the jambs of doorways are often supposed to have been cut in witness to vows; it is, however, probable that some of them were cut to scare away evil spirits and prevent them from crossing the threshold.

[1] External consecration crosses were peculiar to the English rites.

Remains of medieval glass are more numerous but
also more fragmentary than those of the wall-paintings.
The difficulty of dating them has usually been com-

FIG. 76. Thirteenth-century glass, Wilton, in which every piece sepa-
rately leaded is of a single colour. Coloured glass of this period is often
formed into medallions, oblong, circular, or pointed-oval, set in grisaille
(silver-grey) glass in lancet lights.

plicated by the nineteenth-century practice of collecting
fragments of all dates for preservation in a single
window. In the smaller openings high up in the
tracery, however, pieces may often be found in situ

FIG. 77. Panel of fourteenth-century glass, Stanford, Northants, c. 1330, forming one of a band extending round the chancel windows. The leading is less obtrusive, the pieces larger, and much of the detail is painted in yellow stain. The figure shows the 's' curve, the foliage is naturalistic, and the lettering Lombardic.

and may then be approximately dated from the style of the stonework, as in the Lady Chapel of St. Peter's, Oxford. Details of armour and costume, corresponding with those of effigies of known date, will also serve to fix the period of any figures that may be represented. The form of the episcopal mitre is a particularly useful guide: until the fourteenth century it was a low cap with a right-angled point; afterwards it grew steadily taller. Crowns increased in size and height, correspondingly. The size of the principal figures also gives a useful indication; the kings and bishops in the late twelfth-century glass at Dorchester, Oxon., are only about ten inches tall; those of the thirteenth century are usually twice that height, and those of the Perpendicular period may be three feet high or more. Pedestals supporting the figures were introduced late in the fourteenth century. Figures of the Edwardian age rarely stand erect, but have the sinuous lines of the curve of an 's' (Fig. 77). In the fourteenth and fifteenth centuries canopy-work filled a large part of a window and, as it reproduced the contemporary tracery, its period is easily known. Naturalistic foliage, in glass as in stonework, marks the craftsmanship of the fourteenth century (Fig. 78). The royal arms too, a very usual part of the design, will frequently enable us to date other fragments associated with them. Until 1340, when Edward III claimed the French throne, the English kings bore only the three gold leopards on a red shield, first assumed by Richard I. After that date they quartered the arms of France, i.e. divided the shield into four and set their leopards in two of the quarters and the golden fleurs-de-lis of France on a blue ground in the other two; a quartered

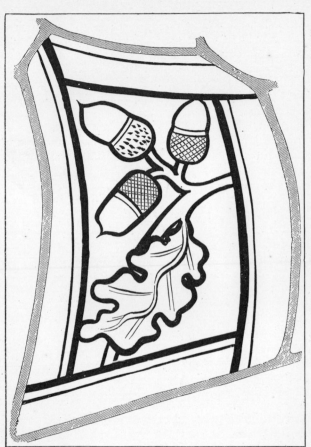

FIG. 78. Early fourteenth-century glass showing naturalistic foliage drawn in enamel on grisaille, forming the background for a band of coloured glass (Fig. 77).

shield may be safely assigned to a date not earlier than the reign of Edward II.[1] The fleurs-de-lis at first were powdered all over the blue, but soon after 1400 were reduced to three. With the Stuarts the red lion of Scotland and the Irish harp came into the royal arms. The king's badge often accompanied the shield; the blazing sun of York, for example, remains in the upper lights of a great number of windows, and dates the glass as belonging to the period 1461–85; so the triple-turreted castle of Castile is found in windows of the reigns of the first two Edwards. The shape of the shield usually gives a clue to its date: the earliest are isosceles, long and acutely pointed; those of the fourteenth century are equilateral; the later are often fantastic in outline and roughly rectangular, so as to allow space for quarterings at the base, for by this time the display of heraldry was the only function of the shield.

The study of glass dated by these and other means (documentary evidence in the case of York Minster for example, and actually dated windows at Merton College), has shown that the technique of glass-making, like that of architecture, falls into well-defined stages, the dates of which practically correspond with those of the Early English, Decorated and Perpendicular periods of Gothic.

Throughout the Middle Ages all pictures and patterns in glass were formed, like a tesselated pavement of mosaic work, by fitting together small pieces of glass of various shapes and colours—a piece of yellow to make a crown, of brown or white for a face, of ruby

[1] With the exception of the lion and castle quartered in the arms of Edward the First's queen.

for a cloak, blue for a robe, and so on. Shadows and lines for details like the eyes and noses of faces or the fingers of hands were obtained by means of opaque enamel put on with a brush and afterwards heated until it fused upon the surface of the glass. The windows were designed in England, but the glass itself, except a certain amount of white or clear glass manufactured at Chiddingfold and in the Chilterns, was made on the Rhine and on the Seine and imported mainly from Antwerp and Rouen.

The first modification of the purely mosaic method was due to the discovery, very early in the fourteenth century, that white glass could be stained yellow by means of silver nitrate painted on it and heated, so that, for example, a face, hair, crown, and halo, could all be shown upon a single piece of glass. The discovery so simplified and reduced the labour of picture-making that painted windows, previously found only in a few churches, became usual in every village throughout the Perpendicular period. Henceforward the pieces forming the mosaic and the figures represented grew alike gradually larger, and the leadwork bands less and less obtrusive until, in the middle of the sixteenth century, the mosaic method was abandoned and pictures were made on sheets of glass by painting upon them in enamel, as an artist paints on canvas.

Glass, like the walls themselves, tended to grow thinner through the successive centuries. The early glass, of the thirteenth century, is very thick and opaque; unless held to the light it might be mistaken for roughly glazed pottery. It was found impossible to make a translucent red and therefore white glass with a film of ruby was used. In the fifteenth century it became a common practice to grind or chip away the ruby 'flash' to any shape required and to stain the exposed white surface with silver nitrate. The golden leopards of England were often set in their red field by this simple means.

Windows should be examined from without as well as from within; most ancient glass shows externally the effect of wind and rain in the corrosion of its surface to a greater or less degree, which is not, however, proportional to its age. Mr. Le Couteur states that corrosion is most noticeable in the glass made in the two or three generations following the Black Death, and suggests that it was due to the shortage of competent workmen.

Since the diamond was not used by glaziers until the seventeenth century, glass cut before that date may be distinguished by its rough edges, caused by the tools with which it was snipped into shape.

On the merits of the glass of the various periods opinions differ. The earlier is more brilliant in colouring; for its very defects, its unequal thickness, and its streakiness, by breaking up the light caused it to sparkle. But its figures were crude and grotesque, with fingers like talons and toes like fingers (Fig. 76). Not until the fifteenth century do we get anything like a portrait in painted glass; naturalness in the human features is therefore as sure a mark of Perpendicular glass as naturalistic foliage is of that of the previous century (Fig. 78). The artists of the Perpendicular period had no doubts of the superiority of their own work, for they rarely, if ever, transferred the older glass to any new windows that they might build.

Fig. 79. Fifteenth-century glass, Woodmansterne, showing realistic treatment of the figure but conventionalized floral ornament. Black-letter inscription.

# XVI. THE PAROCHIAL RECORDS

E V E R Y church had its great chest, for the preservation of its churchwardens' accounts, of the wills of the
parishioners—in which the church was often interested
and which, as a rubric in the Prayer Book (visitation of
the sick) reminds us, were usually made with the advice
and at the admonition of the priest, and, after the
Reformation, of the parish registers and the books of
Protestant doctrine which every parish had to provide;
these last formed the nucleus of the parish library which
most churches seem to have possessed in the sixteenth
century, and of which they have been despoiled. Dench-
worth, Berks., kept its copy of the *Golden Legend*,
printed by Caxton, until 1853, when the vicar sold it
to a dealer for £20. It is now in the Bodleian. Buckland and Sutton in the same county still have a large
number of ill-cared-for books printed in the seventeenth
century. There must also have been still larger chests
for the storage of vestments, like those which still remain in some of the cathedrals; for the memorial
effigies of priests invariably show them vested in rich
and elaborate garments, often in great processional
copes, which could not be folded small. In Aylesbury parish church is a medieval vestment-cupboard
with hanging frames that swing outwards. English
church-embroidery, *opus Anglicanum*, was famous
throughout Christendom. At the Reformation vast
quantities of it were sold and pulled to pieces for
the sake of the gold and jewels with which it was
enriched. Yet a good many churches still possess an

altar frontal or a pulpit cloth made from a medieval cope, and such fragments give us some faint idea of the splendour in which even the humblest parish-priest was

Fig. 80. Thirteenth-century chest, Stoke d'Abernon, showing sunk roundels.

arrayed; not Solomon in all his glory painted on the walls, nor popes and apostles in the glass of the windows, could have compared with him in magnificence of colour.

Chests of every date remain from the twelfth century downwards. The earliest are made by hollowing out a great oak-log; these are often called dug-outs. Those of the Early English period (Fig. 80) may usually be known by their scrolled iron-work, by carved roundels sunk on their faces, and by the absence of iron hinges, those of the Decorated period (Fig. 81) by their elaborate carving or by their heavily banded ironwork; and those of late Gothic date by their linen-fold panelling (Fig. 82). But at all dates, plain unornamented chests were common, and only the expert can decide their period.

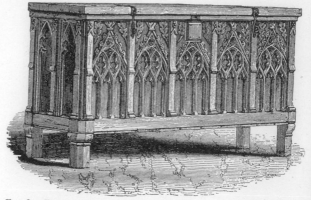

FIG. 81. Fourteenth-century chest, Huttoft, showing panels reproducing the Decorated tracery of contemporary windows.

Of the documents once stored in them a small proportion yet remain; and though now for the most part kept in safes they are still very much at the mercy of a careless incumbent. Very few churches are fortunate enough to have kept a set of registers complete since Henry VIII's Vicar-General in 1538 ordered that every parish priest should 'kepe one boke or registere wherein ye shall write the day and yere of every weddyng, christenyng and buryeng . . . And shall there insert every persons name that shalbe so weddid christened or buried'. The motive behind the order was the imposition of a tax on these sacraments, but the idea provoked so much indignation that it was abandoned. Registration, however, went on; and in 1593 Convocation ordered that all entries should be on parchment, on which earlier registers of paper should be copied,

Fig. 82. Linen-fold panel of early Tudor date.

and that duplicates of future entries should be deposited in the diocesan archives. So it happens that we know the date of Shakespeare's christening from the parchment copy at Stratford, and that the records of many parishes which have lost their early registers can be consulted at the diocesan office.

Besides the names of past generations the registers often contain entries of the highest interest to the student of social conditions. A certain number have been printed and so made accessible, and, which is more important, safe from destruction, by various archaeological societies, but the vast majority of these valuable records are still uncopied. If our millionaires were not, for the most part, bookless materialists, and our cabinet ministers mere politicians, all our parishes would have printed copies of their records, and the originals would be in safe keeping at the Record Office.

Like the registers the parish accounts survive only in a fragmentary state. The office of churchwarden is as old as most of our Norman churches, having been instituted by the Council of London in 1127. But the oldest set of accounts, those of St. Michael's church, Bath, begin only in 1349. A few other parishes have churchwardens' accounts dating from the fourteenth century but none of them has an unbroken series. Those of St. Lawrence, Reading, and of All Saints, Bristol, however, are practically complete since the beginning of the fifteenth century.

The original duties of the wardens were to raise and to administer the funds necessary for the upkeep of the church fabric and its services, and to prosecute offenders against ecclesiastical law, adulterers, sabbath-breakers, and swearers, for example. After the Reformation many purely civil duties were imposed on them, the provision of arms for the militia, the relief of maimed soldiers, the provision of pounds, stocks, and pillories, and the destruction of vermin.

Their accounts of receipts and expenditure show that the churchwarden must have been incomparably the busiest man in the parish. He had to collect the rents of lands and houses left to the church, to farm the church stock of sheep and cattle which those who had no freehold land often bequeathed instead, to sell wool and cheese and other gifts in kind, which he had also to gather in a house-to-house collection, to organize 'church ales', saint's day revels, when ale brewed in the church in the parish utensils was sold and consumed there by the holiday-making parishioners—for it was against the canon to work on a Holy Day. His disbursements of the funds so raised were equally varied, and included, of course, the payment 'for makyng clene of the Church agaynst the day of drynking in the seid Church', which at St. Lawrence's, Reading, in 1506 amounted to 4*d.*, while the 'mete and drynke' consumed by the Taberer on the same occasion cost 9*d.*

Our churchwardens' accounts are the most valuable of all sources for the student of economic history, containing, as they do, information as to wages and prices of almost every kind of commodity since the fourteenth century. Space forbids illustration here, for the entries are so varied that any quotations to be at all representative must be numerous. But considerable numbers have been printed and are thus easily accessible. To those who wish to get a general idea of their contents, the admirable *Churchwardens' Accounts*, by Dr. Cox, in Methuen's Antiquary's Books, can be unreservedly commended.

A certain number of medieval bells remain, usually single, in small towers, for, as they were not intended to be rung in harmony, most of them were melted down at later periods to form peals, which first came into vogue in the seventeenth century and often led to the enlargement of towers. The lettering on a bell gives the clue to its date—Lombardic and black-letter on the earlier, Roman on the later.

Similarly, the small medieval chalices were melted down or sold to provide the larger vessels needed when the Cup was given to the laity after the Reformation.

# INDEX